Contents

FOREWORD:

An Apology to the Printers

It is traditional to address the foreword to the readers, to explain to them what the item they have just bought is about. This seems to me to be a somewhat aimless courtesy, since if they have been prepared to fork out the requisite coinage to carry off the item, they will almost certainly protect their investment by reading it, in which case they will have all the fun *discovering* what it's about.

Also, if you title a thing *The Punch Book of Kids*, there should not be too much confusion in the reader's mind as to what goes on between the covers.

May I, therefore, beg the reader's forbearance, which is the sort of phrase you tend to get in forewords, and use this space to apologise to the printers for the assorted confusion and delays which have attended the gestation of this anthology?

All the material was gathered on time, scrutinised, arranged, prepared, and put in irreproachable shape for publication, before my small daughter started eating it. How she got her hands, and, more to the point, her teeth on it, is a mystery to all except those who have had any experience of one-year-old children.

When at last, dear printers, the manuscripts came back in proof form from your skilled premises, I dutifully made all the minor corrections that have to be made in the margins provided. So did my four-year-old son, who can unlock any desk built and who will be sent out into the world with a mask and a jemmy as soon as he's old enough to carry a sack on which one of my cartoonist colleagues will by then have written SWAG. For the time being, he corrects proofs. He puts cowboys in the margin, and fills in all the letters in the text, and you get a lot of felt-tip aeroplanes drawn in places most calculated to obliterate the copy beneath.

When I eventually took delivery of a second set of proofs, I was much more careful with them; I worked on them in a room the door-handle of which is too high for either of mine to reach, and the only children to see them were school-age citizens who accompanied their parents on visits and who, left to their own devices while the adults nattered about affairs of great moment (such as What Are Children Coming To These Days And Where Will It All End?), would quietly leaf through the sheets and unobtrusively steal such cartoons as would bring a laugh to their friends, fill up the odd page in their holiday-task scrapbook, and enable me to good-humouredly bang my head on the floor and scream when subsequently trying to find them.

And when, at the end of this fraught sequence of vicissitudes, I had finished my proof-reading, I wisely passed the pages to a young cousin down from Oxford for the weekend, who happened to be sponging off us, and who, I thought, would be just the lad to spot errors I had missed; he sat up the night poring over them and then spent the remainder of his stay in bashing tables with his fist and waving scrunched-up pages at me as a method of informing me that schoolchildren and students were nothing to be funny about, did I not realise they were a suppressed minority in no way distinguishable from the black South African mineworker, had I not heard of the Third World and did I not agree that the downtrodden student race was a de facto member of it, and when would geriatrics over the age of twenty-five learn that the world was on the brink of being taken over by a worker-student coalition, and did I not accept that I and writers and cartoonists like me would be laughing on the other side of our faces when Utopia was ushered in on Thursday week and we were all locked in the basement of LSE with our heads nailed to the wall?

And all that, esteemed printers, is what lies behind our myriad setbacks. It's also, now I come to glance at it, what the book is about.

Alan Coren

7

The Younger they are, the Harder they Play

"It gets me there and it brings me back."

KEITH WATERHOUSE on the games that adults never see

Acording to Hoyle, most popular children's games simply do not exist. I suppose this is because their participants, being naturally indolent or illiterate or preferring to climb trees instead of attending committee meetings, have never bothered to write down the rules. It is also true, I believe, that children tend not to congregate in the upper rooms of village pubs, where traditionally the laws of cricket, Association football, Rugby League, ice-hockey, poker and the remainder were drawn up on the backs of menus.

A pity, that, for how many games of conkers or hopscotch have been won by default through ignorance of the complex rules? How many children can recite the Declaration of Intent—a variation of the Hippocratic Oath—that was to have cleaned up the sport of doctors and nurses? What boy is aware of the first law of marbles, which is that although every tournament shall be played for keeps, no tournament shall really be played for keeps always provided that the loser shall throw himself to the ground, drumming his heels and screaming, "'Tisn't fair!"'?

For want of a stub of pencil and half a page torn from an exercise book at the right moment, the rules of many children's games are lost in antiquity. This constitutional void has often led to unseemly be-

haviour on the field. A skipping marathon in East London, for example, recently broke up in disorder because none of the contestants could agree as to the order of the condiments in the skipping rhyme. An elimination standing-on-one-leg competition in Derbyshire was abandoned when one of the semi-finalists challenged the umpire's decision that holding onto the railings was not permitted. The Northern Long-distance Spitting League has been arguing for three generations as to whether the expectoration of licorice juice shall constitute a foul.

These are happily isolated examples. It would be a sad day if children's games in general began to acquire the same ugly reputation as soccer or chess. In order to avoid the escalation of unpleasantness in what should be healthy, competitive sports, I have attempted to jot down a few notes on some of the children's games I remember best. Perhaps some minuscule Hoyle will continue the good work and produce the definitive treatise.

Not Walking on the Cracks of Pavements

This is an essentially urban game, the object being to perambulate a measured stretch of pavement—usually to the nearest sweetshop and back—without stepping on the cracks. The origins of the sport are

9

obscure but there is documentary evidence that it was played by Dr. Johnson, whose shambling gait was said to have been caused by over-meticulous play on a cobbled course.

Rules. 1. A crack in the pavement shall be interpreted as the gap between one paving-stone and another. Faults in the pavement surface or the edges of coal-hole covers are not cracks. 2. All players to set off simultaneously. 3. No bumping or boring. 4. It is permissible to negotiate the course on a scooter, but scooting over a crack will be declared a fault. 5. Last one to the sweetshop is a big sweaty nit.

A player shall be deemed to be dismissed when he or she steps on a crack. In the event of a player being so dismissed, the earth shall open up and swallow that player alive. The game shall continue until all but one of the players shall have been swallowed up alive.

Walking to the End of the Lane with Your Eyes Closed

This was originally a rural version of the game just described. It is said that many years ago a group of yokels were playing Not Walking On The Cracks in a certain village lane. One of them, more observant than the others, noticed that the country lane was not paved, hence that there were no cracks. To enliven what was necessarily a slow-moving match when played in pastoral surroundings, the yokels introduced a new rule: that all contestants must keep their eyes closed until they reach the end of the lane. Thus—in much the same was as Rugger evolved from Soccer when William Webb Ellis first handled the ball in 1823 —an entirely new sport was born.

In essence, the rules of Walking With Your Eyes Closed remain the same as those for Walking On The Cracks, with appropriate adjustments for the variation just described. The most important of these is that a player being dismissed the game shall be carried off by a big furry monster and boiled in a pot, rather than being swallowed up alive as in the traditional version.

Counting up to a Zillion

There are many variations of this exacting sport, ranging from the simple Counting Up To A Million to the more sophisticated and energetic Counting Up To A Million Zillion Trillion. Counting Up To A Zillion has perhaps the most devotees.

Rules. 1. Each player shall count in a high-pitched monotonous voice, beginning at nought (0) and not pausing for breath until he has reached one zillion (1,000,000,000,000,000,000). 2. A player counting under his breath and then claiming to have reached twelve million shall be disqualified. 3. Counting in fives, tens or hundreds shall be disallowed. 4. The use of non-recognised or eccentric numbers such as fifty-twelve or eleventy-ten is not permitted.

A disadvantage of Counting Up To A Zillion is that like the Eton Wall Game it rarely ends with a definite result, the main reason being that it takes twelve years to complete a single innings.

Holding One's Breath

This is often played on Counting Up To A Zillion pitches when the presence of parents or elder sisters may have created unfavourable conditions for any game that cannot be conducted in absolute silence. The object of the game is to see which of a number of players can hold his breath longer than the others. The rules may be subject to many and diverse local variations, but there is a standard Non-Breathing Code laying down the circumstances in which one contestant may examine another to see if his heart has stopped beating. The Code also discourages babes-in-arms from taking part in the game, even as amateurs.

Is-Isn't-Is-Isn't-Is

Played with something of the ritual of Japanese wrestling, this is a battle of wits between two players, requiring great verbal dexterity.

The game commences with one of the players making a statement or *postulation*, e.g., "The moon is flat" or "My dad can beat your dad" or "If you swallow chewing-gum it winds round your heart and you die".

The challenger must then reply with the *response*, which according to the rigid customs of the game shall be "It isn't", or "He can't" or "You don't", according to which may be most appropriate.

The first player then counters with the *assertion*— "It is", "He can", "You do", etc. Immediately, the second player must produce the *contradiction*— "Isn't", "Can't", "Don't", etc.—else he shall have forfeited the game. Note that at this stage the *abbreviation* of the responses has been arrived at—"Isn't" instead of "It isn't", and so on.

This style of play continues until one or other of the players shall introduce the *variation*. There are as many variations as there are moves in chess, and it is necessary to learn them by heart before one can hope to become an accomplished player. A simple sequence of variations might be as follows:—

"Is."

"Isn't."

"Is."

"Isn't, you rotten stinker." (First variation.)

"Rotten stinker yourself." (Second variation.)

"Don't you call me a rotten stinker." (Third variation.)

"Well you are one." (Fourth variation.)

"Aren't." (Fifth variation.)

"Are." (New sequence commences.)

The game continues through many such sequences and concludes with the *assault*, when one player shall have been led to the point of hitting the other one in the mouth.

JUNIOR UNION

by HOLLAND

"My dad wants me to follow him into Hugh Scanlon's Union, but my teacher thinks I might make Clive Jenkins's."

"Did you know we're expected to start as lower-paid workers?"

"My basic rate's the same, but I've got an increased minimum earnings guarantee."

"I suppose if you count woodwork and metalwork we're blue-collar workers."

"It's an Under-Twelves game between the CBI and the TUC."

"My dad's party will bash your dad's union!"

We sit all alone,
  We've nothing to do.
We pick up the phone
  And we call up Peru.

Afar in the Outback
  A telephone rings.
How jolly to shout back,
  Hello, Alice Springs!

Hello there, Manhattan!
  Hello, Bulawayo!
And Daddy will flatten
  Us out any day-o.

My little sister Molly
  Is always out of luck.
She has a pregnant dolly,
  But oh, its zip has stuck!

When Mummy wipes our faces
  As clean as clean can be,
And ties up all our laces,
  We know we're going places,
  Most likely, to run races
  In the Public Libraree.

And what better way of expressing ourselves
Than to shove all the books to the back of the shelves?

Little child beyond the sea,
Arab, Turk or Cherokee,
On your head the sun may shine——
Have you an *au pair* like mine?

Sweetly blows your spicy breeze.
My *au pair* has dimpled knees.
Tropic fruits may bring you bliss——
Little Nubian, what you miss!

Eskimo and Hottentot,
I don't want what you have got.
I'm a happy Hampstead child,
My *au pair* would drive you wild.

A modern child's garden of verse

The BBC came round to chat
  To Annabelle and me,
And though we talked of sex and that
  We never got a fee.

O Devil take the stingy pack,
  And scourge them with a rod!
We just can't wait till they come back
  To ask us about God.

The Hindu child reveres the cow
  Which overturns his pram.
I love the cow no less——but how
  Much happier I am!
A Christian shuns the tinsel gleam
  Of fallacy and sham.
The cow was made to give us cream
  To pour on strawberry jam.

I should like to rise and fly
Like a Jumbo in the sky,
Driving people deaf and dumb.
Meanwhile, I just bang my drum.

And another thing I'd like——
Lord, I want to rev a bike
Night and day till Kingdom Come.
Meanwhile, I just bang my drum.

Daddy says I'll have to wait
Ages till I can create
What he calls an Aural Slum.
Meanwhile, I just bang my drum.

Up into the old oak tree
Who should climb but little me?
If I scream and break the peace,
They will send for the Police.
If I cry and seem afraid,
They will fetch the Fire Brigade,
And the N.S.P.C.C.
Lucky, lucky, lucky me,
Playing in the old oak tree.

Praise God for caffs where pie and beans
And gravy come from slot machines.
We dined at one the other day——
Sid's Pull-Up, on the motorway.
There seemed no reason to dispense
With giving thanks to Providence,
Yet Daddy pulled a dreadful face
When I began reciting grace.

"Daddy doesn't know everything, son."

What Every Schoolboy Knows

By ALAN COREN

With the introduction of sex education into the curriculum of the under-tens, something is likely to happen to the whole fabric of the British school system. In fact, anything is.

THE honeyed sun streamed through the double-glazed mock-mullions of St. Swine's Comprehensive, dappling the upturned faces of the two thousand pupils at morning assembly and making their little bloodshot eyes cringe back into their sallow bags. Many a tiny tongue was furred with the strain of a long night's practical homework, many a small hand trembled involuntarily, many a lustless head lolled on an aching shoulder, all passion spent.

As the last discordant notes of *How Sweet The Name Of Kinsey Sounds* died wearily away, the Headmaster rose, drew his dirty fawn raincoat more majestically around him, and, pausing only to fondle the Senior Mistress, cleared his scrawny throat.

"School," he began, in that distinguished whine so familiar to the smaller girls, on whom it was his habit to press boiled sweets, "I have one extremely pleasant duty to perform before we dismiss. As you know, this is the moment in Assembly at which we offer our thanks and congratulations to those whose achievements above and beyond the call of mere duty have brought honour to the fine name of St. Swine's. Today, I ask you to acknowledge in the traditional manner the success of J. Griswold of the Lower Sixth, through whose selfless and unstinting efforts Millicent Foskett and Anona Rutt of Form 5a have both become pregnant."

13

The staff applauded vigorously, drumming excited feet upon the echoing dais. The school, however, responded merely with a dutiful and brief clapping of limp hands.

Nobody liked a swot.

It was the shrieking laughter from the gymnasium changing-room that proved the illicit mob's undoing. As it rang across the playground and down the musky corridors of the school, it fell inevitably upon the tensed ear of the Senior PT Master, who sprang athletically from the Matron, grabbed his track-suit on the half-leap, and began sprinting towards the fearful noise of joy. He took the gym steps four at a time, as befitted a man who had outdistanced every husband in the neighbourhood, tore open the changing-room door, plunged through the mass of terror-stricken boys and dragged three soaking offenders with their hands upon the very taps out from the shining tiles.

They trembled before his fury, their sin pooling around their feet.

"You disgusting little pigs!" shrieked the Senior PT Master, shaking with such rage that the Matron's ear-ring disentangled itself from his sideburn and rolled away beneath a bench. "So this is what happens when my back is turned! An orgy! An—an unspeakable vileness! To think that St. Swine's boys should be found taking cold showers!"

Biggs of 3b, tiniest of the offenders, began to sob.

"It's—it's not my—f-f-fault, sir," he wept. "I c-c-couldn't help it!"

Veins twanged and knotted on the Master's temple.

"Couldn't help it, Biggs? *Couldn't help it?*" He bent his terrible face to the fast-blueing lecher. "How many times have you been told what a cold shower will do to a healthy young lad, Biggs? What will happen to you if you don't stop doing it?"

"I—I'll g-g-go b-blind, sir," sobbed Biggs.

"Right! And what else?"

"I'll b-b-break out in w-warts."

"And?"

"G-g-go bald. D-d-die in a loony bin."

The Senior PT Master straightened.

"This is the last time I'll tell you," he roared, and his little black eyes drilled into their very souls. "Don't think I don't understand a boy's problems. Don't think I don't know what it's like when the awful wicked urge to have a cold shower comes over a young man. But when that nasty desire takes its terrible hold on you, there's one thing you can do, isn't there? And that's go straight out and . . . what?"

"Get laid, sir!" screamed the boys.

"Right!" roared the Senior PT Master.

Biggs of 3b got home at four in the morning. His eyes rolled in their sockets like a couple of maraschino cherries, and a lard-like sheen coated his saffron skin. He was carrying an enormous teddy-bear, a deflated balloon, and a box of cheap cigars. He fell through the door, and fetched up, gasping, against a radiator. His parents were still up, waiting.

"Where you been this time?" asked his father.

"Educational outing," whispered Biggs of 3b, and dozed off.

"Where to?" shrieked his mother, shaking him.

Biggs of 3b woke.

"Take 'em off!" he yelled. "Take 'em off!"

"Where *to*, Nigel?"

The child licked his lips, regained a sort of consciousness.

"Been on a ramble," he muttered, "to the Greek Street Nudorium and Strip-o-rama. After that, we visited a Fräulein Sadie Bamboo. At least, 3b did. 3a had to try picking birds up on Clapham Common. They got a Proficiency Certificate exam next term. Norman Loom's gone off to Brighton with a retired Chief Petty Officer." The boy yawned. "Norman's working for a Special Paper."

"They're working the lad too hard," said his father to Mrs. Biggs. "All this

"I only just made it before my Dad's vasectomy."

14

*"Oh, be as late as you like . . . but remember,
every minute past midnight hastens us along the treacherous
road to teenage delinquency."*

learning. It don't make up for experience. Filling his brains up with stuff. I left
school at fourteen and had Maureen Hodges in the bus-shelter. Getting out in the
world, that's what does it."

"Werl, you weren't exactly an intellectual, were you?" said his wife. "More
practical. Good with your hands."

"Good with my hands," nodded Mr. Biggs. "More practical. Now, Nigel," he
said kindly to the boy, "off to bed."

Biggs of 3b shook his head wretchedly.

"Can't," he moaned. "Got to do my prep, haven't I? Got to stand up in class
tomorrow and Describe In My Own Words Without Aid of Diagrams, haven't I?"

"Oh," said his father.

"Oh," said his mother.

They looked bleakly at one another. His father sniffed.

"We've not got to help him with his homework again, have we?" he muttered.

His wife sighed heavily.

"We shouldn't stand in the way of his education," she said. "We shouldn't put
our own feelings first."

Her husband stared at the floor.

"It's the fourth time this week," he said.

Gloomily, the trio trooped upstairs.

"It has come to my attention," said the Headmaster, adjusting his dress, "that
books and magazines of the most evil and pernicious kind are circulating in my
school."

Four thousand eyes suddenly homed in on him. Even the Upper Sixth, who had been cramming for A-levels with an intensity that had reduced them to wizened wrecks, thumbed open their eyelids and struggled to focus on their leader.

"Biggs of 3b," bellowed the Headmaster, "was found yesterday in the east lavatories, locked alone in a cubicle . . ."

"Alone!" gasped the School.

". . . reading Volume III of the *Children's Encyclopaedia*! Also in his possession were current copies of the *Economist*, *History Today*, and the *Highway Code*. QUIET!" shouted the Headmaster, as several girls began screaming and fainting. An uneasy silence settled. He went on: "I fail utterly to understand, when we have a school library full of the most healthy, wholesome texts—*The Perfumed Garden*, *Maurice The Human Stallion*, *Last Exit to Brooklyn*, *Portnoy's Complaint*, to name only the most boring—I fail utterly to understand why boys and girls should creep off to dark corners and fill their minds with cheap non-educational trash. Mens sana in corpore sano, School, and anyone caught reading Enid Blyton will not be allowed to undress on the forthcoming outing to Epping Forest!"

In the body of the hall, shunned by his nudging classmates, Biggs of 3b began pitifully to whimper.

The next day, Biggs of 3b would not get up. There was no observable sickness, no evidence of fever; it was merely that Biggs of 3b lay on his back, staring fixedly at the ceiling, and moving only when a nervous tic racked his small silent frame.

"What is it?" said his mother.

"Nothing," said Biggs of 3b.

"But it's Thursday," said his mother. "It's a very important day at school, isn't it?"

"Yes," said Biggs of 3b.

His brain shrank. Two periods of compulsory Swedish, then O-level Flagellation until lunch. After lunch there was a seminar in Plastic Rainwear II, a period of Petting, and then Free Expression until home-time. He was paired for Free Expression with Cheryl Gurth, who stood a head taller than Biggs of 3b and could crack walnuts with her knees.

His mother looked at him.

"I'll send a note," she said gently. "I'll say: 'Please excuse Nigel Biggs of 3b on account of a bilious attack and a severe nose-bleed and a slight chill.'"

She went out and closed the door. Biggs of 3b smiled for the first time in months, and his hands unclenched, and his tic disappeared. A bird sang, and Biggs of 3b closed his grateful eyes.

He was twelve next birthday, and sick of sex.

"Your mother thinks it's time we had a chat about the 'Facts of Life' son."

THELWELL at the

YOUNG FARMERS' CLUB

"*Right! Now I want each of you to describe the weather in your own words.*"

"*No! No! No! Put the shears down and watch me.*"

"*Mr. Parsons has kindly consented to talk to us this evening about muck spreading.*"

"*You're a menace with a hypodermic needle, Philpot.*"

Superkid

By WILLIAM DAVIS

THE *Daily Telegraph*, a reader of that esteemed journal suggested the other day, "is infinitely more harmful" to school-children than *Oz*. It is a point worth debating: if the argument is to be about what corrupts children (and if it isn't, the whole business is really too tedious for words) then we really ought not to confine ourselves to obscenity.

Is the *Telegraph* harmful? I suppose one could argue that its extensive reports of the *Oz* trial, and the aftermath, corrupted many more children than the original issue could ever hope to do. It whetted appetites that should have stayed unwhetted. But let's not talk about sex—or, if we must, let us reflect, in passing, that the *Sun* and *News of the World*, whose distribution to wholesome British homes is somewhat larger than that of *Oz* or *Ink*, have more influence in that department than a whole army of Richard Nevilles.

Where the *Telegraph* could be said to exercise a harmful influence is in its stout defence of Establishment virtues—its class-consciousness, its admiration of conformity, its impatience with anyone who dares to challenge established concepts.

"Stockbroking's a good career. Yes, if I were you I'd marry a stockbroker."

But let us not be nasty to what is, without doubt, a great newspaper. Let us agree that there are many ways of corrupting young minds—that racial intolerance, blind chauvinism, the glorification of war, and arrogance based on nothing more than an accident of birth are, in their way, no less objectionable than smut. Let us agree, too, that it makes a change to talk about the power of the printed word (or drawing) rather than about the menace of TV.

Whatever the majority of children read, it certainly isn't *Oz* or *Ink*. What do they buy, and what influence, if any, does it have on them?

The answer, of course, depends on the age group to which they belong. At five, it's still likely to be Three Blind Mice and Fee Fi Fo Fum. (I was also brought up on the Brothers Grimm and Wilhelm Busch—both every bit as liable to corrupt as Disney.) After that, to the age of fourteen and often beyond, children tend to be hung up on comics. Older boys and girls read magazines like *Honey*, *Petticoat*, and *Romance*. And, of course, all of them pick up the publications brought home by their parents—including *Punch*.

The voluminous correspondence produced by the *Oz* verdict made me curious about the propaganda line taken by the schoolkids' press. So I started by reading through eighteen different comics published last week. My first reaction was one of astonishment at how little they have changed over the years. Do children really still say gosh, crumbs, and golly? Do they talk about "pesky hounds" and use phrases like "Oh, you rotter"? The comics say they do: Billy Bunter, still going strong in *Valiant and Smash*, hasn't got a day older. The villains, too, seem much the same: swots, know-alls, and tell-tales still get into awful trouble.

There is, Judge Argyle will be relieved to hear, no sex in British comics. None whatever. As far as the publishers are concerned, it simply does not exist. American comics tend to be more forthcoming: boys do occasionally fancy girls, and vice versa. In Britain, by golly, even the villains are ever so chaste.

There is no outright colour prejudice either. The only black men I came across were in a publication called *Scorcher and Score*, and they were straight out of the Black and White Minstrel Show. Lord Rumsey, you see, was trying to raise money to save his mansion and his loyal staff, so he formed these good blacks into a football team and . . . but you get the drift. Lord Rumsey, you will not be surprised to hear, has a splendid moustache and wears a solar topee. The Empire lives—in *Scorcher and Score*.

The wars live, too. Fifty-three years have passed since the first world war, and twenty-six since the second, but bi-planes and evil Germans go on forever. *Lion and Thunder* tells us that:

German World War One ace Baron Maxilien von

Klorr, known as Black Max, had trained giant killer-bats to tear British planes from the sky. He captured a recruit pilot, Johnny Crane, and turned him into a "human bat"! Then, using his "mind slave" to help him prepare a trap, Black Max captured his greatest enemy, Lieutenant Tim Wilson!

Another comic, called *Jet*, has an even more devastating tale:

To gain revenge for Germany's defeat in the Second World War, criminal scientist Doctor von Hoffman had invented a gas which enlarged all creatures and insects. He then embarked on a one-man invasion of Britain.

The same issue also has "the kids of Stalag 41" taking on a troop of stupid Gestapo: "I vant," says Herr Kolonel, "these spies captured at vunce! You heard . . . at vunce!"

This sort of thing could, of course, be portrayed as insidious anti-Common Market propaganda. But, of course, this isn't the intention. Germans and Japs make convenient villains; it saves having to draw them from swarthy ethnic minorities or, worse, from the ranks of the British aristocracy.

The impression one is, nevertheless, left with is that most of these strips are drawn by mysterious old men who miss the Empire, resent the need to be friendly with old enemies, want to keep blacks in their proper place, and firmly believe that nearly all problems are best settled by brute force.

Nor do they hold with women's lib. A weekly called *Princess Tina* has a heart-warming tale about Sue Day's Mum, who joined the Women's Liberation Movement and as a first sign of her freedom went for a week's holiday at a health farm. She simply *hated* it, and within a few days was back at the kitchen sink. "And that," Sue reports with a happy smile, "is the last we heard about women's liberation in our house!"

Snobbery seems to produce mixed feelings. On the one hand, we have *Scorcher and Score* giving a new role to royalty:

Bert Lacey, player-manager of Thornton Villa, had discovered that Rudolph Maximilian Rantzberg, the boy-king of Moravia, was a brilliant footballer and he was trying to make sure that Rudi returned to England to play for the Villa. . . .

On the other hand, *Bunty for Girls* does not hold with royal arrogance:

Sally Smith, a scholarship girl at Redford School, was

"Daddy and I have no need of drugs. That's because Daddy and I lead full, rich lives."

told to help Princess Rosetta of Centralia, a new girl. But Sally's job was to take all the punishment earned by Rosetta, who claimed that a princess could not be punished by commoners. . . .

The Princess and Sally are invited to visit the castle of a cockney peer who has made his money from supermarkets, calls them "ducks" and claims to be "ordinary Alf Higgins underneath." The Princess is appalled, and seizes an opportunity to chain him to one of the walls of his dungeon. Sally helps out, the Lord rewards her by taking her picture for a pre-packed food advertisement, and the headmistress arrives just in time to mete out suitable punishment to snooty Rosetta.

It seemed an appropriate moment to me to put aside the comics, and turn to teenage magazines like *Lover* and *Romance*. They are, happily, much less old-fashioned. There are no princesses romping through their pages, and no mad German scientists either. The world of Billy Bunter seems a million miles away. The editors clearly work on the assumption that their teenage readers are more interested in undies, deodorants and the eternal problem of how to keep a boy—or girl—from running off with someone else.

Sex dominates almost every page, but none of the magazines is ever likely to find itself prosecuted at the Old Bailey. "Some Day in Summer", a feature in this month's *Romance*, has a pretty young girl confessing: "I wanted to be sure of Noel—that was why I let him make love to me." But, of course, the episode had the traditional consequence: Janey found herself pregnant. Elsewhere, the magazine offers cunning advice on "How to get your holiday male," but this is tastefully balanced with sub-headings like "You can have the sofa, but be warned—there is a bolt on my door." Judge Argyle, I'm sure, would approve.

In the "heartcry section" of *Lover*, a troubled young lady wants to know if there is something wrong with her, and her boyfriend, because they have never discussed sex. "All the other girls," she explains, "say they're always being asked by their boyfriends to have sex." The reply is reassuring. "Some boys," we are told, "are satisfied to work out a mature and happy going-steady relationship before they think much about the sex bit. Others are different. But often it's a lot of talk. Your boyfriend's normal. You're normal too."

Fabulous, another weekly, defines what "being a girlfriend is":

Not wanting to go to the disco with your work-mates anymore.

Spending your money on aftershave or a T-shirt for him instead of make-up and clothes for you.

Washing your hair on the night that he's at football.

Not wanting him to see you without your make-up.

Being nice to his family and putting up with his friends.

Getting used to the back seat of his scooter or his open top car.

Telling him he's wonderful—when he's happy and when he's down.

Nothing obscene there—unless, perhaps, you read more into that business about the back seat than you ought to. And not much in the way of corruption either.

This, of course, is precisely what magazines like *Oz* reject: the world of supergirl is no less distasteful to them than that of superkid. But it is obviously what young readers want; if not *Lover*, *Romance*, *Fabulous* and all the rest could hardly hold such formidable circulations.

For real protection, I am afraid, you will have to keep your children away not only from the Richard Nevilles, but from the daily stories of our adult world —violence in Northern Ireland, murder in My-Lai, persecution in South Africa, wife-swapping in Peyton Place. It means hiding the *Telegraph* under the sofa and banning the Nine o'clock News; it means explaining that long-haired young people have no monopoly on crassness.

On the other hand, you *could* just let them grow up in their own way.

"*I'm beginning to wonder what sort of dumb cluck we gave birth to, Marge . . . three weeks he's been in there already and STILL he ain't broke out . . .*"

"And naturally as an executive you would be entitled to a Company car."

LITTLE LIES

By HARRY SECOMBE

Court Usher: *"Do you swear to tell the truth, the whole truth and nothing but the truth?"*
Seagoon: *"Yes."*
Usher: *"You're going to be in a right mess then, mate."*

THIS LITTLE EXTRACT from a Spike Milligan Goon Show script* seems to sum up rather succinctly the prevalent attitude towards honesty. We live in the age of the half truth, the slightly bent statistic and the party manifesto, which is a combination of the other two.

One can only write honestly about honesty where it applies to oneself and one's relations with others; so, on the somewhat overworked premise that the child is father of the man, let us look into some of my own youthful encounters with the truth. It's not a pretty sight, I warn you.

When I was a lad I was an avid reader of Arthur Mee's *Children's Newspaper* and *True Confessions*. The first was ordered for us by our parents and the second was read clandestinely when they were out. One was full of tales of honour and Empire and biographies of people like Philip Sydney and Edith Cavell, and the other told of dishonour and seduction, never explicit but hinted at by delicious dots. I must admit that I found the exploits of Mrs. X of Trenton, New Jersey far more exciting than the tribulations of St. Francis of Assisi, who must have spent too much time trying to get the bird lime off his habit to have naughty dishonest thoughts.

*from *The Goon Show Scripts* published by the Woburn Press

"The man we need must have guts, daring and initiative, Mrs. Hempson! Is your son that man?"

However, we were brought up in the belief that it was better to tell the truth and face the consequences than to tell a lie. As a choirboy I remember sitting through a sermon on this theme, nodding sagely with my Young Woodley face on, my mind switching rapidly from thoughts of what was for lunch to agonised speculation on whether I should tell my mother about being caught playing doctors and nurses with Elsie Thomas by her elder sister who now showed signs of wishing to be examined herself. At twelve years of age I was too young to cope with a full surgery, and was avoiding both girls, who, to my mother's surprise, had taken to calling at our house and asking if I could come out to play. I was a junior Dr. Jekyll who was forced to hide. I was saved from a head-on confrontation with the truth by a fortuitous bout of yellow jaundice, during which I abandoned *True Confessions* and settled instead for a less heady diet of *Film Fun* and *The Magnet*. Just after my illness the Thomas sisters discovered an embryonic gynaecologist living in the next street, and I was spared their attentions.

Featured in *The Magnet* were my favourite characters, Bob Cherry and Harry Wharton, two school boys of immaculate character and impeccable honesty, and upon whom I began to model myself. I became an insufferable prig at home, telling the truth about everyone and everything until even my father, the mildest of men, was forced to comment. "If young George Washington doesn't stop his self-sacrificing, I'll sacrifice him myself," he said, waving the carving knife one Sunday lunchtime after I had pointed out that there was more meat on my plate than on my brother's—a most uncharacteristic gesture. Mind you, calling him Pater didn't help filial relations.

This phase came to an abrupt conclusion after an incident in school. I happened to be in a form which was noted for its exuberance, and its rough handling of the unwary teacher. One particular afternoon we decided to play a prank—a word not indigenous to a Swansea Secondary School, indeed until I read *The Magnet* I thought it was Chinese for a piece of wood. The victim was the maths master, a bibulous gentleman who would come back from a liquid lunch, set us some work to do and promptly fall asleep with his mortar board over his face and his feet on the desk.

On this day we waited impatiently for him to go to sleep. When he had done so we blew sneezing powder around the room, dropped two stink bombs and as a pièce de résistance placed a beautifully made imitation of a pile of dog droppings

22

on his open book. Awakened by the sneezing and the smell, he took the mortar board from his face and prepared for battle. However, the sight of the mess on his book unhinged him and he fled the classroom whooping wildly like a Red Indian.

Vengeance was swift, and soon the Headmaster faced a flushed, frightened form.

"Come out the boys who did this," he hissed, glasses glinting. In true Harry Wharton style I stood up and went forward to the front of the class.

"I dropped the stink bomb, sir," I said.

"Of course," said the Headmaster enigmatically. "Anybody else?" I moved aside to make room for the others but nobody volunteered. Twice the head repeated his request, and still no one came forward.

"Am I to believe that there is only one honest boy in the form?" I held my head high, as the rest of the boys shuffled their feet and whistled tunelessly.

"All right," said the beak. "You're all on detention until further notice. You, Secombe, come with me." I left smugly, expecting a lecture and nothing more. When we got to his study the head turned on me in fury.

"You're not honest, you're damned stupid," he said. "Bend over."

It was then that I realised that the truth does indeed hurt. I received on my behind what he thought the class should have had, and with each stroke of the cane I cursed Harry Wharton and Bob Cherry and the whole editorial staff of *The Magnet*.

Afterwards I found it prudent to compromise by crossing my fingers either behind my back or in my pockets whenever I was forced to tell a lie. This led to complications later when I worked in an office where one of my duties was to make tea for the other employees. I provided the tea, sugar and milk and charged a penny a cup. There was one snag—the head of the department would insist on drinking only Typhoo Tea which was expensive and cut down the profit margin. Eventually I hit on the idea of putting a cheaper blend into an empty Typhoo packet and spooning the tea from it into the pot whilst he watched.

The first time I tried it, I brought the teacup and saucer over his desk on a little

"Well, that's the pill for you. Unpredictable side-effects."

tray together with a packet of biscuits. He looked up from the huge ledger in which he was painstakingly writing in different inks all the month's output from the colliery.

"Are you sure that's Typhoo tea?" he asked.

"Yes," I said.

I didn't know whether any reader has ever tried crossing his fingers whilst holding a full tea tray, but I can assure them that it is not possible. The resultant shambles would have had me fired had I not been called up that afternoon for service with the Territorial Army. I must have been one of the few people, apart from Mr. Krupps, who was glad when war broke out.

I still cross my fingers when I go backstage after a not particularly successful first night, and I know I am going to have to be dishonest in order to bolster sagging egos; or when a customs official says "Anything to declare?" My own youthful struggle and eventual compromise with the truth is obviously compatible with most other people's. Which brings me to the inevitable conclusion that all world leaders and statesmen were young themselves once and must have carried into adult life some childhood superstitions.

When Chamberlain waved that piece of paper in the air after Munich, crying "Peace in our time," were his fingers crossed? Why did Napoleon always have one hand inside his jacket? Watch the next political broadcaster on television; if his hands drop out of sight when he's making a solemn promise to the electorate, don't believe him. One thought has just struck me—if you can see that his fingers are at rest, he might be crossing his toes instead. I feel there's no hope for any of us.

"Pay attention to the game, will you!"

"*You're a violent, lying little twit, lad, I can't understand you youngsters these days . . .*"

"*But I come from a broken home, sir, a rat-infested slum dwelling.*"

"*Well, I came from a rat-infested slum dwelling, but I didn't turn out like you.*"

"*But my father was a drunken dope-pedlar who used to beat us up with a pickaxe handle.*"

"*And I suppose your mother was a whisky-sodden prostitute who used to lock you in the coal bunker.*"

"*Er . . . yeah, that's right.*"

25

a PRogRess RePORT on AMERICAN EDUCATION

or How We Get Our Smarts On Nowadays
researched by ARNOLD ROTH

A Horn Book History of American Learning

 A

 B

 C

 D

Hi! I'm Jim! Gimme a dime! 39¢

←This is Jim. He has no EDUCATION. He also has no JOB. He does have a bottle of cheap wine. He drinks it and gets philosophical all over.

Vini Vidi Vino

←This is Balsam. He is a Ph.D. from Yale. He HAS education. He has NO job though. He gets philosophical. Then he drinks cheap wine.

Contemporary Creative Progressive Free Form

Diary of a Child Guerilla

By KEITH WATERHOUSE

Monday, **March 1,** St. David's Day. Got up. Went to school. Came home. Had fish fingers. Went to bed. Started to count up to a billion but only got up to 7,643 for the reason that, my Father made me stop. He said that if he had to come up to my bedroom once more, that he would strangle me. This man is dangerous.

Tuesday, March 2, Got up. Had breakfast. Got

"Hello, Dr. Spock. Say, I hate to bother you, but I've got this Forty-year-old kid."

ticked off by my Father for holding my Breath. People should not get ticked off for holding your breath, for the reason that, it is a free country. Therefore I hate my Father. He thinks he is somebody but he is nobody. Also he have hair coming out of the end of his nose.

Wednesday, March 3, Ember Day. I am going to get my Father. He has been asking for it and now he is going to get it. Just because I was sucking bread. He go purple and bangs the table. If he was Run Over I would be glad. He look like a Jelly and also is Smelly.

Thursday, March 4, moon's first quarter 3.01 a.m. Got up. Went school. Watched telly. Left roller skate on top of stairs, but, it did not work. This only works in comics such as Whizzer and Chips ect., therefore, comics are stupid. They, the people you are trying to get, do not step on the roller skate and go ker-bam-bam-bam-bam-bam-bam-kkkklunk-splat-aaaargh. Instead of this, they just pick up the roller skate and say (This house getting more like a pig-sty every day.) He is Potty and also Grotty.

Friday, March 5, Today I said I was going to John's house but I did not, I went to the Pet Shop to buy a poisonous snake, but they did not have one. The copperhead, the Rattlesnake, the cobra and the Mamba are among the poisonous snakes to be found in the world. The man in the Pet Shop just laughed and tried to sell me a hamster. I am going to get him after I have got my Father.

Saturday, March 6, sun rises 7.35. I have got an Idea from watching Telly. It is where they were in a certain foreign country and he, the Tall one, invents this special kind of warfare. It comes to pass that this Warfare is something nobody else knows about, therefore he wins it. It is called (long word) warfare. (Long word) warfare is where, they do not fight with guns, tanks, also armoured cars, thus killing them, you fight a person's mind so therefore he will do what they tell them. It begins with the letter P. This I am going to do to my Father.

Sunday, March 7, 2nd in Lent, 1st day of Operation Stare. Operation Stare is where, you just look at your Father. You do not say anything, you just Look. This was when he was reading the paper, also when he was painting chest of drawers. He did not know I was there until, he saw me. I was just Staring at him. This is Operation Stare. It is (long word) warfare. It did not work, as he said (If you nothing to do you can tidy up your room). Another example of the poisonous snake is, the sea-snake. He has spots all on his neck. He is Spotty and also Potty.

Monday, March 8, On this important day I invented the art of making yourself cry. You have to pretend that you have a dog. This could be a Sheepdog or numerous others, it is called Zebadee. You have to pretend that it runs away in the park and, you come to this swamp and it rescues you and die. After you have gone into the swamp to get it out, the (dog). It dies and you are sorry. This can make you cry, but my Father just say, (Stop snivelling or I will give you something snivel about).

Tuesday, March 9, Nothing happened. I am still going to get my Father. I will make him Crack.

Wednesday, March 10, birthday of Prince Edward. Today I got my Father to think that I could not move my left arm, also that I could not feel anything in it, it was Dead. I thought this would make him sorry and it did. He went all white and call me Son. He pinch my arm and asked if I could feel it, I replied that (I could not.) We had better see Dr. Murray!!! he exclaimed, but just as he was helping me on with my coat to go Dr. Murray, he sticks a pin in my arm accidentally on purpose. This hurt me so I said (Oh.) He went all purple and call me Lad.

Thursday, March 11, Got up. Decided to Lie Low.

Friday, March 12, full moon 3.34 a.m. On this day Operation Blink came into being. You just blink your eyes all the time, it drive him Potty. Also, at the same time, you must screw your nose sideways and also make your mouth go down, while you are blinking your eyes. I did this all the time, until my Father Went Out.

Saturday, March 13, An unlucky day for my Father. On this, the 2nd day of the famous victorious Operation Blink, he take me to see (The Railway Children). I was sick on the bus going, also in the cinema. When we came out, he asked, (Are you feeling better now). I replied that I was, therefore, we went on the bus. I was sick. My Father does not know it, but, I did it on purpose. I have discovered the art of being Sick. It is my secret. I was Sick all over his shoes. The (Railway Children) is a good picture, it better than Rolf Harris. He is Cracking.

Sunday, March 14, 3rd in Lent. Operation Blink and Operation Sick are still in being. I said I was going to Get him and I have got him. If you keep sniffling, he does not say anything but you can tell he does not like it, this big Vein stands out in his forehead and sort of goes throb-throb. This is Operation Sniffle. This morning I heard him say to Mr. Baker (Are they born like it or what, I don't know what I am going to do with him.) This means that I have won. He knew that I was holding my breath all through lunch time, but he does not say anything, he just Went Out. This also means, that I have won. Today I have started counting up to a billion and have got up to 10,500. I have got to get up to 25,000 before going to bed, or it will mean that I have lost the Battle. He has come back in and, he knows that I am counting up to a billion but, he is just staring at wall and drinking the whisky. It is 3.10 p.m. on Sunday, March 14, the day of Victory. He has Cracked, and must sign my Terms.

"Mamma! Mamma!"

"Who are you? What you want with my Joey?"

"Mrs. Frenelli, Joey killed a cop tonight. C'mon, kid!"

"No! My Joey's a good boy. Don't take him. He's a good boy." ·

"Mrs. Frenelli, we need good boys like Joey in the Mafia!"

"As a child psychologist of twenty years' experience, my considered opinion is that two rounds with Henry Cooper would do him the world of good."

Collapse of Small Party

By STANLEY REYNOLDS

TOMORROW, you were told, you are going to So and So's birthday party. "That will be exciting, dear. A magician is being hired. Maybe there'll be pony rides. Passing the parcel." You had been out playing on the railway tracks, jumping off the roof of an empty house or searching for that place along the river bank where they said there was quicksand (and where there *were* rattlesnakes) and you are now supposed to get excited about passing the parcel. Children's parties were something like church and school that had to be endured.

The best children's party I ever went to was in 1938 or 39 when something called a gyroplane, which was the forerunner of the helicopter, suddenly crashed in the river and freed all of us from the supervised ennui of hunt-the-slipper or blind man's buff. We raced to the river bank in search of blood and gore. It is, of course, the sort of entertainment that only the richest of parents could hope to provide; besides, the sight of aeries is nothing now, every good sized town has an airfield near it where kids can go any day in the week in the hopes of something exciting coming up, or, rather, coming down.

The second best children's party I attended was some time in the 'forties when we boys of nine or ten started to get interested in what we wore—and that was mainly trying to look like the gangsters in the movies. We went in at that time for well oiled quiffs (soap was the best actually) and flashy jewellery: a three-inch long sword tie pin with a gleaming glass ruby, worn about two inches down from the tie knot so it could be seen even with the suit coat buttoned or with your overcoat on.

This party was held in the backroom of an Italian restaurant and I remember spaghetti being thrown up on the chandelier. Do restaurants still have back rooms as opposed to private dining rooms? We still, of course, have "back-room boys" but the whole ambience of the backroom seems to have died in this century of the common man and equality, lingering only in old songs like Marlene Dietrich's "See What The Boys In The Backroom Will Have." If you have ever seen the

American Al Capone cops and wops series, *The Untouchables*, on ITV and have seen the gangsters sitting around in the backroom of the Hotsie Totsie Club in Chicago discussing in a very business-like manner who is going to get rubbed out next, you will have some sort of idea of the ambience this birthday party managed to create. Because of this special thing, I guess this party was the first trendy children's party I ever attended.

But the truth perhaps is that all children's parties have always been trendy. Traditionally the entertainments you offered children at parties have been a means of demonstrating your status and class. In the past parents followed a certain trend by affecting poshness: the hired entertainers, the pony rides, the visits to the theatre. Since the youth cult burst upon us in the Swinging Sixties parents have changed the pattern of the way they entertain their offspring on ritual occasions. They now wish to prove something other than the fact that they are rich and posh. Children's parties nowadays are the parents' means of demonstrating their own youth and sense of fun. Because of the general affluence it is no longer necessary to show that you are well off, because newspapers and magazines supply ready references on "good taste" it is no longer necessary (or, indeed, easy) to demonstrate your good taste at your child's party. What the trendy party does now is demonstrate that the parent is young in heart and taste. One can imagine the horrors of boredom this means for the child. Instead of parents supervising the games, they have started joining in as if they meant it. It makes one happy that one's own childhood parties meant stiff, starched clothes and adults who did not pay much attention to you but merely shoved you into a room where idiot games were in process. If any adult ever did join in the games it was a pretty safe bet that he or she was loaded.

We have had—quite by accident, I must say—some trendy children's parties. A pop guitarist of some note shares the same birthday as my eldest boy and he attended and sang one year. Another year a pop poet of much fame ran the party games. They both made absolutely no impression on the guests although they certainly wowed the other parents who recognised them off the telly. (Afterwards one parent asked me how much the pop poet charged to come and organise the games at a children's party and I wondered which was the least offensively trendy thing to say: that he cost me a tenner or that he had just happened along.) Since then I have often thought that trendy people could make rather a good thing out of hiring out their kids to the parties of the less than trendy, with the star turn coming when the trendy person himself comes to pick up the kid at the end of the day. How much impression this will make on the children themselves I do not know. F. Scott Fitzgerald, who knew all about this sort of stuff, opened his last novel, *The Last Tycoon*, with a snobbish reference to such a children's party. It is a line that is often quoted: "Rudolph Valentino came to my fifth birthday party." The trouble is the line is almost always misquoted—I have never heard it quoted properly—it should be, "Rudolph Valentino came to my fifth birthday party—or so I was told." And there you see it, the kid did not give a damn.

The important thing to remember in arranging a children's party is that it will hardly ever live up to their expectations, although you could buy them, I suppose, something like free parachute jumps. I am convinced that kids themselves do not like the things except for the presents and that they continue just because your child has been invited to one and you feel you must return the treat. One year my first son asked to be taken out to a night club. I thought he was "getting older" and wanted to see the way grownups live. We took him and he fell asleep on the table. Months later I happened upon a notebook of his in which he had written: "My bruthday comeing soon. Shall it be a knight club? or diner at the Cabaleer Stake Bar?"

It dawned on me then that he had been sitting in the restaurant watching the cabaret and waiting for the men in armour to come out. The Cavalier Steak Bar, which is what they removed the local pub's bowling green to build and which is a sort of Wimpy Bar, perhaps sounded even grander to him than a "knight club" when you consider that at the time he spelled "bear" as "bar." Could he have thought the place would be filled with Cavaliers driving stakes through bears?

Children do, of course, want to get let in on the mysteries of the adult world and I am sure, if the law and other parents permitted, you could give the kids a great day out by taking them to see a matinee of *Oh! Calcutta!* with a pack of grown ups up there on the stage in their bare skins. There is nothing like the sight of a bare backside to set children off roaring with laughter; it shows just what crude wit these kids have.

I have been thinking that a cheaper and more therapeutic trendy thing to do, considering the current vogue for W. C. Fields, would be to hire a W. C. Fields impersonator to come along and insult the kiddies. Fields, well beloved of NWI, was a passionate child hater, saying once: "When I was a poor and hungry boy, I vowed when I was rich and famous I would help out the poor and hungry children of the world. Then I did get rich and I thought, To hell with the little bastards anyway." He would be the perfect parent surrogate upon whom the little bastards could vent their infantile resentment—after all, Mummy and Daddy are so trendy and young these days you can't really communicate with them any more.

Pamela : ' How's your wife, Peter?'
Peter : ' She died last Tuesday.'
Pamela : ' Are you sorry?'
Peter : ' Sorry? Of course I'm sorry. I *LIKED* the woman.' [1927]

Mickey Mouse— The Rumours

By JOHN WELLS

MICKEY MOUSE, the veteran American comic, is back in London. He is here to launch the forthcoming series of his best comedies, to be shown here by the BBC in 1971.

Still wearing the big-buttoned Bermuda shorts, round-topped shoes and stitch-back gloves that made him famous, he greeted me in the foyer at Claridges with a sprightly grace that belied his seventy-one years. A simple "Hi Pal!" a gentle wave of introduction to his wife Minnie, sixty-nine, looking charming in a mauve veil, a mauve 'thirties-look handbag and mauve accessories with big high-heeled shoes, and we were sunk deep in the generous sofas, sipping martinis and talking nostalgically about the Good Old Days with Pluto, Donald, Goofy and the Twins.

But the years since Hollywood's most successful husband and wife team set audiences all over the world laughing at their zany, madcap antics have not been easy, and Mickey spoke movingly of the storms that have threatened to wreck both his career and his marriage.

"You have to remember that in those days, way back in the 'thirties, Minnie and I were called upon to project an image of extraordinary naivety. Fundamentally it was one of mischievous innocence, consistent with the behaviour of a normal, well-adjusted ten-

year-old white Anglo-Saxon Protestant American child belonging to what you would call our successful middle class." He hooked a thumb in his wide braces and frowned thoughtfully. "No liquor, no violence, no sex, and above all no social comment.

"Now Minnie and I have always been deeply committed to this whole anti-war thing, whether it was against Mussolini's Germany, or Vietnam or whatever."

"We believe war is a very terrible thing," she agreed, nodding and fluttering her endless eyelashes with a very real sincerity, "and we've always been against it, right from the very start." Mickey finished his martini and ordered another round. "But how could we convince the kids? We tried introducing satirical lines into the script, I even wanted to do a whole anti-war movie where Mickey got his call-up papers and was shot up by the Japanese, just to illustrate the whole goddam futility of it, but the studios said they'd throw us out on our ear. And we had the Twins to think of," Minnie added by way of justification, "what could we do?"

"Then it was like I said." Mickey lit a long cigar and brooded into the middle distance, musing on an old wound. "There was the strain of keeping up the image off of the set. Neither Minnie nor I ever drank excessively, but the gossip writers started in on us, and

34

boy, there wasn't a tabloid in the States didn't have some pictures of one of us being thrown out of some club or other. It got so we couldn't go out in the evening." Minnie seemed relieved to hear her husband talking so freely, and urged him to go on. "Tell him about Pluto."

Mickey took a long pull on his cigar, drained his martini, and turned to look me in the eye, his big ears silhouetted against the light.

"There was this story going around about me and Pluto. I know how it started, but there was nothing I could do about it, and it caused Minnie here a great deal of distress." Minnie nodded again, and almost whispered, "Sure, I went through hell." "So okay. Goofy was a faggot, and he didn't care who knew it. He was made that way, I guess. So okay, he used to ask Pluto and me round to the gay clubs to keep him company when he was depressed: he'd sit there at the bar with his great big teeth hanging out and his little hat all crumpled up over one eye, and we used to just drink with him. That's all there was to it. But not for those newspaper guys. Boy, they really had a ball."

This was Mickey's lowest moment, and it was a cruel twist of fate that the younger generation should choose exactly that time to turn against him. "I couldn't do a thing right. I was accused of blacking up. They used to call me Uncle Tom Mouse. They said I'd sold out and betrayed my race and class. Even my name was wrong. They said I was sneering at the Irish." Minnie laid a hand on her husband's gently shaking shoulder and ordered another round of martinis. "He even tried to join the Black Power people. He offered to change his name to Mustapha Ben Mouse, but they laughed in his face."

After that every studio in the United States was closed to him.

Today, Mickey Mouse is a sad but dignified old trooper. "We still have the Twins. They're both married, for the second time, and this is for keeps, I know. We're both very happy to be in London, and we're only sorry that Donald (now Governor Duck of California) can't be here with us. I guess we should have learned from him, really: we just never understood politics."

' AND WHY AREN'T YOU GOING TO SUNDAY SCHOOL ? '
' 'COS IT'S 'AROLD'S TURN FOR THE COLLAR.' [1920]

*"This is a hi-jack, proceed at once to Hinchley
Junior School and step on it!"*

Let Them Drink Gin

MAHOOD reports on the fightback by parents, teachers
and councils against the Tories' ban on free school milk

36

"And now children, time for 'Fire'!"

IN CASE OF EMERGENCY BREAK GLASS

"Only one of them qualifies for free milk but there is nothing in the law to say he can't share it."

"Suddenly, every school in the country wants a herd of Jersey cows for their biology class."

"Milk . . . Milk . . . Milk . . . !"

Mr & Mrs Tom Brown's Schooldays
By ALAN COREN

"The Inner London Education Authority said that crèches for schoolgirl mothers were being considered. 'With the prospect of the raising of the school-leaving age and more and more people getting married, many education experts are expecting schools to develop into family centres.'" *The Times*

"SIR! SIR!"

Mr. Griswold, cantankerous (yet lovable) Latin master of Greyfriars School, turned irritably from his blackboard, declensions hanging half-finished and dropping chalk dust. He glared at the Classics Fifth furiously. Little Bob Cherry had his hand up. A particularly obnoxious boy, Cherry, thought Mr. Griswold.

"What is it now, Cherry?"

"Please, sir, Foskett Minor's having an affair with my wife!"

The class gasped.

"Sneak!" they cried.

"SILENCE!" roared Mr. Griswold. He fixed Foskett Minor, a sloe-eyed, dissipated youth, with his eagly glower. "Is this true, Foskett?"

"Please, sir, it wasn't me, sir."

The master stepped down from his dais, and took two threatening paces into the room.

"What is that you have in your hand, Foskett?" he said.

"Me, sir? Nothing, sir."

"He's lying, sir!" shrieked Cherry. "He's got my wife's knee, sir!"

"COME OUT HERE!"

There was some confused shuffling, at the end of which Foskett Minor eased himself out of the double-desk he shared with nubile hockey queen Raquel Cherry for convenience (they were both left-handed), and walked sheepishly up the aisle.

"I do not believe you, Foskett," muttered Mr. Griswold. "You will stay behind after school and sterilise teats for the entire Economics Sixth."

"Please, sir, he can't, sir." It was careworn, faded Maureen Foskett Minor who spoke, ace O-level candidate, whose assiduous nocturnal studying had bitten so deep into the Foskett Minor marriage. "He's bathing the kids tonight on account of me doing a map showing the principal exports of Java, plus the digestive organs of the toad for Miss Borner."

Mr. Griswold sighed. He had left Balliol forty years before in order to bring the mellifluence of Virgil to generations of impressionable young ears. That was what teaching was. He ached for retirement.

"Very well, Foskett. You will write out one hundred times I MUST NOT CARRY ON WITH MRS. CHERRY."

"Yes, sir, thank you, sir," said Foskett Minor. He returned to his seat. Raquel Cherry pinched his thigh sympathetically. The class settled. Maureen Foskett Minor sobbed, once.

"Amo, amas, amat," incated Mr. Griswold, wearily, "amamus, amatis . . ."

"I say, you fellows!"

The Famous Five were lolling in the Remove, filling in their family allowance applications, fiddling tax rebates, ironing nappies, advertising for au pairs, dis-

"We were relieved to find a school that wasn't soft on uniforms."

39

"I think he's swallowed his father."

cussing the shortcomings of the inter-uterine loop, and generally behaving as schoolboys anywhere behave, when the Fat Owl burst in upon them.

"What is it now, Bunter?" cried Harry Wharton, cheery pink-cheeked rugger captain and father of four.

"Still waiting for that postal order, old fat man?" enquired sturdy prop forward Johnny Bull, glancing up from the bootee he was knitting.

"As a matter of fact, it's due any minute," said Bunter, blinking, "and I was wondering if you chaps could see your way clear to lending me £743 11s 8d until the end of the week."

"£743 11s 8d!" exclaimed Bob Cherry, who was still rankling from the fact that his wife, having left Foskett Minor, had now gone off to Le Touquet with the board monitor from 3a. "Isn't that a bit steep?"

"The bitsteepfulness of it is terrific," said Hurree Jamset Ram Singh, whose normal dusky jollity was somewhat dimmed by the recent news that three of his wives were pregnant again, and the cricket season six months away. "What is all this money for, I am asking myself?"

"Three months' outstanding interest on the mortgage, £156, three months' insurance premiums, £87 10s," moaned Bunter, "a hundred guineas for the gynaecologist, ten days in the maternity ward at £12 a day, three months' nanny salary in advance, £120, pram, bath, crib, cot, washing machine, spin-drier, three doz. nappies . . ."

"I say!" cried Frank Nugent, "Mrs. Bunter's in pod again!"

"Can't keep off it, can you, old fat man?" shouted Johnny Bull.

"The can'tkeepofffulness is terrific!" exclaimed Inky.

"What say we bump him?" yelled Harry Wharton.

With shouts of glee, the Famous Five laid hold of their podgy partner. Bunter hurtled ceilingwards!

"Leggo!" he cried, "Yarroo!"

Downstairs, the row interrupted the rest period of Mr. Quelch, scourge of the Remove, doyen of beaks.

"Wretched boys!" he muttered, "Where's my cane?"

40

"It's where we left it, ducky," murmured Raquel Cherry, who had returned from Le Touquet on the noon flight.

"Of course, of course!" snapped Quelch, snatching it from the bed. "And take those spurs off at once, wretched girl! That eiderdown is the property of the GLC."

"So I said to him, I said, it's no good you coming home and expecting a cooked dinner, putting your feet up in front of *Jackanory* and not even taken your cap off, I said, leaving your jar of frog spawn on the landing where anyone can trip over it, I said, and expecting your cod briquettes to appear out of thin air, and me stuck up 4b all day, seven months gone and studying chemistry and civics and bleeding calculus, I said, you don't want a wife, I said, you want a bloody skivvy, so he hit me with his satchel."

The other members of the Fourth Form Girls' Open Discussion Seminar sucked in their breath. Freda Wharton paused in her tale to blow her nose on her gymslip.

"And then he said, I'll be late tomorrow night again, he said, so I said that's the third time this week what is it this time, so he sort of looked away, you know the way they do——"

The Fourth Form Girls nodded sympathetically.

"——and he said, it's the Model Railway Appreciation Society, he said, and I said Oh is it really, a bit, you know, sarky, is it really, I said, last night it was the Cigarette Card Club, and the night before it was the Dinky Toy Collectors Circle, I didn't realise what a busy little bee you were, I said, are you sure it's not that bitch in 5a?"

The Seminar knitted furiously, urging her on. Outside, a lone netball slapped the concrete, as the sole unpregnant player trained toute seule.

"What *her*? he said, *her*? har-har-har don't make me laugh, she's nearly four-teen, he said, I wouldn't touch an old banger like *her*, so I said, what's that on your collar, red biro, and he said, yes as a matter of fact it is, only I can tell when he's lying, his acne starts swelling up, and I said you're a fibber, I said, right to his face, and that got him, I can tell you, so he turned to me and he said yah boo sucks knickers, he said——"

"Oh!" gasped the girls.

"——true as I'm sitting here, so I said how dare you use that filthy language in this house, I said, I'm not staying here, I'm going to me mum's and I'm taking the kids with me."

She broke down, weeping.

"So what did he say?" asked Winifred Nugent.

"He——he s-said good riddance to bad rubbish and no returns," she said, and buried her face in her sopping cardigan.

"It's always the woman who pays," said Millicent Grove, darkly.

She had been Madcap Millie Grove, once. But that was before her divorce. She was thirteen now, and life held few surprises, these days.

"It was a very expensive doll, but I think she should be made aware that two thirds of the world is starving!"

AND NOW FOR SOMEONE COMPLETELY DIFFERENT

A profile of the Prince of Wales by ANN LESLIE

AT the age of five he was voted one of the eleven best-dressed men in Europe, since when, sartorially at any rate, his career has been downhill all the way. But apart from that minor skid in his progress, you could say that things have improved no end for the Prince of Wales image-wise since the days when his career seemed littered with embarrassments such as the Stornoway Cherry Brandy incident and the Case of the Missing Exercise Book.

He admits he took life far too seriously as a little boy and even used to cry when he read some of the more patronisingly cruel remarks made about him in the press. For popular myth had it that the Royal Heir was a gawky, jug-eared little chap, dull and faintly stupid, plodding dutifully in the wake of his supercharged, flashy Boy's Own hero of a dad, making touching attempts to imitate his mannerisms and match his boundless boyhood achievements.

According to this wither-wringing press fairy-tale, the pale, puddingy, introspective little prince was flung up north into the Scottish fogs to be toughened up by Gordonstoun. And then, in case there was still some cissiness left in him, slung out east to become a cobber among the Aussies, a heartier, jock-strappier race than which it would be hard to imagine.

In fact, in spite of initial home-sickness, the Prince rather enjoyed Gordonstoun, did well and became head boy. As for all those cold showers, he insists he actually enjoyed them. Has had one voluntarily every morning ever since; shivering visitors to his Hicks-decorated Palace study maintain he still preserves a pretty Gordonstounian attitude to fresh air as well.

What's more, he adored Australia and got on extremely well with the Aussies who showered him with endearments like Pommy Bastard. After which of course he proceeded against all the odds to moderately enchant some of his least loyal subjects, the dour tomato-slinging Welsh nationalists who were thick as thistles around the Royal heels at Aberystwyth.

The point is that he revels in the tough outdoor life. He recently "fell in love" with Kenya by going on a camel safari, an example he says of the "enlightened masochism" he goes in for. Once he even leapt "like a mountain goat" according to an equerry, to the top of a 3,500-ft. Welsh mountain, followed by the press—a

"Well, at least I don't have to worry about my son's future, he's selfish, dirtyminded, mean, and heartless."

breed normally averse to leaping like mountain goats towards anything other than bars and telephones—puffing up crossly in his wake.

In fact, ever since Prince Charles was officially unveiled on the Royal stage as a star in his own right with a major speaking role, all that stuff about the dull, shy, introspective prince has been chucked overboard and a general ecstasy over the wit and brilliance of the chap has taken over instead. To do him justice, he seems almost as embarrassed by some of the excesses of the new image as he was depressed by the old.

He has but to play a passable cello and one might think from the gasps and sighs of admiration that we have a royal Casals on our hands, secretly straining at the leash to hit the concert circuits of the world, or that some dazzling cultural Camelot is about to break upon the amiable philistinism of Buckingham Palace.

In fact he took up the cello in his first year at Cambridge, dropped it in his second to take up acting, and has not played the instrument since. He enjoyed the cello—and indeed the acting—partly because of the sheer pleasure it gave him to be part of a working team to which he belonged by merit rather than by social status.

No sooner had he proved that he was a more than adequate student, scholastically worthy of his place at Cambridge, than it was instantly touted around that he was by nature a frustrated academic. He's recently been described as having "the gentlemanly tranquillity, almost softness, of an intellectual" and one of his tutors thought that given half a chance "he would have made a very good schoolmaster." He himself laughs at the idea that all he really longed to do was become some sort of earnest academician in a Fair-isle cardy, listening to Vivaldi and scratching out interminable theses on cargo cults in central Papua. Three years of academic life he feels were just about his lot. . . .

If he hadn't been born into his present job he admits he might have liked to have been a farmer, his real passion being the countryside, and indeed one can best imagine him in some bucolic setting, striding amiably about in ancient brogues, exchanging pleasantries with tenants, accompanied by muddy gun-dogs with blood and feathers in their teeth. But even that job would not have been enough: he'd want to do other things as well.

He is temperamentally prone to dart from one quiet enthusiasm to another but manages to go about all his varied activities with an air of conscientiousness rather than of gay abandon, which somehow protects him from any suggestion of unsuitable light-mindedness.

Of course in theory, being pretty good at most things but outstanding at nothing is unfashionable in a technological age where ideally a bright young man

"You're supposed to blow them out!"

is expected to grab a white coat and specialise brilliantly in something like low-temperature physics, and never mind that he can't tie his shoelaces or tell one breed of cow from another. But in fact one of the secrets of Prince Charles's success with his public lies precisely in the fact that he does everything rather well, but nothing *offensively* well.

With varying degrees of skill he can fly, shoot, fish, play polo, the cello, and the trumpet, act a little, speak Welsh and, when called upon, make jolly and apposite speeches on any subject from the importance of float-glass making to the future of the herring industry—and do so with a practised ease which is perhaps a trifle chilling in a twenty-two year old.

But although he's lost his early shyness, he still has a tendency to blush which reminds you, if you think he's a little too polished to be true, that he is after all just a very nice, perhaps even vulnerable young man who is bearing up extraordinarily well to the demands of a faintly ridiculous, rather lonely and often skull-crushingly boring job. Indeed the one thing he really is very good at is, mercifully, the job into which he was born, that of being principal understudy to the head of the most successful and indefatigable team of professional garden-party givers, tape-snippers and ceremonial tree-planters in the world.

Whether he intends to be or not, he is often thoroughly disarming. He disarmed one tough lady journalist I know who, after weeks of hacking her way up the Palace beanstalk past thickets of courtiers, finally won an interview with him, jammed into a half-hour space between official engagements. As she was about to thank him for sparing her the time, he forestalled her by saying disingenuously "I'm so glad you could spare the time to see me—I know how busy you journalists are. I do hope you won't think it's been wasted."

Well, yes I know it's not subtle but it worked. She was struck all of a loyal heap, dimpled prettily and somehow forgot to ask all those gritty abrasive questions she'd thought up while cleaning her teeth back home in fearless republican Hampstead.

He is of course constantly accused of being too remote from everyday life as she is lived in Surbiton or the Balls Pond Road, and indeed mocked the cliché himself in a sketch he wrote for the Cambridge revue in which he stood beneath an umbrella and intoned "I lead a sheltered life." Of course he's remote, he admits, but he tries as hard as possible not to be.

One story frequently repeated to prove how vastly out of touch the future King of England is with his subjects-to-be, recalls how, during a tour of Welsh colliery country, he asked a large lady holding two children by the hand whether she was their nanny. Even Prince Charles however is not so remote as to imagine that nannies are a normal fixture among the slag-heaps of pit villages. His courtiers worked themselves into interesting knots attempting to explain that what the Prince had *really* meant to say was that the lady was their *granny*, thus displaying impeccable local knowledge, because you see "nanny" in certain areas actually means "granny" and it was thus a compliment to . . . etc. etc.

In fact it was simply a Royal Joke gone wrong. (On the whole he feels his spell in comic revue was a help in learning how to time and deliver a Royal Joke successfully.) The Royal Joke, at least as delivered by Prince Charles, is again by his own admission, a rather light-hearted facetious thing which loses whatever esprit it might have had when seized in the relentless butterfly net of the press and set down in concrete for posterity.

He is not witty, and would have to watch it if he were—wit, as opposed to "having a sense of humour" being regarded as somewhat smart-alecky in Royals, even a bit un-English.

One suspects that Prince Charles's personal salvation has been the discovery of the private and public uses of a sense of humour. Beneath the jaunty, self-deprecating badinage, he takes his job as seriously as ever, but by mocking it publicly largely disarms criticism. In fact the mockery shouldn't fool anyone—if he didn't believe in his job he couldn't possibly be as good at it as he is. Grand ritual these days always trembles on the edge of the theatre of the absurd, and the only reason, to my mind, that the Investiture didn't degenerate into High Camp, despite the trendy

"See if you can find a fire-engine—he wants one for his birthday."

perspex sets and Lord Snowdon's bottle-green jump-suit with its theatre-curtain tassels, was the utter belief in the goings-on on the part of the two principals concerned.

Obviously he is hardly typical of most other members of his generation. He really does believe in the old-fashioned Service virtues of leadership and devotion to duty and his spell in the Navy is thus not a decision imposed upon him by his family against his will.

He doesn't even look much like other young men of his age either, but then he is a PRO for an institution and it is bad PR to antagonise half one's squarer clients by looking too way-out. But in any case there simply isn't a frustrated hippie longing to burst out of the shapeless hacking jackets at which the mandarins of the *Tailor and Cutter* like to point their scissors in scorn. He *likes* baggy clothes, seems to have an ideological commitment to turn-ups not even shared by his father, and says long hair is uncomfortable. Besides one is forced to admit that long hair would indeed look somewhat foolish trailing out like lily roots from beneath some of the more absurd regimental head-gear he is obliged to don from time to time.

In fact, all his tastes and attitudes are rather touchingly reminiscent of the sort of young men who, decades ago, marched forth to become dedicated District Commissioners in the African bush. Even his slang smacks more of Greyfriars school than of the Woodstock generation—"rozzers" for "police" instead of "fuzz." In his study he has, among other things, bound copies of the old schoolboy comics, Lion and Tiger.

He has none of the rather seedy glamour, the café-society charisma of the Snowdons, nor the strong-willed, sometimes rather surly sex-appeal of his sister. He is as conscientious and dedicated as his mother, but with a greater social ease. He adores and respects his father whom he once described as "the wisest man I've ever met," resembles him in many ways, and shares some of his outspokenness—he recently roundly ticked off a photographer for being a litter-lout in a Kenya game reserve. On the other hand, he has none of the faintly petulant naval commander's irritability towards "bloody stupid questions" which is inclined to make his father one of the less popular royals with Grub Street, whose denizens can be remarkably thin-skinned and react like scalded cats to royal wisecracks.

He is not particularly extrovert by nature, admitting that at home among friends he is never the one to dominate the conversation by sheer force of personality. Oddly enough, he finds public occasions easier to deal with than private ones: at least in the former his role is clearly defined. In private social occasions the ambivalence of attitudes towards him disturbs him because it disturbs those around him.

Which is why perhaps the suggestion made to the Prince by Lord Butler that he should enter the Foreign Office rather than the Services was rejected. The presence of the Prince of Wales as a lowly Third Secretary would be disruptive, it was felt, to the life of the Embassy. The services are at least used to having Royalty in their midst.

This ambivalence in social attitudes towards him has made him a rather lonely young man: few people at school or university wished to be accused of toadying to a prince and most tended to steer clear of him. Up till a year or so ago this loneliness still upset him somewhat but now he is far too busy for it to disturb him much. Besides as he once pointed out, he's pretty used to it by now and really rather enjoys the pleasure of his own company, which is why he loves the solitary joys of fishing so much. In any case, despite his apparent ease and openness, close friends of the family say there is an inner remoteness in his personality, a secret still-centre which makes him ultimately difficult to get to know very intimately.

His romantic life, if any, is both discreet and of necessity, circumscribed. In theory he is the most eligible date in the world, but as he must have learnt to his cost by now, some girls do not view the privilege of being taken to, say, the theatre, by a royal prince with unalloyed pleasure, accompanied as it is by a wild hailstorm of flashbulbs and gossip-column speculation.

He is most unlikely to marry any stylish miss totally unsuited to the job of being Queen. As he pointed out once "the advantages of marrying a princess for instance, or someone from a royal family is that they do know what happens."

His great great grandfather, poor Prince Bertie, burst into tears when presented on the morning of his seventeenth birthday with a memo from his parents which said "Life is composed of Duties"—and then tried to drown the knowledge in years of raffish high-living. One suspects that Bertie's great great grandson is not only resigned to a life composed of duties, decently and devotedly performed, but actually rather looks forward to the prospect. . . .

"And what have you been doing with yourself since you left school?"

45

"Good morning, madam. Do you have any children that want to be doctors?"

For Fear of Finding Something Worse ...

ALAN BRIEN on a world without Nannies

THE way I heard it, Prince Charles was on a progress round Wales when he stopped to speak to this ordinary kid holding the hand of an old woman in black, and he asked the boy—"Is she your Nanny?". Now the left-wing journalist, an Old Etonian, creased himself at the idea of Charles not realising that ordinary kids do not have Nannies. But the right-wing journalist, who's been to an elementary school, pointed out that the Prince obviously knew that ordinary kids often called their grandmother "Nanny", and creased himself at the idea of a left-wing journalist not realising this. It is difficult to adjudicate on the merits of the two interpretations without consulting Prince Charles which I have not been able to do.

Where I come from, grandmothers are usually called "Nanna", and if Prince Charles had chosen to wander around up there the dispute could not have arisen. I wonder if there is a best-seller in The Rise and Fall of the British Nanna? Or is it essential to have a name like Jonathan Gathorne-Hardy with its agreeable sound of a small person tobogganing downstairs on a tin tray?

I didn't actually have a Nanna myself, being the last drop in a downpour of children, arriving after everyone thought the storm was over. But most of my friends and neighbours seemed to have two. The grandfathers having bleached, dried up and been carried away on the breeze, like the surplus spouses of spiders, the Nannas left behind felt obliged to divide male and female roles between them.

One would have a face like a shillelagh, as wiry as a footballer in a cassock, a cross between Old Mother Riley and Canon Collins, with Lowry feet and Francis Bacon eyes. It was not so much that she was mannish, as human-ish, an active principle of nature which had progressed beyond such petty distinctions as gender.

This one never appeared to sleep, but simply to hibernate for half an hour or so, semi-upright in an uncomfortable armchair, suspended by an invisible thread like a chrysalis. The rest of the time, she would materialise on and off, like a flashing bulb in an old-fashioned electric sign, all over the house, at the front door, the back door, at an upstairs window, at the bottom of the backyard, a character in a kitchen-sink farce.

Her language was appalling. Having survived beyond all taboos about sex, excretion, money and class, she spoke the dialect of the unconscious, using the most direct word for the thing, regardless of the inhibition and modesties of her listeners. I remember a Nanna-in-law who, much to our delight, would scrutinise any visitor clinically, like a consultant surgeon, and say suddenly—"What's the matter with you? Do you want the shit-house? It's outside."

As a substitute child-minder, a stand-in for your careful, conscientious mother, this Nanna was in another dimension. Nothing was allowed to interrupt her random trajectory, her restless rearrangement of her few possessions against the arrival of Death, and we knew she would have out-faced and up-staged the Archangel Gabriel, just as she did the rent-man, the school inspector and the election canvasser who might just as well have been emissaries from Mars or runaway, mad axemen from Broadmoor. The myth was that, having brought up one generation, she must be exceptionally equipped to look after the next. But this was little more than a convenient fiction, believed by none of us.

The other Nanna was fat, somnolent, permanently enthroned, a Lady Buddha in gutta-percha, an inflatable Queen Victoria with a slight leak. She conferred

"Never mind lad, we'll try for a Government loan."

47

sweets, sticky and unnaturally warm, from some kind of kangaroo pouch situated under her buttocks, as if they were orders and decorations. She was content that children should stay out of sight, and unheard, so long as they clocked in from time to time, such as on their birthdays. She spoke with distant condescension of her rival Nanna, as of some upstart Lambert Simnel or Perkin Warbeck who was forever raising rebel bands in the marches or on the borders but would never dare approach the imperial capital.

Occasionally, she would convene a durbar, when tributary princelings were expected to file through her court, bearing small gifts, usually something picked up in her ante-room, before being subjected to a ritual examination of ears, socks and underwear, to the kettle-drum rattle of a clicking tongue, like an Ann Miller tap dance. It was not an onerous duty, we discovered, as the same two or three obsequious, and relatively clean, descendants could be continually presented.

My only Nanna-in-blood was my father's elder sister, Auntie Polly, who combined the functions and powers of both species. Perhaps because of her name, I always thought of her as some kind of supernatural parrot. She hopped around her house, from perch to perch, jangling the decor as she moved, halting only to give us a sharp, affectionate nip to keep us alert.

When I first began to take an interest in politics, dividing the town into Capulets and Montagues, I was shocked to discover that she was the darling of the local Tory organisation, collected every polling day to be taken to vote in a large car, ferried on to the pictures and then returned home at the end of the double feature. She was a prize exhibit as a proletarian Conservative. But my father insisted that she had never been known to support anything but Labour. One day, I asked her if this was true. "Sssh", she said. "How many motors have we got to drive an old lady around? The ballot is secret."

I'm afraid there is no dramatic pattern in the rise and fall of the working-class Nanna. They were there in the beginning, are now and ever shall be—safety nets and long-stops, umpire, referee and buffer in the match between the generations. The upper classes should be so lucky as to have them. The middle-class granny has a blue rinse, goes off on cruises, and only baby-sits if it's a good night and there's colour telly. I doubt whether I could stretch my material into a book. Who, I wonder, was the Pope's Nanny?

"There's always Tory politics of course, depending on how
attractive your wife is."

CHRISTMAS KIDSBOOKS

from the Michael Heath bookshop

① THE MOST INTERESTING CHILDREN'S (OR SHORT PEOPLE, AS THEY PREFER TO BE CALLED) BOOK THIS YEAR IS "THE NIGHT PORTER". ALL ABOUT A BOY WHO SLEEPWALKS THROUGH THE WORLD OF FRITZ LANG. AND MEETS AND BEFRIENDS PETER LORRE. JUST BEFORE THE CLIMAX, THE BOY WAKES UP TO FIND THAT HE'S STUCK IN HIS POTTY. THIS WONDERFUL BOOK HAS WON EVERY AWARD GOING IN AMERICA. IT'S A PITY THAT ALL CHILDREN IN THEIR RIGHT MIND HATE IT. THE GUILT PRESS £2.85.

② NEXT, I REALLY MUST RECOMMEND A SERIES OF BOOKS FOR THE VERY YOUNG, FROM YUGOSLAVIA. DECEPTIVELY SIMPLE, THESE BOOKS REALLY ARE VERY SIMPLE. THAMES & JUMP PRESS 35p.

③ THE NEW COMBINE "LIBERATED CHILD'S MEDIA" HAVE PRODUCED SOME BEAUTIFUL CHILDREN'S (DEPRIVED ADULTS AS THEY CALL THEMSELVES) BOOKS FOR THE 3-5 YEAR OLD. NO PRICE-YOU ARE TO STEAL THEM.

④ TO BALANCE THIS. WHY NOT BUY THE "TED HEATH CHILDREN'S BED-SIDE BOOK," CAPITALIST PRESS £9.95? CONTAINS SOME FINE UPLIFTING STORIES TO BE READ BY NANNY.

THIS IS A RATHER SAD BOOK AS THE DUCK IS SHOT IN THE END. STILL I THINK MOST HEALTHY. CHILDREN WILL FIND IT UPLIFTING.

EVERYTHING THE KING TOUCHES TURNS TO GOLD AND HE GETS HAPPIER AND HAPPIER, IN FACT HE DIES LAUGHING.

⑤ THE "POP UP POLLUTION BOOK" SHOULD BE NICE UNTIDY REMINDER FOR YOUR CHILDREN THIS POLLUTED CHRISTMAS. AWARE PRESS £1.50

HEATH

The Very Young Ones

By ANGELA MILNE

HAVE you ever thought that children seem to be starting life awfully early these days? A visit to Mr. and Mrs. Trend's family would convince you. Not one of this numerous brood is a teenager yet, but all, in the words of their father, haven't wasted any time getting with it.

When I called at the rambling North London house little Jacko lay asleep in his carry-cot after a day at the studios. He had been having his voice filmed, said his proud mother. "You'll hear him as the fretful yell the nervy housewife hears before she uses the quick furniture polish, and the contented gurgle after. And he's lined up next week for a margarine pram sequence. It's hard work getting him and the other two around—but I love it," laughed Mrs. Trend, stuffing pound notes into a jug.

Josephine and Sam bounced up and I was asked if I recognised them. They did look vaguely familiar and I could accept their father's claim that they had been shouted "Belt up" at by viewers most often of any children in Britain. "But the rainwear in the women's mag ads are Josephine's real thing," said Mrs. Trend. "Tell how you keep your figure, dear."

Josephine said she ate everything, especially all those free cereals, but wore a foundation garment as one could not start too young. She was fond of pets but had no time for boy friends. No, she would not mind starting school in 1964 though it would be hard giving up £2,000 a year and the perks and she'd heard primary schoolchildren were forbidden wigs. Sam, still absent-mindedly wearing his working spectacles, took them off to show me they were only frames. "I wear them when I talk about ingredients," he explained.

Sam's twin Moira was not at home and from an excited babel I learnt of her good luck. "The answer to little Katharine Douglas, that's what her rich auntie's grooming her for," beamed Mrs. Trend. "Sable boiler-suit, rocket flight, tea with President Ayub Khan, I don't know what isn't planned for that lucky child!"

"Got the VIP lounge walk after only a week's rehearsals," nodded Mr. Trend from his armchair. I asked him if his children's successes had enabled him to retire but he said No; he happened to be on strike for a shorter week, needing the overtime to keep Sarah and Jean in hair-styles. Those two were a proper

Man in School by Larry

drug on the market with their education and beauty care. As if to prove his words the girls burst into the room, flinging down satchels, showing me their platinum-rinsed, elaborately dressed heads—"we just love Maison Twinge now they've done it up like a coffee-bar with rubber plants and a rocking-horse"— and settling in a corner with earphones and radio. "They always listen now it isn't called *Children's Hour*," said their mother. "That was a fine way to treat seven- and eight-year-olds! But the BBC's got a bit of psychology now."

There was a rhythmic thumping from the next room and somebody said Graham was back. We found him, a stocky crew-cut boy of ten, crouching by a gramophone. "Having to work it by hand because the autochange has gone again," whispered Mrs. Trend. "And after a hard day at school! No wonder he looks pale. Of course he looks even paler at week-ends in his black jeans and black leather jacket. But fancy, only ten and he knows the names of all the Shadows!"

Between "She's Not You" and "Sealed With A Kiss" I asked Graham what fascinated him so about pop music, since it could not possibly be the words. He mumbled something that sounded like "What words?" and seemed to be in a kind of trance; but at tea, at which he did not appear, Sarah put away the free lipstick she had received with her *Teenbeat Girl* and said that what got Graham got her. Pop music was always the same, that was why you liked it, you tuned to Lux and there you were all evening with endless records, all cosy and secure.

Mr. Trend nodded and said young people needed security. Hadn't had enough of it, with these child-rearing books that told a mum how to act and talk, which she did, all sweet and forbearing, then broke out *her* way so the poor children didn't know where

they were. All these strikes, he added, had started him thinking. Mrs. Trend said yes, and was telling us about a lovely new pop singer just Graham's age when we were joined by Yvonne, a strapping girl with straight dark hair and no lipstick. Surely, I inquired, here was a teenager?

"Well yes, I suppose I am," confessed Yvonne, easing her shoes off and taking a non-fattening biscuit. "Though I won't actually *be* twelve till Thursday. Oh! it'll be wonderful to be grown up. All I can do now is get sent home from school for wearing my charm bracelet round my ankle. But soon I'll be on the important things like World Youth Week records with twenty-three of us in one dustbin and holding umbrellas up at Prom last nights . . . What do I want with my life? You mean careerwise? I'm writing a biology textbook, they say textbooks are the big money in the literary world now. But I want to do some real writing too, so I've put in for reviewing on *Disc*."

As we watched Sam and Josephine on TV ("their teeth are worth money, *they* don't eat these toffee bars they go on about") I heard how the whole of this go-ahead family frequently appeared on the screen. Thomas, aged eleven, who wore real spectacles and had slipped into the room unnoticed, played the harpsichord like Bobby Darin and led a talent prize quartet. Yvonne was often seen in quizzes—"You remember her, she's the one who's read *Lorna Doone*" —while Sarah, Jean and Graham (Yvonne considered herself too old) were regular members of the *Juke Box Jury* audience, the girls being in special demand for their Fair Isle jumpers and dopey expressions. "Though I'd like to get that cameraman who does the feet," said Mrs. Trend angrily. "The way he lingers over my two's sling-back stilettos and ankle-socks you'd think he was a health-shoe specialist doing propaganda!"

The same three had also acted in *The Young Ones*, being exactly the age for Cliff Richard fans, and had also been engaged by a cinema manager, when the film was generally released, to attend as many performances as possible. "Me in a kid's Wyatt Earp hat," said Graham bitterly. "But we earned our free LPs—we stamped and squealed like in the film and the odd grown-up that was there would blink in a square old way as if" —his solemn face showed the hint of a smile— "as if we were *too young*."

It did seem a funny thing to say of this bustling family, pressing ever towards the new horizons opened by astute business minds. As we said goodbye Mrs. Trend cooed over the carry-cot "I wonder what lies ahead for little Jacko!" Who doesn't?

51

Children –
This Concerns You!

How to make use of the proposed Schools Ombudsman

by HANDELSMAN

*"Now you listen to **me**, Mrs. Thatcher. Either we get that milk first thing tomorrow, or you'll be out of a job quicker than you can say 'Party Political Broadcast'."*

"Not only do you exploit children; you are a traitor to your sex, a veritable 'Doris Day'. Go!— and never teach needlework again."

"We are glad to report that you are less sadistic than last term, but there has been no significant improvement in your views, which remain deplorably stodgy. In the matter of personal appearance, we note with disapproval that you persist in cutting your hair."

"I was against voluntary schooling, but I must admit it facilitates individual instruction."

$$x + x + x + x = 4x$$

"Oh! Don't stop! This is even more fun than the other way."

"When we get an ombudsfrog, we can go to a biology class and dissect somebody."

SMALL VIEW

BASIL BOOTHROYD

I'm practically walking,
So next it's going to be talking.

By May
I'll have a few things to say.

If you want a sample,
Take the pram jams, for example:
First thing everybody seems to get after a marriage
Is a baby-carriage,
For parking al fresco
Outside Marks and Sparks or Tesco,
And passers-by who have to walk in the gutter
Probably don't think we hear the remarks they utter.
What?
No, they're certainly *not*
Things I'd care to repeat . . .
Though I suppose you have to make allowances for
     people when a bus runs over their feet,
Even if
The whiff
Of general adult resentment serves
To shred a kiddy's nerves.
And from where I sit, I must say,
There's plenty of resentment around today;
I don't see why;
They seem to buy
Anything that catches their eye
While I

Have to watch them staggering out with it
And piling me up to the snout with it.
As it invariably includes,
Besides frozen foods
(And damned cold they can be
Stacked on a person's knee),
Sharp-cornered Kleenex for Men,
Miracle cleansers with free ballpoint pen,
Monster packs
Of TV snacks,
Fruit
Oozing into your woolly boot,
Beer
On your ear,
And something with an unidentifiable smell
Propped on your fontanelle . . .
You could contract a phobia,
Spending half your waking hours under this blasted
     cornucopia,
No wonder when a stranger with a face like a
     kangaroo
Bends over and says boo,
Baby girls and boys
Reply with a rude noise.

We need a spokesman, that's our trouble,
And I'll be it, once I can spoke anything but a
     bubble,
What we need for the good of our tiny Ids,
Is fewer people and more kids,
Which would suit us fine,
Oh, yes—and a ban on all prams but mine,
(Which happens to represent my Pa's
Views on cars).

No,
Though,
Taking the broader spectrum . . .
If I can just shift this impulse-bought aerosol
     suede-cleaner out of my rectrum . . .
If you ask me
I don't see
Why the what's-its-name, affluent society
Is such a mass of anxiety.
Good grief,
It's nothing but beef, beef, beef.
You'd think with a full belly,
Colour telly,

*"Well, if they **don't** go 'chuff-chuff
anymore, how **do** they go?"*

Cleaner,
Cortina,
Hi-
Fi,
National Health feet,
Central heat,
The amazing
Boon of double-glazing,
And all
The things you have to scratch along without if
    you're one of the starving millions of Bengal,
That it'd be sweetness and light
All day and night.

Not so,
Though.

They worry all the time,
About crime,
Drugs,
Bugs,
Squeezes and freezes,
Fatal diseases,
The rotten standard of BBC comics,
Flare-ups at the London School of Economics,
Natural gas
Or something equally crass
Like should someone disembowel
Enoch Powell,
Or is the Commonwealth a failure
And, if so, is the Queen wasting her time in New
    Zealand and Australia?
It makes a tot
Go hot
The way they prickle
Over Tasmanian nickel,
Or Willy Brandt not knowing how to get in
To East Berlin,
And everyone being at you
About where, given the say-so, you'd personally
    stick the Churchill statue,
And what's all this fuss about the Asians for?
I mean, I get on great with little Mukund next door.

Mind you, I blame half these agitations
On what they call modern communications,
Chiefly the papers'
Capers:
Not that I read them, but
I've got ears in my nut
And you'd never believe the beating they're handed
Whenever I'm in range of someone opening the
    Mirror, *News* or *Standard*,
"Madman Slays Three—
Honey, that's terrible, could have been you, Baby,
    and me!"

(Never mind that the item referred
To some remote Kurd
Unlikely to repeat
The performance up our particular street) . . .
"It says here a man in Manila
Was eaten by a pet gorilla,
Also his daughter,
They think it was something in the water . . ."
"What dear?
I didn't hear,
I was reading where it says there's a change in the
    four-minute warning,
It's down to two, as of this morning . . ."
What's it to them, I mean, if Mia Farrow
Strays off the straight and narrow,
Or Archbishops in Cyprus
Get shot at by snyprus?
It's time to worry about rabies
When it starts getting the babies.
Ah, well, there we are. It's going to take a lot of
    arranging,
But it isn't only us kids that need changing.
The minute I can talk I shall start a ginger-group on
    Mummy:
And you know something? She'll be in like a shot
    with that perishing dummy.

Well, you wait,
Mate.

I suppose I've got to go through the Beanstalk,
    Three Bears and Little Jack Horner—
After that, watch it: I'll be at Speakers Corner.

*"I've never been a great believer in all that child
psychology stuff . . ."*

Babes in the Wood

LARRY'S
School Outing

The Fig Generation

ROBERT MORLEY

IN Folkestone I still expect to be patted, to be recognised as the little boy who delighted them all in my sailor suit. I like to return whenever I feel the shadows beginning to lengthen, to ring the doorbells of the houses and explain to whoever opens the door that this was where I lived when I was a child. We were always moving round in Folkestone. We left The Leas and set ourselves up in Augusta Road. We had a house in Earls Avenue and another in Turketel Road, not at the same time, of course. We weren't rich by Folkestone standards. If there's one thing young people lack today I am afraid it is Folkestone standards. It may well be what's wrong with the country. Who today rides in a bath-chair? "I think," the doctor would say, soon after the spots disappeared, the rash faded, the temperature subsided, "I think he could go out for a little, in a bath-chair." And in a bath-chair I went. The very best Folkestone bath-chairs had folding mahogany shutters with windows through which one looked out on to the patient back of the attendant, silently plodding ahead. With the shutters drawn one was insulated from the noise, a silent world with the delicious uncertainty that one might have suddenly become stone deaf. It was necessary sometimes to open the shutters and shout, just to reassure oneself. Mother steered from the back. Convalescence was achieved slowly, thoroughly, but achieved. Young people nowadays never get a chance to get better in bath-chairs. What's lacking is "style."

On Sundays the bands played on The Leas. The bandstands were situated at some distance from one another, but it was possible, by positioning one's bath-chair accurately, to listen to the Grenadiers with the right ear, while the Marines enchanted the left. No wonder I am not fond of discotheques. I was spoilt in my youth by the real thing.

What gave Folkestone, and in a sense myself, character, were the cliff hangers, the lifts. I travelled in them on an average at least once a week, always my heart was in my mouth. It is this sense of danger that makes life sweet. I am numbed by the blaseness of astronauts, those laconic voices revealing their boredom. Even their names appear to me subnormal—Pete, Greg. My sister, who is called Margaret, and I, who was christened Adolf, used to scream loudly just before take off. Countdown was signalled by closing the sliding doors, and then there would be the terrifying surge of water. We would look up at the seagulls circling far, far overhead, at the tiny figures in the car which was about to crash down on our heads, and scream. Of course it never really hit us. We used to pass the car halfway.

Sometimes it would be quite full, whereas our lift would contain only my sister, myself and our governess. I always wondered whether they adjusted the weight of the water, how it was that we rose and they sank without unseemly haste, while the balance was so unequal. At the top, splashdown was always carried out without a hitch. The car was accurately positioned to enable us to step out of it and hurry home to tea. Our governess was called Miss Faithful. She was called a lot of other things as well, by which I mean she didn't keep changing her name, it was we who changed our governess. My sister and I simply couldn't keep a governess. They came and went. We used to stick pins in them. What idiots they must have been to desert their posts, to cry halt. What trouble they caused my parents by deserting so frequently. But despite the incessant upheavals, the comings and goings, dismissals, resignations and engagements, my father and mother never lost hope, never surrendered to the modern and quite ridiculous assumption that parents can raise their own offsprings. What singles my generation out is this lack of coarseness so prevalent today. Young people are no longer refined. They never had a governess to show them how it should be done. For if our governesses had anything in common besides a deadly loathing for my sister and myself, it was this air of ineffable refinement, evinced in every action which they allowed us to observe, and which they encouraged us to emulate. The washing of hands, for instance before every meal. They never held their fingers under the tap, or left a smudge on the towel. Soup spoons travelled outwards across the plate, bread was crumbled, toast was cut, butter was spread evenly. Tidiness was maintained, handkerchiefs were kept in sachets, pins arranged symmetrically in pincushions, bookmarkers placed between pages. Our governesses were always prepared for inspection, and they tried to keep us similarly at the ready. I wonder sometimes what was the reason behind the rule. Why did they insist on everything always being in its proper place? Was it only because when it was time for them to pack and go, they would know where everything was? And why did they go so often? There are pictures still in existence of my sister and me at various ages—dear, jolly little things we seemed—but not to our governesses. When I undress at night I let all my clothes slide on to the floor—the big shelf, Miss Kipps used to call it—and there they stay until morning. My clothes seem to last as long as everyone else's. They may have to go to the cleaners more often, but I have saved hours of my life through defying Miss Kipps and not arranging them neatly on a chair, or hanging them in a cupboard. But what of the generation who never knew Miss Kipps? What pleasure would it be for them in middle age to let their clothes lie around? Or if it comes to that, to hold their hands under a tap, or not even to wash them at all? They will be simply doing what they have always done. They will never know the pleasure of not doing what they were brought up to do.

For in the tight little world in which I was hatched and reared, there was tremendous security, a security, largely unknown today, and based I think on three great faiths—Keplers, Dr. Parrish and Syrup of Figs. These were the three great patent medicines which no household could afford to be without. Keplers was imbibed after breakfast. There was a special Kepler spoon kept in the medicine cupboard. A delicious treacly substance which wound itself out of the jar and down the gullet. Parrish's Chemical Food was taken through a glass tube, otherwise, legend has it, one's teeth turned black. The excitement of this ceremony could hardly be exaggerated. As the tube was clenched between the teeth, one entered the world of Jules Verne, H. G. Wells and R. L. Stevenson. The mixture thus assimilated, one handed the tube back and hurried to the glass to examine one's teeth. Syrup of Figs never quite managed the rapture of the others. It was always offered in a spoon over-large for the mouth, had a tendency to spill and stain the pyjamas, and because one had already cleaned one's teeth, was seldom followed by a sweet. One had to content oneself with a throat pastille. Bath-chairs, governesses, patent medicines made me what I am today. How sad that the younger generations would infinitely prefer to be without any of us.

The Two-Father Family

CLEMENT FREUD, who has lost all faith in Santa, explains

WHEN I was a child I thought as a child . . . but my parents were radical agnostic intellectuals, always more prone to look at the psycho/economical aspects of the festive season than believe in Father Christmas.

Presents arrived in orderly profusion but there was limited magic.

When I became a parent I determined that the order of things would be changed. I did not buy a Father Christmas set or open an account with Rent-a-beard . . . but we encouraged spirited mid-December talk on the subject of reindeers and on the appointed day I did my damnedest to properly perpetuate the myths. I recall way back in 1956 dialling 0 for a 3 am call and being told that 0 no longer dealt with calls, one now dialled INF and INF said "3 am eh? Do your children suffer from insomnia; I did the stockings before I went on the night shift."

"Each man must fight the good fight within the context of his conscience—Karl Marx," I said to the man, to which he replied "You're a proper little . . ." the last word seemed to me to have no place at all in a yuletide vocabulary.

If my child did wake, I argued, her vision of Father Christmas would be one of bemused voluminous shuffling . . . I was then rather fat, took sleeping pills, drank more than I do now and sported a reversible dressing gown—the B side being red. We also had this rather smart thing of buying socks in pairs, giving our daughter sock no. one to lay at the end of her bed and replacing it at the appointed hour by sock no. two which necessitated no more than a smart substitution instead of a prolonged filling. It is regrettable to report that no one was fooled for long.

I recall successive Christmas breakfasts at which my logical children (more came as Christmases went by) appeared, complaining that Father Christmas had about as much idea of the order of things as, well, as Dad.

"I mean honestly, everyone knows that Matthew doesn't like tangerines."

My wife, always quick on the uptake was on that occasion heard to remark "does that mean Matt got the nail scissors and the silver-mesh tights; I told you I should have done it."

I let it pass pleading that Father Christmas, what with one thing and another a lot of this, quite apart from a profusion of that, may have become confused but as Matt had indeed received those very things, the dread Mrs. F. was therein after appointed officer i/c distribution while my job was more that of exchequer, without portfolio or much power. Since our first child and our optimum efforts to do all the right things Christmases have actually become more rewarding.

Two years ago, a small face appeared at the door of my study at around 11.30 pm with the words "I say, Dad, shouldn't Father Christmas have struck by now?" I asked him to sit down and argued that as our postman, milkman, and dustmen always started at the Maida Vale end of the road, the chances were that Father Christmas worked to a similar plan.

He listened attentively, yawned politely and said "well, don't be long; the others are waiting up."

I like to think that the seeds of disillusionment were planted by a man in John Barnes department store who once snapped at a bright-eyed daughter to "get yer ticket at the far counter" if she wanted a present from him . . . "and he smelt of Guinness" said our mother's help, who was something of a wine snob. But I may be wrong. It just could be that progressive schools and picture books in which mummies and daddies are seen in beds on top of one another with the caption of "this is how people do it" have replaced the need for pushing the responsibility of minor gifts on to anonymous doppelgänger.

"Oh my God! . . . his report says he might be Prime Minister one day!"

*"She's playing abortion clinics and wants you to be a taxi-driver
at London Airport."*

NO GAP AT ALL

PATRICK RYAN

BUT by the millennial creep of evolution, naked apes don't
change. It's just the environment and its passing shibboleths that alter. There is no
new generation gap. Its sudden novelty is the invention of harassed chaps whose
early purgatory it is to fill with something the hungry page, the silent minute, the
empty screen. Youth has always cocked its non-conforming snook at age. The old
bulls have ever feared the young bulls, knowing in their rheumy bones that their
offspring will one day take control of the herd and cast them out into the wilderness, the private hotel, or the old folks' home.

This atavistic trepidation is tinged, however, for this antique bull with overtones
of pity. Though the mighty-thighed dollies affright me, I feel truly sorry for the
current crop of young males. They are, poor loves, the Deprived Generation.

Compared with the primordial days of my youth—the 'thirties down the Old
Kent Road and the 'forties around High Street, Cassino—the lads just seem to have
had it too comfortable. They've been cheated by the welfare state of their due share
of adversity, and deprived by progress of their self-righteous war. Though
science has made this-happy-band-of-brothers warfare obsolete, human evolution
hasn't advanced to the point where the masculine young can forgo the blessed
release of violence. There are today no Hitler or Mussolini, no wicked enemies
assailing our Beloved Country, in repulsion of whom our Dear Brave Boys may
smash things up with the approbation of the adult establishment. Legally demolish-
ing towns or driving tanks across other people's front gardens is a capital way of
working the dirty water off the adolescent id. Particularly if they're foreigners'
front gardens.

Thus deprived of outlet for animal aggression, our callow blades are forced to rampage around universities to the detriment of their later earning potential, pick fights on football terraces instead of watching the game, and spend their Sundays trying to provoke the police to be brutal to them in Trafalgar Square. The principal difference between the police, then and now, is that if you hit a copper when I was hirsute, he didn't smile indulgently; he hit you smartly back. I have only once hit a policeman and that was during the General Strike of 1926 when I was ten and he was dissuading the then balding generation from overturning trams in the Tower Bridge Road. He retaliated so swiftly with his folded cape that the imprint of his number—L 24—can still be seen on my left temple in moments of apoplexy.

The deprived boyos of the 'sixties, no matter how they may boast, don't have it so good on sex. In the 'thirties, before equal pay became infectious, a nubile popsie earning but a pittance was only too pleased to allow back-row liberties to young bulls who would pay for her pictures and egg-and-chips afterwards. Today, the pendulum has swung with a vengeance and affluent maidens can now make more contemplating typewriters than graduate lads can earn grooming computers. The girls have grown independent of impoverished masculine company and seem content to go around with other females in their own income group. With the loss of his God-given financial superiority, the young male has lost his confidence. In desperate efforts to get the damsels to notice him, he has been driven to wearing his crowning glory like a golliwog, growing Pancho Villa moustachios, endangering his potency in strangulating trousers, and sweating cobblestones inside his mum's old fur coat. It truly is a shame and the girls must try to take a little time off from admiring the older men and give the adolescent lads a break.

But even if, by lucky chance, young Mr. Now gets a dolly to go out with him, he can't be sure just how much of her is for real. In my hunting days, but for a dab of lipstick and a bit of rouge to cheer up their anaemia, you could broadly see what you were getting for your egg-and-chips. Today, however, Olivier played Lear in less cosmetic foliage than mademoiselle puts on to face the 8.25. Having donned her lanolin impasto, false eyelashes, foam-enriched bra, undetectable hairpiece, artificial fingernails and death's-head pupil-shadow, when she looks in the mirror, she thinks she's got burglars. I have met my own eighteen-year-old daughter, flesh of my flesh, fruit of my loins, with her full evening warpaint on and never even knew she lived down our street.

Wreaking wicked wills on little honeys is also a much harder problem for space-age Lotharios. Without pressing detail beyond the pale of a magazine for family reading, let it be said that the 'thirties were the heyday of the liberal-minded and unimpeding cami-knickers. Indecisive maidens could then fall in moments of rural abandon and lightning affairs could be conducted to mutual satisfaction between sportive lift-passengers in the taller office buildings. Today, buckled into her firm-control pantie-girdle, reinforced by elastometic briefs and all-enveloping tights, young chastity has never been so formidably defended since the Crusades. It is just not sartorially practical for anything decisive to happen in moments of unpremeditated passion. I have it from a frustrated nephew who hunts Streatham Common that to lower the defences of an indecisive young lady before she goes off the boil, you need a couple of quick-fingered Suomi wrestlers lurking in the nearby undergrowth and ready to haul away by numbers. It may be a permissive society, but it's the birds who have to give the permission.

And such is likely to be the rule of later life for our unlucky lads in more things than loving. Gynarchy, which in my balding time has been remorselessly on the trot, is now gathering pace for the final gallop home. Indira Gandhi commands India; Barbara Castle rules Britain; Golda Meir has just taken over Israel, and lovely, agate-eyed ladies lead the Vietcong. The wealth of America has steadily passed into female ownership as thrombosis and ulcers rub out dynamic husbands. And Messrs. McKinsey and their demented mates are actively furthering the same object over here. Matriarchy is on the double march; the reign of Big Mummy is at hand; it will soon be a woman's world and the poor dear boys are welcome to it.

And what can we do, concludes my brief, about the generation gap? . . . Nothing but to accept its inevitability and try to avoid actual fisticuffs. Parents should give up trying to communicate with their offspring. Kids don't want to communicate with their begetters; they just want to have rows with them. Don't try to understand the young, because they don't want to be understood. Unless they are actually impeding your path or hitting you with something heavy, the best way to get on with the juveniles is to ignore them.

Never give them advice unless they ask for it eleven times. Most of the trouble between parents and offspring is caused by the former offering the latter unrequested advice on present action based on outdated experience. Guilt-ridden mums and dads should abstain from trying to prevent their grown-up children making mistakes. The only true liberty any of us have here below is the right to make our own mistakes. Nobody ever learnt from advice; only from misery experienced.

The stupidest words that come from old lips in the battle of the generation gap are, "When I was your age, my boy, I was . . . so-and-so and this-and-that . . ." And the tritest chant that comes back from the junior trenches is, "Just look at the mess your generation left the world in . . ." But choke back your anger, purpling pa, and remember that in the eyes of its successors, every generation since Adam has made a right balls of things. And take further comfort that your present accuser, in twenty-five years' time, will be whining to his offspring, "When I was your age, my boy, I was . . . so-and-so and this-and-that." And his kid will be moaning back, "Just look at the mess your generation left the world in . . ."

Fings, fundamentally, remain what they used to be, for ever and ever, amen.

"For my part, I won't feel safe until every kid is in jail."

No point teaching children something unless there's an exam at the end of it, is there?

GENERAL CERTIFICATE OF EDUCATION

June 1971

Ordinary Level

SEX

Three hours   (Questions 1 and 2 are compulsory. Answer TWO others. Be gentle.)

1. *Read the following passage carefully, and answer the questions below:*

When the ****** descends on the *********** the pressure within the ******* is rapidly reduced; also, as the ***** ****** past the sideways position, the leverage is reduced so that, beyond a certain point, little useful *** is being done. Advantage is taken to increase ********* by arranging for the ****** to open before the **** reaches bottom dead centre, so that the remaining pressure assists in expelling the ****** from the ******. The latter process is known as **********. Finally, in order to encourage the rapid influx of fresh *******, the ******* is opened before the end of the ******** stroke, so that the outgoing **** of ******* creates a follow through effect. To complete the *******, the ****** is not closed until a little after top dead centre. It will be noted that for a short period both **** and ****** are open simultaneously, and this is known as **** overlap. The ***** and ***** are shaped to reduce the tendency for the incoming **** to escape via the ******.

   (i) How does the author keep up your interest?
   (ii) What influences, literary or otherwise, can you trace in the style?
   (iii) Can you fill in the asterisks?
   (iv) Does the passage now seem an accurate account?
   (v) Could you describe it in your own words?
   (vi) Would you be surprised to learn that it was taken from *The Penguin Car Handbook*, p. 34?
   (vii) Why?

2. Write an essay of not more than five hundred words on ONE of the following:

   (i) What I did in the holidays *OR* What I'm going to have to do about it.
   (ii) A bird in the hand is worth two in the bush.
   (iii) "Choose thou whatever suits the line: call me Sappho!" (S. T. Coleridge)
   (iv) "Pat-a-cake, pat-a-cake, baker's man,
   Bake me a cake as fast as you can;
   Pat it, and prick it, and mark it with B,
   Put it in the oven for baby and me!"
   (v) My favourite form mistress *OR* My favourite mistress's form.

3. "Oscar Wilde was a great writer but a bad queen." Discuss.

4. According to Macaulay, Catherine the Great of Russia frequently entertained young subalterns on the sideboard. Will you draw the sideboard, and answer any THREE of the following by marking the details on your sketch?

   (i) When the Seven Years' War broke out on August 29, 1756, what was Catherine the Great's position?
   (ii) Do you consider her to have been too close to the bookcase?
   (iii) Was the candlestick a "heroic gesture that all but succeeded" (Brückner) or a "tactical error of the first magnitude" (Waliszewski)?
   (iv) When Vasili Mirovitch attempted to restore the imprisoned emperor Ivan VI in 1764, how did Catherine come between them?
   (v) How often?
   (vi) Where was the fifth riding-boot, and whose was it?

5. Answer any TWO of the following:

   (i) Tom is taller than Maureen, but shorter than Mary. Mary is shorter than Arthur, but thinner than Jim. Freda is fatter than Jim, but taller than Tom or Arthur or Eric. Eric is twice as fat as Mary, but shorter than Freda or Horace. Horace prefers Jim to Maureen, but Maureen prefers Arthur and Eric to Tom. Tom prefers May to Freda, but Eric to Maureen. Jim is left-handed. Draw a diagram in which everyone in bed is happy.
   (ii) Two vans are approaching one another. Van A is travelling at 30 mph, van B is travelling at 45 mph, and the vans are nine miles apart. In the back of van A are Maurice and Beryl, who normally reach a satisfactory conclusion after 8 minutes 7 seconds. In the back of van B are Herbert and Winifred, who normally take 6 minutes 8 seconds. What will be the distance between the two vans when
   (a) Maurice and Beryl finish?
   (b) Herbert and Winifred finish?
   (iii) Edward is fifteen years younger than his father, but two years older than his sister and one year younger than his twin brothers. The sum of the ages of their mothers is the same as the age of their paternal grandfather, which is two-and-a-half times that of their father. How old is their father?

6. Find the odd man out in the following groups, illustrating, where necessary, the reasons for your choice:

   (i) Troilus and Cressida; Dido and Aeneas, Abelard and Eloise: Mr. and Mrs. Jilly Cooper.
   (ii) T. E. Lawrence; T. E. Shaw; J. H. Ross; Peter O'Toole.
   (iii) Parkinson's Disease; Reiter's Syndrome; Bell's Palsy; Portnoy's Complaint; Todd's Paralysis.

"I'm waiting till he's old enough to say whether he wants to be legitimate."

RALPH SCHOENSTEIN:
Tell Me, Daddy, About th

"THIS," said a California newspaper, "is war."

What triggered such belligerence from the Anaheim *Bulletin*? Was it the theft of a ship that belonged to the Seventh Fleet? No, it was a seventh grade probe of a subversive act called intercourse.

While millions of American parents have been seeing such films as *I, A Woman* and *I Am Curious (Yellow)*, millions of others are opposing the teaching of the curious callow, teaching that has turned the three r's into four by adding reproduction. In nervous cities across the nation, people are rattling sabres over sex education. Should we teach our grade schoolchildren how to make other children or should we just let them drift along with their innocent ids, each one a tiny Columbus on a tittilating voyage into puberty?

The very battle itself shows the distance we have come since the medieval days of my youth, when I learned about sex not in a grammar school but in the University of the Gutter. The foes of sex education insist it belongs neither in school nor gutter but only in the home, a point that would be valid if most parents had the skill to turn their children's eyes from the TV to the ovary. Although my own parents gave it a touching try, their abbreviated guidance was really the ideal birth control: they prepared me for little more than hygienic kissing.

The sexual briefing that I got from my father was memorable for the way that it avoided textbook jargon and came directly to the point: he took me into the library one day when I was twelve and solemnly told me that the time had come for me to know that I was never to use a men's room in the Broadway subway. Since this dissertation left a certain gap in the story of procreation, my mother tried to fill in by also taking me to the library, this time the public one, where she spent more than an hour trying to find a book that explained how I'd been brewed; but in those dark days, the secret was never published for tiny eyes.

My teachers did no better than my parents in telling me about the birds and the bees. Not only was there never a word about the passions of my own species, but even the birds and the bees were handled platonically. Once when I returned to school after having been sick for several days, I heard a rumour that one of the teachers had told a suggestive story about a rooster; but from that day on, in spite of the strain of my innocent ears for some juicy stuff on crows or canaries, I heard nary a bawdy word.

It remained for a pal named Mickey Higgins to take me into an alley one day during the Battle of Midway and reveal the facts of life in all their ageless beauty.

"It's somethin' your mother 'n' father do to each other," said Mickey, carefully choosing his words. "Your mother 'n' father—they're definitely the ones involved. Y'see . . . well, y'see . . ." And here he smiled with embarrassment and disbelief. "Well, this is gonna *kill* ya 'cause believe me it's really *stupid* . . ."

The story didn't kill me, but it left me with a wound, for the earthy scholarship of that little curbstone

ees and the Fleas

Kinsey moulded my view of amour. Perhaps it was Mickey's Rabelaisian presentation or perhaps his story *was* inherently silly: I only know that no matter how sweetly the violins are playing, I can never approach love without also approaching laughter. At least I have the comfort of knowing that Richard Burton shares my affliction, for his wife has said that he also laughs in bed. Was there a day in Wales when a Mickey ruined him, too?

Although Mickey's romantic tale fell somewhat short of *Ivanhoe*, it was good that he told me how the population explodes because I went on to have two little pops of my own. By loosely following his instructions, I managed to sire two daughters, one of whom has just requested the flaming facts from *me*, the facts that every father hates to declassify. One day last week, Eve-Lynn, my eight-year-old, came to me and said, "Daddy, what's *mating*?"

There it was: the new American trigger word; and for a moment I felt like joining the militants called POSE: Parents Opposing Sex Education. I was silent for several seconds after Eve-Lynn's question, but not because I didn't know the answer, for mating was something that I almost understood, I was silent because I didn't know if some racy little two-reeler from the Board of Education—perhaps something called *I, A Mommy*—was already playing in her classroom. And so I made a quick decision: I would explain only *external* fertilization and let all other thrills come from the teacher.

"Honey," I said, "mating is when two bees or fleas or fish decide to make *more* bees and fleas and fish."

It was hardly a marriage manual, but it was prettier than Mickey's tale. Carefully remaining on a low zoological level, I went on to deliver a veterinary *Kama Sutra*, shrewdly avoiding pauses for questions; and by the time that I was done, Eve-Lynn knew exactly how to keep herself from ever being compromised by a lobster.

I couldn't have gone any further and still protected the American way of life, for I've recently learned from leading conservatives that sex education was invented by Karl Marx to wreck the family unit, corrupt the young, and destroy the domino theory. Moreover, it has now been established that for the past two decades, the Communists have been following a programme of conquest by pornography, distributing French postcards whenever political subversion has failed, while Americans in the silent majority have looked to prayer and impotence for a patriotic counter-attack.

"The long-range plan to bring sex education into the American public schools for children from kindergarten to the twelfth grade is part of a giant Communist conspiracy," says the Reverend Billy Hargis, for whom POSE also means Preacher Opposing Socialist Erotica.

And so I gave Eve-Lynn just enough information to satisfy her curiosity while still keeping her loyal. All the naughtier details will have to come from the Vietcong.

Unfortunately, however, I now have a problem with my older daughter, Jill, who may well be headed down the road to socialised hormones. Yesterday Jill's class saw a movie that told how cows are born. When I asked her about it, she said she'd explain the whole business to me when I take all the THINK AMERICA stickers off her books.

"*I'm fed up with being a nuclear family, we should be living in a commune!*"

"*Did you plan it, or goof it?*"

CHILD POWER
BY HEATH

"*Oh, don't come the old 'you're not too old to be spanked' unk! You lack authority and you've always lacked authority!*"

"*I'd have left home years ago—but my paren need me around to hold the marriage together*"

"*Can you imagine what it will be like in a few years' time— I'll be slopping around the house full of pills, and you'll be wondering where you went wrong, plus the fact that we won't be able to communicate . . .*"

"*Look, you need me as much as I need you, let's neither of us rock the boat too much*"

"*Listen mate! I didn't ask to be born but since you brought me into this mess the least you can do is stuff me full of sweets.*"

ALL GOD'S CHILLUN

JOAN LITTLEWOOD
imagines herself
Secretary of
State for
Education

I CAN only say now, without attempting to vindicate myself in the eyes of history, that I got off to a rather poor start. I had, in a weak moment, agreed to accompany Dr. Miller, Minister of Transport, on a bus ride as he wanted to get the feel of things, first hand, and we had as a result been living in one of the lesser jams for the entire week-end. He had wisely provided himself with some protein simulacrae, a lady tourist had some tea bags and thank goodness the milkman got through regularly by a little dexterous roof-climbing, so we weren't entirely without comfort. In fact when we glanced out at the contactual stress mounting hourly among the pavement multitudes we considered ourselves fortunate.

I was finally delivered by Mr. Short, who offered me a lift on the cross bar of his bicycle, and the last I saw of Dr. Miller he was taking samples of air at the mouth of Oxford Circus tube. He was later carried on the backs of the crowd to Middlesex Hospital and I am relieved to learn from this morning's paper that he is now out of the oxygen tent.

Merry, my secretary, had been holding the fort, undismayed by my absence. In spite of the disparity in our ages, she understands me. She had remembered to feed the canary, unpacked Horace and Virgil who are my constant companions and placed them between the precious bookends carved from the oaks of my grandfather's country seat. My office overlooks the sweet Thames. I wonder if I shall ever see it flow again, as it was prophesied by our Prime Minister. I can only pray that we shall all be restored to health and the pollution-carts will cease to rattle through our streets at night.

Merry cannot work without her little transistor—she says she uses it as a soundbreak, but I insisted on having it off while we worked on my filing system—it's of my own devising. I've broken up the whole country into areas under the headings "Social Foci," "Social scatter," "Aesthetic fixes," and of course one needs to concentrate if things are not to go into the wrong pigeon holes. Merry meanwhile mounts moves on my wall map with little flags. . . . The phone rang.

"It's someone beyond the Tower of London."

"Oh! Well, see what they want."

"It's another school burned down."

"Good gracious. How did it happen this time?"

"The headmaster was locked in a cupboard, the gas taps were turned on . . . and pouf!"

"I shall need a complete report!"

"They're now burning the furniture and throwing books on the fire . . ."

"We may even have to have a short, sharp enquiry."

"The police and fire brigade are trying to bring the situation under control."

"Guess what, dear—Nigel got Katmandu today!"

"Well, there's nothing we can do dear. Don't look so worried, it doesn't help."

"One of the children said the place was too dull to be endured."

"Well I don't suppose it'll get beyond the local press. Now where's my S . . . Surbiton . . . P . . . Primaries. We'll have to forget *them*!"

"Beyond the Tower, warehouses fired, swastikas daubed on public conveniences, windows smashed. Snipers terrorise elderly couplies in quiet street."

"It's a twilight area, dear, it'll be gone soon."

"A clip from Manchester—'Sixth form schoolboys riot because they object to being prepared for dull university curriculum.'"

"What to do? What are the army doing at present?"

"Well, there's Ulster."

"Yes, good, useful training! Of course there they are fighting over something important like religion, here it's just war for war's sake. I was only thinking of dear Field Marshal Montgomery as I gazed at the dreaming spires of the Army and Navy Stores. He would be just the man for this job."

"You mean it's not a matter for our department, Miss Littlewood?"

"Of course not. The War Office will have to take over."

At this moment the door opened and a gentleman with a patch over one eye appeared unannounced.

"Madam," he said, "I am your problem."

"Are you? Pray sit down!" But he could not, for his trousers were rigid with sticks, canes and whips which had been thrust down his legs. His fingers were fire crackers and one of his feet was a cloven stump. I'm afraid he caught me peeping.

"Lost, lady, fighting for my country," he said, "and no medals for it!"

"Oh, how did it happen?"

"Blown up, by one of us own, ma'am."

The visitor strode away and unbuckled his leather belt which caused a great clatter of falling things.

"What we need ma'am, is a bit of the old one-two."

"A good old-fashioned war? I've already thought of that. You could lead one side and"—but he wasn't listening—he was playing with a contraption.

"There's a lot of under-used land up north that would do for war games," said Merry.

"Boys," he said, "are all evil. They are a wicked, obscene, deceitful, cunning and cowardly lot, usurpers all! What are they there for but to usurp us? They have spies, they know what we will do before we know it ourselves . . ."

"Some teachers love their pupils, Sir."

"Yes, as guards love their prisoners! Now I have invented this."

"What is it?"

"A flogging machine. It does them all at once.

Discipline, ma'am, the only way to get the country back on its feet. It's yours and the price I ask is small."

But at that moment a stink bomb of evil proportion burst upon us, heaven knows where it came from, and I fled to the canteen to do my sums: £171 million for all schools excluding universities, £11 million for the renovation of school buildings, £2,200 million in all. Well, we're going to *have* to cut £100 million of that for a start!

One can always rely on some stimulating conversation in the canteen. Over my baked beans and Eccles cake I heard all about the new cultural events and was lucky enough to be given a ticket for *Guys and Dolls* which features the story of Lilian Bayliss. Somehow I felt cheered, our theatre and our beloved Arts Council are still the real heart's blood of the nation. No other country can match us in this aspect of education. But back to the grind, by an ancient passage, one which avoids the crowd.

"Give me something nice," I said, and she offered me a chocolate drop. "No, work, work, something encouraging."

"Well here's a pretty postcard from Oxford," she said, chewing.

I sighed. Oh for those days of tranquillity! The postcard was bright and gay and the handwriting a little eccentric but nice. Every word a different colour.

"Deep down she is a kind and considerate daughter—she's gone!"

SUGGESTIONS 4 ATTENSHUN OF MRS. MINSTER, it read. WE WOULD LIKE TO PACE OUTSELVES AT WORK AND TO HAVE A BIT MORE FLEXABILITY AND MAKE UP OUR OWN GAMES AND LAWS. WE HELD A TRIAL AND THE OTHER DAY AND WENT INTO FINGS AND WHO DO YOU FINK WE FOUND GUILTY? US. BUT DO YOU FINK WE CAN TALK TO OUR TEACHER? NO, ITD BE EASIER TO GET FROO TO THE MOON. WE HAVE A NEW BUILDING 4 OUR STUDIES ITS GOING TO LAST TILI 2020 AND WE FINK IT IS ROTTEN COS WELL BE GRAND FAVERS THEN AND OPE KIDSLL HAVE A BETTER TIME JACKIE FINLAY AGE 12.

"My new boyfriend says that programmed learning needs teachers and teachers need programmed learning, if only to save them the boredom of repeating everything," said Merry. "Then, my boyfriend says, teachers might perk up and learn a thing or two themselves."

"How, pray?" I asked rather coldly. She has become too cocky, ever since she took up with that romantic cybernetician in Richmond.

"Well if I wanted to teach I'd learn to play, Miss Littlewood. I'd think up schemes and maybe the kids would think up better ones, and we'd analyse them and throw out the dull unnecessary bits, and invent new ways of saying and doing things."

"What things?"

"All the new jobs waiting to be invented."

"Where are your classrooms?"

"Everywhere. The whole world perhaps. In the courts and streets and banks and factories and churches—everywhere where the theatre of learning lives, and when we need to be private and work alone we'll have a carrel, quiet as a monk's hood. We could even carry it about with us, it would be sacred."

"Oh dear, what a ship of fools has sailed my way today. Is every day to be like this?"

"Worse," said a sharp voice which seemed to come from the top of the wardrobe, and suddenly a long Edwardian coat materialised in the midst of us and two downtrodden shoes came flapping across my carpet.

The visitor brandished an enormous scroll and carried a pair of Wellington boots and a very large black portfolio—its lank hair fell across its grey face and angry eyes that looked as if they'd never closed stared at me. "Time is short," it said. "I must fly." And pulling out a pair of dusty wings it attempted to mount the parapet outside our balcony, slightly impeded by a paunch and the effort of throwing the scroll at me. Merry unrolled it.

"What is it?" I asked, for the legend was quite unintelligible.

"Desolation, unchanged since the nineteenth century," muttered the apparition.

"It looks like a spider's web."

"That's the system is it?" asked Merry.

But the creature was swaying perilously on the balustrade adjusting its nose to a miniature theodolite, at least I took it to be one.

"Disaster area," it croaked, "Hartlepools to Cardigan Bay, West to Southminster."

"Project Thinkbelt," it said, and put a plug in its ear which seemed to be attached to a battery in its sock.

"An improvement in the quality of life," Merry said, finding a simple phrase in the rather quixotic orthography of the scroll. "Less pedigree-shrouded patterns!"

The apparition nearly overbalanced at this point, and we both rushed to clutch its feet, only to find that he was bending and adjusting some mini-binoculars to survey Barbara Castle sunning herself on the terrace with a whole bevy of parliamentary pin-ups.

"Do come down, please," I said, "and explain what this cipher means."

"Explain!" said Leonardo da Vinci, "it's all there."

"Flexibility, mobility," Merry read on, as he threw his wings in the river and prowled the room tapping the panels. "If food, clothes, gadgets, motorcars and lovers are a matter of personal predilection, why not buildings, why not learning, why not universities?"

"What's a collection of books?" said the prophet and drank all the water in my daffodil vase. "If education is to be a continuous human servicing run by the community, it must be provided with the same lack of peculiarity as the supply of drinking water or free teeth." At which it took out a small denture and threw it at me. I am used to eccentrics, so I ducked the missile and pretended to listen to Merry, but kept a close eye on the curious personage.

"Education must be a major industry, a source of employment, wealth and delight, planted and supplanted with the minimum amount of fuss. Think what happened to that little East Anglia market town," muttered the toothless one chewing on a murderous-looking cheroot.

At this point my diary goes blank—Merry tells me that I did look a little strange—it must have been too much! The first thing I remember was the Prime Minister's voice! Where was that friendly sun tanned gaiety—where the—Ah well, I think I offered my resignation with the coolness and dignity which will give me some little spot in the footnotes of history.

A Frank Address to the Old School

By JOHN BETJEMAN

MY dear boys, it was kind and wise of your Headmaster to choose me to address you. Just when I was reaching the port stage of my excellent dinner with him last night, you were supposed to be dropping off to sleep in your dormitories and those of you who had not strings fastened to your toes to wake you if you snored, or who were not suspended by your feet from the rafters for not being good enough at football, were no doubt trying to get some rest.

I like an early cup of tea in the morning, and at seven, when mine was brought, the well-known sound of the bell woke you from dreams of home to the more familiar whitewashed walls of school, the rows of iron bedsteads, each bed with its pale burden under the red blankets. I think there must be some educational supply company which has a monopoly of school bells. Their note is always the same, not so irritating as the telephone, but more terrifying; not so mellow as the church bell, but more ominous; not so evocative of excitement as a fire alarm, but conveying the relentless monotony to which it calls you.

As I lay in bed wondering what I was going to say to you, I heard your merry little feet pattering over cool linoleum to some healthy cold tubs to freshen you up for the day's work. It was raining hard outside and I was imagining that you would soon have to be hurrying away from a hasty breakfast, across wet courts and under windy arches to classrooms smelling of ink, old boots, old biscuits and bat oil, there to bluff your way through the morning, trying to prevent your form master finding out that you had not done last night's preparation. By this time my breakfast was brought to me in bed on a tray, grapefruit, eggs and bacon, toast, coffee, marmalade, and *no porridge whatsoever*.

Do not imagine, however, I am trying to make you envious. I have got up after a nice hot bath and at a reasonable hour and can see things clearly. You will only be able to have these privileges by becoming so ill that you have to be moved to the sanatorium. But even then you will get well again and it will be doubly hard to adjust yourselves to the rigours of the school curriculum.

And, dear boys, let me remind you of the date. We are early in October. Christmas is a long way off. The Christmas holidays are short; then comes that terrible term when it is so cold that you have chilblains on your toes as well as on your fingers. Then there are even shorter holidays at Easter and after that the long, long summer term with its unspeakably boring hours of grilling cricket followed by the dangers and the duckings of the bathing place.

But I am anticipating. I wonder how many of you will survive unscathed until the summer term? Looking round at this sea of faces, I wonder how many of you will be expelled; how many times each of you will be beaten by the prefects for leaving your clothes about, by your housemasters for not doing enough work, by the Headmaster for more serious crimes. Some of you I see already have spots. During the term, owing to the difference in the food from what you are accustomed to at home, these spots will grow angrier and boils will appear on the backs of your necks. But these are not complaints bad enough to earn you a rest in the sanatorium.

Well, it is time for me to go now. Your Headmaster has kindly put his car at my disposal to take me to the airport. I am taking a 'plane to a diplomatic mission in Bermuda. Besides having ample private means, I am paid by the Minister of Commonwealth Relations, for whom I am a sort of roving ambassador, at £5,000 a year with hotel bills and expenses extra. I shall stay at the best place in whatever is the capital of Bermuda, and I shall be away for some months as my work is of national, nay global, significance. Perhaps your Headmaster would like me to talk to you again next summer and if I have the time I will come. But I am a busy man.

71

STAGE ONE: GUILT

"*Oh, Fred! We've actually done it— we've brought a new human being into the world! How can we make it up to him?*"

"*Nancy, if you insist on staying up with the grownups—and of course we're delighted to have you—you must allow us to make an occasional remark that goes over your head.*"

"*I wouldn't worry too much about Jonathan's desire to conform. It's probably just an attention-getting device.*"

"*Look, I don't know if there's a God, so how can Ruthie Philips be so damned sure?*"

We Americans (at least of a certain class, which, as we have a classless society, includes everybody except those who don't count) bring up our children more permissively than you English do. We don't shush them or cane them or force our views on them or make them wear a tie or send them to bed before they're ready. We feel that if a child is a fascist at four, it will be out of his system by the time he reaches maturity (ten). And the accusation—prompted by his psychoanalyst—of "You never gave me limits!" will be no worse than any other. So we leave the limits to Mayor Daley, and the final solution to the draft board.

STAGE TWO: GUILT

"Oh, let him smash his guitar! It makes him feel grown up and professional."

"I don't approve of your taking drugs, not that I suppose you're interested in my opinion, but if **I** wanted to try, let's say LSD, er, don't tell your mother I asked you this, but where . . ."

"You want a motorcycle? You can **have** a motorcycle. You want to kick your mother? **Kick** your mother. Only finish high school."

"Bye-bye, Mommy and Daddy! Thank you for a lovely childhood."

Out of the Mouths of Babes Comes Gibberish

By STANLEY REYNOLDS

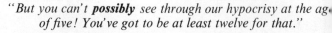

*"But you can't **possibly** see through our hypocrisy at the age of five! You've got to be at least twelve for that."*

THE next time you get browned off with the boss and get to wondering what devious plot in the Cosmos set you to a lifetime of selling double-glazing, hewing wood or drawing water, spare a thought for the way Mr. Gordon Wells of Bristol earns his readies and you will soon find yourself back whistling, perhaps even dancing, over your life's work.

Mr. Wells is head of the Education Department at Bristol University, which sounds a cosy little rut with plenty of time off for good behaviour. But there is a rub. Mr. Wells, according to the *Sunday Times,* is also head of something called the Social Sciences Research Council and as such he has arranged to have 100 children electronically bugged so their conversation can be recorded and Mr. Wells can then sit down and listen to it with an eye, or an ear rather, to discovering how children learn to put words together.

Apparently most research of this nature has been done with only small groups of kids and over a short space of time. Mr. Wells is evidently out to find if the American Noam Chomsky is correct when he says that "syntax is the product of fixed inherited patterns in the human brain."

Into such heady realms I do not wish to step, not even on tippy-toes. My mind is boggled enough by the idea of Mr. Wells leaving his own wife and kiddi-winkles in the morning to drive to the office and put in eight hours listening to baby talk. The experiment is going to go on for two years and one wonders what at the end of it Mr. Wells's own speech is going to be like. I'll bet when he goes beddy byes he'll be hearing the kiddies talking in his sleepykins.

Being, myself, the author of occasional light pieces, I have, of course, got myself kitted out with the standard two-year-old brat who just says the darndest things for gosh sakes. In fact I've had several of these two-year-old brats in my time and if it wasn't for the wife I'd have left home long ago. As a famous Dublin barmaid once said, "Kids are death on conversation and they never tip."

But to the point. I think Mr. Wells has got it all wrong. In fact I rather suspect he is a bachelor, otherwise he'd know that every child invents his own language, and that it may sound like someone trying to talk Lower Serbo-Croat with a Welsh accent to outsiders but is perfectly, almost cruelly, understandable to all members of the family. For example, when I dragged my latest two-year-old into the tobacconist's the other day, the kindly white-haired old lady behind the counter looked down at his wildly curly head and said,

"Give me a big kiss, sweetie."

To this, he said, "Get a lock a mena."

The dear old soul smiled sweetly at this babyish talk little realising he had just told her "Get, lost, menace." Where he picked that sort of talk up is anybody's guess. TV, I suppose.

Right now, dear readerkins, this same little fellow is standing outside the door which is locked so Daddykins and readerkins can be alone together.

"Dad? You in there, Dad?"

"Yes, Sandy."

"Dad?"

"Yes?"

"Hello, Dad."

"Hello."

"Dad?"

"Yes."

"You in there, Dad?"

(A long pause. This conversation is boring even him.)

"Dad?"

"Yes."

"Pooka dog."

Unfortunately this child is not the youngest. There is another one right behind him.

"Yes, Sandy, old man, Pooka is a dog." Ha ha! Kids.

"Dad? You in there, Dad?"

"Get lost, menace."

Where was I? Oh, yes, what poor Mr. Wells is going to get when he sits down to listen to his two years' worth of tape recorded kiddiwinkles is two years' worth of unintelligible gibberish—and that'll be the good stuff. The understandable children's talk is going to be the thing that gets Mr. Wells rubbing his eyes, drinking pots of strong coffee, and reaching for the pep pills.

Outside the door again:

"Dad?"

"Yes, Sandy?"

"Tenna ball rabat."

"That's tennis racquet, son. Racquet."

"Tenna ball rabat shoe, tenna ball rabat sock."

He's got my tennis racquet, the little chap has, and my tennis shoes and socks.

"Dadims"—Dadims! I ask you? In my wildest dreams did I ever imagine I would end up being Dadims?—"Dadims, where the bang bang?"

This is bad news. The bang bang is the hammer and that tennis racquet is a brand new Jack Kramer Autograph which cost me £12.

The insidious thing about baby talk, of course, is that it becomes the lingua franca of the family. Long after the kid has grown up and becomes a hulking, and often surly, teenager who only grunts at you occasionally when he wants to borrow money or your new bell bottom flares, Mummy and Dadims are still using those sickeningly cute little private words that sonny made up when he was learning to talk. Mummikins and I when we started out on life's road together were not going to go in for any of that baby talk ourselves. *Our* children were going to be addressed in solid, respectable sentences. Simple declarative ones, certainly, for a start but none of that icky googums yum yum baby talk. But now, like the fat lady who gives up and heaves her corset into the dustbin, we have thrown in the verbal sponge.

Outside the door:

"The Daddan, you in there?"

"No, I'm not in here, This is a tape recorded announcement for crying out loud."

I can hear him twanging the strings of the £12 a copy Jack Kramer Autograph. He's using it as a guitar, which in Sandyspeak is called primitively "for song."

Sandy (singing): "Pooka Pooka Pooka Pooka Pooka Pooooo KA."

It's always the same, this song: five quick Pookas with the sixth elongated, ending on a high note. It's been known to go on for thirty minutes on a family drive. The second verse is about Lucky, the cat, and it goes: Lucky Lucky Lucky LucKEEEEEE.

Another Sandy number, which was written in honour of Wimbledon Fortnight, goes a little something like this:

Tenna ball man
Tenna ball rabat
Tenna ball shoe
Tenna ball shoe sock etc etc

and then he sat down and wrote:

Crika ball man
Crika ball ball shoe
Crika ball bat
Crika ball ball shoe sock.

If there's anything in this for Mr. Wells, he's welcome to it. From such evidence he, or you or I or the dustman, might well be able to deduce the sorts of environmental influence which stimulate the speech patterns of two-year-old Reynolds children. Further, I dare say, when he is sifting through the accumulated verbal jottings of his subjects he will also find strong signs of the relative contemporary influences of Tony Blackburn, Bugs Bunny, and the baked beans commercials, and how he is going to plough through that lot to come up with a sound theory of syntax is a case study in itself.

As for the Daddan, some nights he doesn't seem to have the energy left to watch the telly and it's all the old Dadims can do to climb the wooden hills to Bedfordshire for some nightie pitie bobos.

WHICH SCHOOL?

By MALCOLM BRADBURY

IN my last two years at grammar school, when I was in the sixth form, I developed the habits of sporting my cap, with its prefect's tassel, on one side of my head, wearing brown trousers, and staying in bed until noon at week-ends. The processes of maturity had me in a grim stranglehold; I had strange urges, poetic thoughts rushed to my head like wine, and the joys of the intellectual life were beginning to overwhelm me. I had been overcome by the conviction that I was different from other people—larger, somehow; more noble; with rarer, finer passions. Also, I needed more sleep than anyone else. I have settled my passions, and modified my convictions, somewhat since then (though I still need more sleep than everyone else); but at the time they ruled my conduct with an iron hand.

For I was growing into that strange creature, the grammar school intellectual. My hair was long and dark and flopped over my eyes. "He looks like some big soft girl," my father used to cry, when I came home in the evening. My arms and legs were thin, but my head was growing big and round; and more than once my name appeared in print over articles in local newspapers and in little poetry magazines. These were months of self-realisation; I had found myself; it was all a vindication of my earlier years in the school when, amid the cruel wastes of those harsh, over-sportified days before school certificate, I used to evade the games period by hiding my pimply self in a corner of the library and so, out of sheer boredom, had started reading books. These years before the sixth form are, in the modest grammar school, terrible years—the years in which children are at their most vile and when, full of a new power, they seek to socialise one another. The society they make is one filled with violence; and so these are the years of one's life one could not bear to live again.

But now a member of the sixth form, a prefect, one of the survivors, I found myself a figure in a new *élite*—the *élite* of the university entrants. My character was divided between a taste for rebellion, protest, bohemianism—hence the brown trousers—and a sense that, given enough social responsibility, I could solve human problems and handle men—hence the prefect's tassel. It is conventional now to mock the morality of the school prefect (and one gathers from Mr. Jonathan Miller that this whole new satirical organisation called "The Establishment" has been founded to destroy this cardboard figure). But the prefect in the grammar school is surely not a comic but a sad creature of our time—the Butler man, the meritocrat, the person who has his feet directed to the first rung of the social ladder only to discover that, already, the world is planning to take the ladder away. He is a creature hung between two systems, between the past and the future. And it is indeed during these two short years in the sixth form that the meritocrat is made. A way through the world is marked out for him; there is a system to answer to; he has his meaning and his use. His mind and his curiosity are at the heart of his prowess, and they expand within the limits of such ideas and stimuli as are provided. The limits, as far as I was concerned, were clear enough; and I drew all I could from the sixth-form world. I had a taste for the arts, a fancy for intellectual discussion, and a rolling eye for the girls.

My grammar school, I should explain, was a co-educational one; and in this

76

fact lay the rudiments of another kind of training, in the social and sexual arts, which also needed thought and dedication. Every evening when the lights throughout the building went out I could be seen, wheeling my bicycle, escorting down to the bus-stop a tall, delectable, dark-haired girl whom I fancied enormously. I scarcely saw her at any other time, but in those slim ten minutes a wealth of things happened. The pedals on my bike would keep coming round and hitting my shins as we walked between the suburban villas, with their stained-glass hall windows, and I begged her to run away with me to some Mediterranean paradise where we would live on bananas, chianti and the profits of my writing (which, by great good fortune, had started to mount as high as ten or even fifteen pounds a year). At week-ends, too, I expanded myself; when at last I could be inveigled into getting up ("You'll get bedsores," my father used to shout from the bottom of the stairs), I would go on solitary bicycle rides, my tyres hissing round the accessible countryside. "He's bone idle," my father constantly complained, and so I was; for all this was twelve years ago, before the teenage revolution, and there was nothing for such people as I to do. The coffee bar was still a twinkle in some Soho man's eye, the badge of CND was as yet undesigned, and jazz was still music and not a form of protest.

In fact, I spent these two formative years in a singular isolation from the world in general, and I doubt if I would have wanted to go on marches or gone to jazz-clubs if I could. It all sounded too like fun, moral and emotional indulgence. At the same time, however, I found my isolation disturbing. The ten minutes each day at the bus-stop with the dark-haired girl was sparse time in which to mature a relationship. I knew few people. Now and again, for companionship, I joined in the hockey games; and on Saturday mornings I could be seen in goal, blue and shivering, stick at the ready, stopping the ball inexpertly by turning round and addressing it with my buttocks whenever the opposing team broke through our defence. But our team was so good that goal-keeping proved another formalised kind of isolation; and when I turned out I used to tuck the morning paper in my cap so that I could have something to do out there. I also appeared with the cricket team as twelfth man and scorer, pencils sharp, scorepad under my arm; but this was another private role, and my little white face peering out of the high window of the scorebox, nodding acknowledgement to the signals of the umpire, was the face of a man in prison.

In 1950, however, all this training came to its culmination, when I got on a train with a suitcase full of new pyjamas and went off to the Redbrick which had admitted me. There had been some talk of my staying for a third year in the sixth and trying for Oxbridge, but my father couldn't stand the thought of another year of my agonised idleness, and so off I went to the natural development of the grammar school. I bought a college scarf, a gown, a pair of even browner trousers. I seem to have spent the first year of my studenthood bicycling madly against the wind from my digs to college, five miles away. During the day, as I sat in the lectures, I could see, glancing outside, that the wind was gradually changing direction in time to catch me for my evening ride back to the lodgings again. In the second year, thanks to a move into a hall of residence, I managed to gain some mastery over, some proper relationship with, my environment; I began to be seen about the college, wearing bow-ties, correcting proofs; and finally I inherited the editorship of the college literary magazine and also of the newspaper from a bespectacled lad named Orsler. I introduced visiting speakers to societies; I kept a notebook of my thoughts; I bought floppier and floppier bow-ties. I began to smoke Sobranies, and the smell of scented ash guided me in darkness to my room when, as occasionally happened, I came back late from a bout of dalliance.

I believe I have told before in these pages of the grim moment of reckoning that came when, finals over, I realised that life, with hooked claws, was reaching out for me. I was about to be sucked into advertising when something happened which ought to have happened—since it constitutes, I think, the logical fulfilment of the model career I have described up to now. Let us call it the meritocrat's reward. For, remember, I was taken and shaped into modern man by grammar and Redbrick; I was deracinated by brick-built premises, made by the echoing halls and lecture-rooms of institutions, laboriously constructed by the effort and the spirit of those educational ziggurats that stand out high above every suburban plain. In short, what the workhouse and the orphanage was to the nineteenth century, so was the grammar and Redbrick to me. In an age which has abolished fathers, education is important. I say this with a demeanour not of dissatisfaction but of explanation; for institutions become havens, and it is hard to leave them. And here was where fortune was kind; for the institution kept me—I was given a research scholarship. I went to Bloomsbury and worked in the British Museum, filling dozens of Oxford pads with notes for a thesis. When the thesis was done, a new field of space opened to one side of me—the western side. I went to America and taught for a while, encouraging midwestern freshmen in the use of the comma. Then there was more research, and more America; and now if you catch the train and come and look at me you will find that I am still a Redbrick man, teaching in just such an institution as made me.

It is an unexceptional history. Perhaps there is in one aspect of it a touch of the success story—for when I emerged from the sixth form in 1950 and put away my prefect's tassel for the last time, it was assumed that the job I now do was a job for not the Redbrick but the Oxbridge product. But the world has opened even more in the past ten years, and the old boy of the State school need not expect to find his road too hard if he possesses the approved intellectual equipment. I suppose all of us who are the products of State schools, whether they slipped away or dropped out at fifteen or sixteen or eighteen or twenty-one or never, must recollect the force of them as institutions, offering, in stages, a way into the life of the time. The State school, as Richard Hoggart points out somewhere, provides for most of those who go to it a second set of standards, a second character for oneself. The longer one has this character, the more one is conscious of the parental role of these institutions—and good parents they are, trying to impose on the disorder and violence of youth some sort of standards, a manageable set of passions, and some sort of native critical apparatus. However I must confess that I find it hard—as the product of a local grammar school—not to be convinced of the extent of my own provinciality, not to be convinced that my own thought lies outside the mainstream.

And this, conventionally, would be the moment to complain that still our educational system has not evolved a means of eliminating its inequalities. However, perversely, my mind runs off in another direction; I have no passions to raise on that score. For behind the figure of myself, institutional man, I can't help seeing the figure of another self, the self made not in the institution but in the family; and I can't help associating recurrent feelings of indirection and helplessness with the discontinuousness of the whole process. The heritage of lower middle-class values —of doing the right thing, counting the change, looking and acting decently, being your own man, doing a good job of work, and speaking the truth when it needs to be spoken—goes with the family self; institutional man speaks with the voice of the declassed professional, able to describe anyone's dilemmas for him but incapable, as Robert Frost has lately put it, of taking his own side in an argument.

But discontinuity is, it seems, the great professional advantage, and the necessary psychological and moral equipment for a world going into the great new age that hovers before us. No one can be spared the traumas of modern man; the world goes as it goes. The State school boy—the archetypal State school boy—is thus, I think, characteristically divided between past and future, between hope and reaction. Or, possibly, this stage in the game is over, and now resolves itself into the two characteristic Redbrick types—the conformists, the getters on; and the protesters, the sitters down. As for me, you will still see me with my tie neatly tied; but with my brown trousers browner than ever.

YOUNG MEN FORGET

By V. S. NAIPAUL

I CAN hardly remember my home life until I was fourteen years and three months old. For a writer still in his twenties this is something of a disadvantage. The things I remember are books and school. From about the age of eight my school life was steady and I can measure the progress of the war by happenings at school—the savage beatings of May and September, 1940, and again of July and December, 1941. But although I went home every day I cannot say what happened outside the school gates. I have every reason for believing that my childhood was unhappy. But what can a writer do with an unhappy childhood he doesn't remember?

It is a relief that unhappy childhoods are out these days. Happy childhoods are the thing. Even so I lose. A year or so ago a poet published a book about his experiences as a happy boy of five. He described, among other things, having tea at the home of a poorer boy and distinctly remembering "the taste of the missing butter." The phrase was applauded in *The Times Literary Supplement*. Deprived of childhood's clear perceptions, I am liable to misinterpret any writer who talks about "the taste of the missing butter." It makes me think of a schoolboy detective story.

In compensation I have ridiculously clear memories of babyhood. I am told this is rare. I find it useless. I cannot see how, with the liveliest imagination, I can spin out my adventures as a baby to seventy thousand words.

So the richest part of my short life has been forgotten. The rest has been unadventurous. I have hardly moved outside my family, or needed to. For this family wasn't like the scrubby growths I see around me in Muswell Hill—two adults and two children—but one of those restlessly expanding Hindu conglomerations. I am on intimate terms with forty-two cousins and about two dozen aunts and uncles. I know where to go if I want to drink whisky, if I want to drink rum, or if I want to hear it proved again that Plato and Aristotle and Pythagoras and everybody else took their ideas from the Hindus. Without having to meet a stranger I became acquainted with a variety of intellects, temperaments and professions. I know a moron or two, a number of vagrants and casual labourers, three full-time pundits, four lawyers, two doctors, two dentists, two politicians, six taxi-drivers (some of them part-time pundits), a few businessmen, any number of "students," and a warden at the Port of Spain lunatic asylum, known more directly over there as the Mad House. I am also related to a mosquito-killer.*

With such large forces at one's disposal family politics are almost a career.

* * * * *

It is the fashion these days to bring out "little reviews" devoted to the problems rather than the productions of the young writer. Latterly there has been a tendency to consider the problems of the young critic as well. It is high time *Punch* devoted some space to the problems of the young humorous writer. It is unusual for anyone but his publisher to take him seriously. If he is lucky he will of course have *The Times Literary Supplement* talking romantically about the sadness of the clown and the tears behind the laughter. But in the meantime, reading all but the most perceptive reviews, I get the impression that I have written my novels with unsuppressed mirth on the backs of envelopes during a long rush-hour journey on the Underground. I have been accused of writing about the farcical adventures of Trinidadian eccentrics. This is wounding, and unjust.

* This is no longer true. He is a shy man; when I went back to Trinidad in 1956 it was his mother who told me of his promotion: "Killing rats now."

"An O-level in Domestic Science, I see . . . Have you considered jumping out of cakes at stag dinners?"

Come with me on a brief tour of Port of Spain. We will start in Marine Square. That big building with the dirty sea-green windows is the Treasury. It is pretty and modern. The original Treasury was burned down in 1933. We leave Marine Square and walk north along Frederick Street, the main shopping centre. There are modern buildings on either side. A few months ago a fire disposed of the remaining old ones. In a square on your left you will observe a big old building that has been burnt out and fenced round with corrugated iron. That is the Town Hall. Let us continue northwards until we come to the Royal Victoria Institute in the War Memorial Square. It is the local museum and we might find some explanation there. Outside the Institute a rustless ship's anchor stands embedded in concrete. A sign says it is Columbus's anchor. Drawing rapid conclusions, we go inside. Among the Carib middens, preserved with despairing piety, there are gowns worn at Government House balls at the turn of the century. That, more or less, is the history of Trinidad: it hardly exists. Spare a thought, then, for the people who are commissioned to create folk-dances and folk-costumes to entertain visiting royalty.

In fact all you have in Trinidad are people of many races thrown together for a comparatively short time on a small island. Their ambition is to make money and be thought modern. Unfortunately they have no standards of modern behaviour, language or house furnishings. So they invent. Take language. Trinidad English is full of French phrases, one of the most common being *à force de*. The proletariat say "*A force* I was tired, I took a taxi." (Only the proletariat use taxis.) I have heard this refined and modernized to: "Ah! First I was tired . . ." Jock-strap becomes jerk-strap, clerk clurkist, furniture furnitures. Take now one small aspect of social behaviour: the serving of marshmallows. In England the problem has been settled; variations undoubtedly exist, but they are not important. In Trinidad marshmallow-serving still offers much room for experiment. At one house they are served speared on the antlers of a deer.

This material is too rich. The writer has to reject, simplify, tone down.

*   *   *   *   *

Still, I suppose I could have kept my characters off marshmallows and written haunting little colonial tragedies. I tried. It didn't work. The missing childhood, that family, that background—they couldn't be ignored.

I was encouraged in my light-heartedness by an early drift into literature. It became my duty to read short stories and plays from the Caribbean. One thinks of people laughing and doing abandoned folk-dances on palm-fringed beaches; the stories I read showed a people obsessed with sudden death. A good seventy per cent of the characters died within their allotted two-thousand-word span. They simply dropped dead at the end of the story, or were drowned, pushed off precipitous cliffs, cutlassed, knifed, shot, bludgeoned, run over, hacked by ship's propellers, pursued and eaten by sharks. Anything was a story provided there was a death in it. A story might begin with a happy family sitting down to dinner. They eat; they talk. Suddenly they are dynamited. End.

Wading in this gore three days a week every week for two years I found it increasingly difficult to take a serious view of the human condition. In particular I developed an unconquerable allergy to any drama about the race problem in the Caribbean. There are all degrees of racial and—equally important—religious antagonisms on those sunny islands. Yet people will pick on the crudest, the most worn and the least important: the negro-white relationship. And the only approved treatment is in the American style, something with a nice part for Harry Belafonte or Cy Grant. The depressing result, so false and vulgar, is supposed to remove prejudice. I can think of few things more likely to inflame it. I would also have thought it embarrassing to the people it was meant to emancipate. But no. Week after week I had to put up with radio dramas on "the problem," in prose, poetic prose (". . . then I saw thy ebon frame scarred with whip and glinting in tropic noon . . ."), Elizabethan verse, rhyming couplets.

There are three plots. The first is set in London. The suburban girl is at first repelled by the Caribbean negro; then she sees him carrying books about and is captivated by his self-pity and exquisite manners. The time soon comes for the girl to visit her aunt at Carshalton.

AUNT: Another cup? Milk in first. I know. What's this I hear about you being engaged?
GIRL: Oh, that was what I wanted to talk to you about. I am engaged to a negro.
EFFECT: *Dropping of tea-cup.*

You can see the rest: tears, suicide, the speech at the end.

The Elizabethan verse drama is set in the Caribbean. The hero is the strike leader, the villain the Police Commissioner, the complication the Commissioner's daughter, Esther. Raiding the union's headquarters the Commissioner, a pistol in either hand, sees a couple embracing.

COMMISSIONER: Good God! 'Tis true! Alas! Too true!
ESTHER: Hullo, Daddy.

What follows can be recounted briefly: the death of the strike leader, the death of Esther as she tries to shield her lover, the Commissioner's grief, insanity and suicide, the long speech at the end by the progressive Colonial Secretary.

The third type of drama is more pastoral. At a cricket match in Tobago the Englishwoman sees the young negro getting nine wickets before lunch—it would look like propaganda if he got more. The negro opens the innings for his own side and remains firm while the wickets tumble. He makes 210 (run out) and stumps are drawn. That evening at a reception for the cricketers the woman meets the negro. He refuses to talk about the match. He is urged to play something on the piano. He demurs.

WOMAN: Play something—for me.
NEGRO: Oh, very well. But I am out of practice.
   (Grams: *Schnabel—Hammerklavier Sonata. Play for three minutes, then hold under*).
WOMAN: How well you play!
NEGRO: Thank you.

Love is born, runs its course, and is only cut short by some minor tragedy—drowning, say.

No, "the problem" has too many devotees; and apart from that analysis of a flourishing branch of Caribbean drama, it would be impertinent for me to add anything.

       *   *   *   *   *

So I can give no account of harrowing childhood, no mention of "the taste of the missing butter," no strong drama of race. I suppose I am really far too irresponsible. But I don't see how that can be helped. Perhaps it is because I have been too insulated: through no fault of my own I have never—except for ten fatiguing weeks—had to do a ten-to-four job. Perhaps it is because I know the absurdity of my own position too well. I have lived eight years in England. I have never been to India. And there is little now to attract me back to Trinidad. Uncles and aunts have died. Cousins have gone to Canada, America and back to India. One, imperfectly disguised by a Spanish name, is an illegal immigrant in Venezuela. The latest news from Trinidad is that one uncle has in his old age reverted to violently orthodox Hinduism. I used to hear him singing "When there's a rainbow on the river." Now he is wearing caste marks, cultivating the hairs in his ears and refusing to talk English.

English is the only language I know. I work in an alcove that overlooks a bowling green. The men are in shirt-sleeves. The women wear white jackets and panama hats. Their chatter rises above the clack of the bowls. All around are the flowers of the English spring. I have only recently got to know their names. My senses, numbed for so long by tropical profusion, have begun to react to them.

"You'll always find the odd one who isn't in touch with the realities of this world."

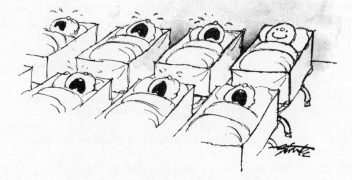

FATHER'S LIB

By ALAN COREN

"The City University of New York has offered its male staff paternity leave on the same terms as female staff get maternity leave. It is believed to be the first time such a provision has been offered in an American labour contract."
The Times

THERE are a number of things that are going to be wrong with this article.

Some of them will be noticeable—a certain sogginess here and there; a tendency, uncharacteristic in the author, to use one word where two would normally do; arguments, if you can call them that, which start, falter, then peter emptily out; odd bits of disconnected filler, such as laundry lists, a reader's letter or two, notes from the inside cover of my driving licence, a transcript of my tailor's label; that sort of thing.

There will be phrases like "that sort of thing."

Some of the things that are going to be wrong will not be noticeable—the fact that the writer has a tendency to fall off his chair between paragraphs; to knock his coffee into his desk drawer; to rip the trapped ribbon from his typewriter and tear it to shreds, moaning and oathing; to wake up with a start to find the impression 1QA"ZWS/XED@CRF£V on his forehead where it has fallen into the keys; to light a cigarette while one is still ticking over in the ashtray; to stop dead, wondering where his next syllable is coming from.

Nor will you notice, since the typographer, sturdy lad, will be backing up the young author like a seasoned RSM shoring a pubescent subaltern before Mons, that a good half of the words are misspelled, if there are two "s's" in "misspelled," that is; and if it shouldn't be "mis(s)pelt," anyway.

I'm glad that sentence is over; if it was a sentence. Was there a verb there?

But, for once, ineptitude will be its own defence; inadequacy its own argument. The very fact that readers this week are about to receive (have, indeed, already in part received) a substandard article with the tacks showing and the sawdust trickling out the back only proves the writer's thesis: which is that the concept of paternity leave has been a long time a-coming. That it has come to the United States, pioneer of the ring-pull can, automatic transmission, monosodium glutamate, the Sidewinder missile, and sundry other humanitarian breakthroughs should be no surprise to anyone; what is grievous is that there is little sign that the blessed concession is to be adopted on this side of the Atlantic.

Not in time for me, anyhow. And—hang on, that little light on the bottle-warmer that goes out when the teated goody reaches the required temperature has just done so. All I have to do now is unscrew the cap on the bottle, reverse the teat, replace the cap, shake the air out, nip upstairs, prise apart the kipping gums before she's had a chance to wake up and scream the plaster off the wall, whang in the teat, sit back, and,

Dropped it on the bloody floor.

That's what I like about the three a.m. feed—that deftness in the fingers that only comes after two hours deep untrouble sleep, the clarity of the eyes rasping around behind the resinous lash-crust, the milk underfoot due to inability to find slipper and fear of turning on light in bedroom to search for same in case wife wakes up, thereby destroying entire point of self-groping around in first place.

I'll come back to the argument in a minute. Now have to boil teat, mix new feed, screw, light goes on, light goes off, unscrew, reteat, rescrew, shake, nip upstairs, prise apart kipping gums, correction, prise apart screaming gums, that's my daughter, five weeks old and more accurate than a Rolex Oyster, it must be 3.01, must get feed done by 3.05, it takes exactly four minutes from first scream for three-year-old son to wake up, where's my panda, where's my fire-engine, I'm thirsty, I'm going to be sick, news that he's going to be sick delivered on high C, thereby waking up wife at 3.09 exactly, wife shouts What's going on? where-

82

*"You and your laying down a crate of
brown ale for him at birth!"*

upon son shouts Mummy, father shouts Shut up, lights start going on in neighbouring houses . . .

3.04 and fifty seconds, breath coming short and croaky from stairs, got feed mixed, teat boiled, all screwed down, whip out miniature daughter with .001 to spare, pop in teat, falls on it like Peter Cushing on an unguarded throat. I lean back in nursery chair, feet tacky from old milk, left fag burning beside typewriter on kitchen table, know fag will burn down on ashtray rim, like Chinese torture in *Boy's Own Paper*— "When frame leaches thong, Blitish dog, thong tighten on tligger, burret brow blains out, heh, heh, heh!"— fag will fall off ashtray, burn hole in table, possibly burn down house, Family Flee In Nightclothes.

I am actually writing this an hour later, madness recollected in tranquillity, if you can call tranquillity thing involving cat which has woken up in filthy mood to find milk on floor, therefore licking up milk off floor, therefore in middle of floor when I come back to kitchen, therefore trodden on.

Anyhow, back to an hour ago, still feeding daughter, she beginning to drop off halfway through feed, terrible sign meaning can't go on with feed since daughter asleep, can't not go on, because if she goes down half-full, she'll be up again at 4.38, screaming, son up at 4.42, where's my panda, where's my fire-engine, wife up at 4.46, saying If you're incapable of doing a simple thing like a feed etcetera to sleeping form, thereby transforming it into waking form, fall

out of bed in netherworld confusion, thinking fag burning house down, look around for something to Flee In, since don't wear Nightclothes, sub-editors all change headlines for 5 am edition, Nude Phantom Terrorises Hampstead Third Night Running.

Wake daughter up, she cries, must be colic, hoist on shoulder, legs all colicky-kicking (I'd like to see James Joyce change a nappy), pat on back, crying goes up umpteen decibels, bring her down again, mad gums grab teat, bottle empties like a Behan pint, relief.

Change daughter, all dry, smooth, cooing, give final burp with little rub, daughter hiccups, sick drenches dressing-gown sleeve, daughter's nightdress, change daughter again, can't find new nightdress, walk around numb and sicky, daughter shrieking now, since, having displaced part of feed, requires topping up, else valves will grind or crankshaft seize up, or something, back downstairs with daughter on shoulder wailing, feel like mad bagpiper, mix new feed one-handed, screw, light goes on, light goes off, unscrew, reteat, rescrew, shake, carry out with daughter, slam kitchen door with foot. Wake up cat.

Get upstairs, son wandering about on landing with dismembered bunny, I want a pee, can't explain holding daughter and feeding same is priority, since Spock says AVOID SUCH CLASHES THIS WAY TO JEALOUSY ETCETERA, lead son to lavatory with spare hand, holding bottle against daughter, daughter can now see bottle like vulture over Gobi, windows rattle with renewed shrieking, leave son peeing in sleepy inaccuracy on seat, back to nursery, finish feeding daughter, son roars I CAN'T GET MY PYJAMA TROUSERS UP, try to rise with daughter, bottle falls, teat gets hairy, hammers start in skull, but thanks, dear God, daughter now full, asleep, plonk in crib, turn out light, hurtle sonwards, son not there.

Son in bedroom, shaking wife, I CAN'T GET MY PYJAMA TROUSERS UP.

I creep, broken, downstairs. You know about treading on the cat. I look at the garbling in the typewriter. It stops at "hang on, that little light on the bottle-warmer that goes out." Sit down, smelling of regurgitation and panic, stare at keyboard, listen to dawn chorus going mad, man next door coughing his lung into the receptacle provided, far loos flushing, new day creaking in on its benders.

What I was going to write about before I was so rudely interrupted was, I see from the first tatty gropings, an article about how enlightened America was to introduce paternity leave for new fathers so that they wouldn't have to work for the first few weeks and could help cope with the latest novelty item, instead of going off to the office, the shop, the surgery, the factory.

Or the typewriter.

I had all these great arguments in favour of introducing the system over here, I had all the points worked out, it was all so lucid, so right, so uncounterable: I should bring about an instant revolution.

What arguments they were!

And if I only had the strength left to get them down on paper.

"Boy oh boy! Is he repressed!"

Slap, Tickle, Pop

DAVID TAYLOR finds himself in the club again

YOUTH Club night was on a Monday. With all of us spent up after the week-end pictures and bored at the thought of another five days, you got more people in that night. Chiefly, you got Daphne who was never any good at ping-pong all the time she was there but was a wonderfully large girl and always came along nicely done up, in the hope of getting undone afterwards, walking home. It wasn't much of a hut we assembled in, even after the brief refurbishing scheme we called Clean-Up '62 and which finished up as one wall painted purple and some coloured light-bulbs up the record-player end. Still, it was nice enough and dim enough for what we at least then thought of as the main purpose of the club—an evening's slouching about where we couldn't be got at, the chance of a bracing moan amongst pals with a beaker of Coke and the stories about school and work and girls. It was the kind of studied aimlessness which was reckoned to refresh.

For the more successful amongst us, it might perhaps happen that they got a feel at Daph over *Be-bop-a-lula* (and there were several went all funny over Buddy Holly) but it was never a demanding time. We were content for the most part to just stand and chat, sizing up the form, some perhaps undecided whether to push off home or hit someone. Seldom, as I remember, that it ever got really rough. There was a mild excitement when some big lads came on over after the *Crystal* ballroom and *Bali Hi Dive* shut and we would occasionally get the Kidsgrove heavies look in on the way home to smash up the chairs. There were no more darts for a while after that but there never was much anyway you could call a youth facility, just a corner for a drink made out of coffee bags—and unique as far as I know—shove-halfpenny for the cissy ones, ping-pong everybody else, and the insistent, thumping bedrock din which was a group from time to time and made your ears sing in bed. I think that once there was a jumble sale. Social education was not much talked about then.

And now, going back to them, youth clubs seem to talk of little else. What it means is that youth clubs seem to have got a far better grasp of how to twist restlessness and boredom into some kind of useful purpose. All the old generalities we had about it being a useful place where young people can come together and learn about themselves, find a field in which he can be accepted, where she can develop an insight into her own social needs, where they can choose from many and varied pursuits and use their freedom to effect (that is to say throw the ball, pal, and keep your nose out of trouble) all that seems at last to have been replaced by some more constructive thinking on what social education ought to be, and what it's likely to be, given that there isn't any cash to splash about. Flexibility, the leaders like to call it, and it can take in anything from the still-useful stand-bys like cycling proficiency and campcraft and outings to the sea through to the more immediate schemes such as rounding up the young drifters left in London after hours, tackling drugs, and any amount of self-directed project work. What has to be stressed now is that the kids themselves decide.

Youth leaders, more than ever aware that it is something of a triumph to have got the members to turn up at all in the currently fashionable climate of a youthful fingers-up at anything they sense is organised, see social education as letting them organise themselves. If it turns out that in some cases the considered opinion is that what they want is simply recreational, well that's fine just so long as they decided it. The nub of it all is persuading them to think, for ping-pong therapy is not what it was.

Which is all very well in theory. What hasn't changed to match is the look of the clubs themselves. A Wednesday night this time (spending patterns must have altered as well) and the sounds are of *Hot Love* and of progressive bangs and whistling noise. Otherwise, the feel of an East End basement youth club last week was much as I remember the Potteries hut (though we called it a venue even then) some ten years previous. The same dingy corridor in, painted brick, and the unsettling feel that any minute now the regulars may start up the familiar bumps-a-daisy barging routine that hints you may be new around here. I hadn't supposed that I was that much past it but it is a less than one-of-the-crowd shove that puts me inside (I expect that's their own policy) into the same kind of fair-sized and very multi-purpose room, finished in orange over blue, with the cranked up table and a sag in the net, music everywhere whether you like it or not. Same just hanging about apparently. Probably somewhere there's a girl called Daph. Despite the best intentions to turn this or any other typical venue into a useful centre for self-expression, one thing sticks out: the youth service is miserably short of cash.

It is typically so. The regular pattern is for the simplest of set-ups, often a business of persuading the curate to push out the Bright and Happy Club one or two nights a week from the recreational church hall. There are pitifully few purpose-built centres. Maybe the local authority can provide a well-equipped permanent base, maybe the area can provide enough skilled volunteers to supplement the needs. Maybe. The youth service has learnt to muck through as best it may, well aware that whatever it would like to see develop in social education and recreational cure, there will still be large numbers booting it about the streets and not very tempted by the twice-weekly shindigs in the church hall. The national association has learnt it to the extent of recognising a potential affiliate in a harmless enough group of lads in studded jackets who patrol the seedier caffs of the North Circular and from time to time fight off the attentions of visiting Satan's Slaves and Road Rats Anonymous. All such colourful characters are indisputably youth and, in their own worked-out fashion, a club.

Youth leaders stress that they are ready to take on the hang-ups of *all* young people but nearly all of the time what we're talking about is just this rougher end of the market: the C streams at school, the neglected at home, the confused and bored unimaginative ones trying to work it all off on a motor-bike. And despite any claim that the modern strain of potential hooligan is clearly more sophisticated, or senselessly renegade, impossible, worthless tat or whatever prejudice appeals, they're still just after some place to kick around in where they won't feel as if they've joined the Brownies and where they will feel that there is perhaps something they can do, and do it well. Better still, tell somebody about it, so they'll know.

With the present set-up, their chances of finding it depend partly on the continued enthusiasm of imaginative leaders (and that at least seems reasonably assured) and partly on the financial support of the public, a public which responds less well to so woolly a cause as "the needs of youth" than to something more specific like a handicapped donkey. One thing is certain, though. Youth clubs may look much the same as they always have, but there are fewer people in them who suppose that with a decent set of ping-pong bats to hand, the problem of what to do with youth will just grow up and go away.

EUROPE GOES TO SCHOOL

Look. MILES KINGTON and GEOFFREY DICKINSON
have been to Brussels. They have been to see the European
School. What is the European School?
Keep quiet and listen

THE address of the school is 42, rue du Vert Chasseur, a long quiet street in the south of Brussels lined with prosperous private houses in their own prosperous grounds. The gateway to 42 is much like the others, with a drive leading to a large house and not much else visible in the trees. As the *Punch* Expedition to the European School fell out of its ruinously expensive Belgian taxi and stood staring down the muddy drive, it had a vision of a souped-up finishing school in a posh suburb, and it sighed.

It wasn't a badly qualified expedition as journalistic double acts go. Dickinson had spent ten years of his life teaching in South London, and even today is approached in pubs by complete strangers who clap him on the back and say they never forgot what he taught them about perspective. He also married into a French family. I myself went through modern languages at

university, which left me with a complete grasp of medieval French. Between us we reckoned we had come to a pretty dud outfit.

We spent two days finding out how wrong we were.

A French class of seven- and eight-year-olds. The teacher is showing them slides of a story set in Brittany. They discuss the twists and turns of the plot. But there is just one odd thing about that class of chattering French children. They aren't French, they are German. You couldn't tell from listening, though. Not a word of German was spoken; excuses, hesitations, explanations, even jokes were all in French.

Which brings us to the question that everyone seems to ask about the European School: which main language is used? The answer is simple: none. The school was set up for the children of those Market officials who are more or less permanently in Brussels, which means a mixture of Dutch, French, German and Italian speakers, and the authorities quite sensibly decided from the start that each one should receive the bulk of his or her education in his or her mother tongue. So, from the time they arrive in the primary school at 6 to the day they leave the secondary school at 18, they are put in the Dutch, French, German or Italian sections. They all cover the same ground, but in their own language.

But (and this is where the school starts being different from other schools) the system lays as much stress on international education as is feasible without sabotaging their national upbringing. At 6 they have to start learning a second language immediately—the choice at present is between French and German, though English will soon be added. More of that later. At the age of 12 they start learning some subjects, such as history and geography, *in their second language*. And the next year they start learning English.

The fact that history gets taught in a child's second language, incidentally, answers the question about their view of history. If you get a class of Germans, Dutch and Italians being taught history in French by a Belgian, you automatically get a fairly balanced view of history.

It also explains why those German seven-year-olds were chattering away in French. They were in their second year of learning their second language.

If that sounds complex, take it from me that I have over-simplified the whole system. The assistant head, the genial M. Desmadryl, takes it on himself to produce a chart each term to cover each class taught which resembles nothing so much as one of those horrific timetables which enable British Rail to get us all home without crashing into one another. As you wander down the corridors of the European School and hear English being taught to Dutch and Germans, biology being taught in French, physics taught in German and, outside, football being played in four simultaneous tongues, you diagnose chaos. It's not true. You might as well look at the crowds on Victoria Station each night and forecast multiple train disasters. Somebody, somewhere, has worked it all out, and it works.

There are six European Schools altogether, scattered round the Market. This one started in 1958, but the first, an off-shoot of the original European Coal and Steel Community in Luxembourg, goes back to 1953. In all of them they try to preserve the pupil's native traditions, while expanding his horizons in a

"If a 32 ton lorry can transport 50,000 bottles of Beaujolais to London in two days—how much faster and cheaper would a 43 ton lorry . . .?"

Saint Nicholas (Mr Terhorst)
visits the Italian primary
section.

way that could never happen at a French or English or German school. To begin with, they stick pretty much to their own national groupings but at about 9 art, music and sport are taught to very mixed classes.

A German master: For the first few weeks they still stick to their own groups, but then it begins to break down. The Germans, for instance, will form their own basket-ball team. After about a month they notice perhaps that they haven't won any games. So they invite a rather good French player to join them . . .

A Dutch master: The older they get, the more they mix. Not just because classes throw them together more, but because love starts to cross barriers . . .

Yes, it's completely co-educational, and pretty informal too. No uniforms, unless you count jeans. Trying to pick out nationalities by studying the dress is hopeless—the only boy I would have sworn was French, with beautifully tidy clothes and neatest of haircuts, was English. He said he had been at the school since six years. Now, "since six years" is not English, it's the French phrase *depuis six ans* translated literally, but I know how he felt.

Now for some geography, in English.

As soon as the *Punch* Expedition burst through the first belt of trees beyond the muddy drive, it found a long, low, seemingly endless complex of modern buildings. In 1958 the site was a beautiful park and there were 500 pupils. Now there are an amazing 2,500 and although there are lots of trees left, the park is mostly built over with more going up, which causes pangs to those who remember its spacious, family-scale beginnings. Down at the far end is the primary school (the 6–11 group) and it is here that the English section has just started, the small landing-party in advance of next year's big invasion. There are three teachers. Two are Mr. and Mrs. Black, late of Watford.

Mrs. Black: I'm teaching the first year, the six-year-olds. The big problem is that up to now they have all been in Belgian schools, taught by French methods, which means something very different from what we're used to in England. The French seem to believe in teaching by rote, in strict repetition of lessons, and as a result these children don't have the initiative yet that we expect in English schools. The books they used had no story in them, the paintings they do are what you would expect from a four- or five-year-old back home. They've been systematised.

Little boy: Please, Mrs. Black, how do you draw an open desk?

Mrs. Black: Just go and get a box, open it and draw it as you see it. *(To us.)* You see? They think there's one special way to draw an open desk, which they have to learn. We're getting better, though . . .

The arrival of the three new nations next year means a new English section, more problems, more space to be found, more buildings to build, and new dimensions on the already hideously complicated chart hanging in M. Desmadryl's room. (Most of the rest of the decor is genuine African; he was head for eight years of a Belgian school in Elizabethville.) And yet the arrival of the English is generally and genuinely welcome.

Difficult to say why, exactly. Perhaps Herr Mittler, the twinkling head of the primary school, put his finger on it when he said that there are more differences between English and Continental teaching than between any of the European nations. The school is already a fairly liberal mixture of traditions, but by comparison with us they have far fewer periods of sport, they depend more on texts and blackboards in science (the French and Italians are reckoned the main offenders), they have less freedom in the way of experiments and projects. We contrast most strongly with the French tradition, which some feel has perhaps exerted a little too much influence at the school.

But the biggest difference between us and them is that in England we specialise so much earlier and more radically. The sort of specialisation needed for "A" levels doesn't occur on the Continent until University. Even at the European School, which represents some sort of compromise, they are still taking eleven or twelve subjects in their last year. England may specialise too early, but there it seems too late.

The curious thing is that most of the Continental teachers we talked to were envious of the freedom in English education, while the English teachers I have talked to since returning feel it has gone too far. A primary teacher in a church school says: Giving children the freedom to muck around and create is all very well, but where are the standards and discipline coming from? The ex-headmaster of a secondary school says: Our enlightened methods work very well

for the bright 25%, but what about the 75% who are thick, thick, thick?

I think one of the things I like most about the European School is that it is likely to hit the right compromise.

Their tough exam, the *Baccalauréat Européen*, entitles them to enter universities anywhere in the EEC. That means they have to satisfy all the countries. Any normal student only has to satisfy one.

German art teacher: My job isn't really teaching art so much, in my opinion, as giving the children a chance to unwind. At this age *(about fourteen)* their other classes involve them in what can be an intensive reproductive learning system *(that was all one word in German)* so here I try to give their minds a rest. At first it is hard. They make very exact, systematic models or do very figurative drawings. But after a while they begin to relax and then it's possible to get them to indulge in fantasy.

Dickinson: The art rooms are so bloody *tidy*. They should be overflowing with stuff.

Me (to Herr Mittler): Everything is geared to university, isn't it? There's no feeling of children slipping off at school leaving age and getting a job. They all want to go to university.

Herr Mittler: Not quite. Their *parents want* them to go there.

And when you think of it, the school is for the sons and daughters of EEC officials, which means professional career people. That's where a lot of the pressure comes from. And yet the extraordinary thing is that the children aren't haggard, studious nervous wrecks; they race and shout and giggle and knock your hat off with a football like any normal school child. The teachers present their problems to you on a plate, as do all teachers; they are also one of the nicest, most humorous bunch of people I've met for a long time. Dickinson has a nose, after ten years, for spotting a good teacher, and in all those classes where we eavesdropped there were a few dull ones and a lot of good

90

ones. Mme. Martinez, for instance, whipping her class of Italians into a veritable storm of information about a Daudet story for us . . . the Dutch lady whose second year English class spoke with a perfect accent, even if "Come in, old boy" and "I say, Tony" are not the most obvious English phrases to learn . . . the music teacher who had let his class write their own modal composition in 5/4 time which they performed eloquently for us.

I suppose the biggest danger in a school like that is that the international or supranational ideals may be swamped by the system. It doesn't seem to have happened yet. The second day we were there was December 5th, which as you know is St. Nicholas's Day. Well, you would know if you were at the European School, because there is a very strong Dutch (to a lesser extent also German) custom that on that day presents are exchanged together with suitable poems, and that St. Nicholas comes round with his two faithful *Schwarze Peter* to distribute largesse.

If it's good enough for Holland, it's good enough for the European School, and on the morning of the 5th we duly saw St. Nicholas, acted in four different languages by a Dutch master, touring the primary school with his blacked up servants. The Dutch and German classes took it pretty well, but the young Italians had never seen anything like it; luckily, Dickinson was there to capture the moment for posterity, and in case there might be too much solemnity, the two *Schwarze Peter* were there to fling nuts and sweets round and cause instant chaos.

Despite all which, the thought that still worried me at the end was the possibility that the system might turn out faceless Europeans, that after twelve years of European education all national characteristics might be muted. Take, for instance, the two boys we talked to at the end, both of whom had just taken exams to get to Cambridge. One was an Italian medical student who had been at the school since he was six, but had been all that time in the Dutch section. The other was an Icelandic boy who had always been in the German section. To us they talked in English. Chatting to each other, they used French. Didn't this sort of situation confuse all of their national characteristics?

Patrick Sigurdsson: Not at all. Everyone behaves very much according to national habits. The Italians, for instance, you can always recognise—they dress a bit more fancifully, they have cravats and bits of decoration, their trousers are always beautifully creased. The ones with the most sense of national pride are not the French or the Germans, it's the Dutch—and the Dutch are also the most progressive. The French and Germans are generally content to let things stay as they are; all moves for change come from the Dutch.

S. Bottari: You can usually tell a class's nationality from the way it treats the teacher. The Germans are fairly respectful, but the French and Italians have the most discipline, the most formality. It's partly because of their own tradition, partly because the parents are very careful to demand it. The Dutch, on the other hand, treat class very informally, almost casually. I've been in the Dutch section all my life, and I've never really got used to the way the Dutch treat their teachers more like, well, brothers.

And it was just about at that point that the door burst open and in swept St. Nicholas, bearing not only gifts for the two English journalists but a poem that he must have sat up half the night working on, in English, which was duly solemnly recited to the assembled audience of Dutch, Italian, English, Icelandic and the Belgian headmaster.

At least, I think he was Belgian. He may be French.

After two days at the European School you get confused.

What's good about the place, of course, is that we were the only confused people there. Anyone who has been through the European School can take somewhere like that in his stride. And that means, on a larger scale, somewhere like Europe.

Peter Pan and Windy

By JOHN WELLS

Professor Graham Hough, 62, Professor of English at Cambridge, this week attacked what he called "Peter Pan Dons," university teachers over 40 who refuse to accept the fact that they are no longer young and foster the "myth of general student revolution." When the sentences on the undergraduates involved in the Garden House Hotel riot were announced, Professor Hough was in a pub in Essex, where, he says in the magazine *Granta*, "the whole bar went up in a roar of delight: the only regret was that the sentences were not longer." The following recently discovered dramatisation of J. M. Barrie's classic goes some way towards supporting the Professor's views.

"*Once upon a time . . .*"

SCENE ONE

A suite of book-lined rooms in Cambridge. The Red Banana, a one-piece pop group of indeterminate gender with a face-obscuring mop of ginger hair and an ankle-length red fox-fur overcoat, is sitting by the fire. It is known simply as "The 'Nana." Windy, in a long blond wig and a white nightdress, is sitting up in bed, his chin cupped in his hands. He is 62.

'Nana: Like Socrates just makes me flip, man. For me, you know, he is Beethoven and Ho Chi Minh and Fats Domino all rolled into one.

Windy: 'Nana, you are boring me to distraction. Your tutorial ended seven hours, three minutes and five seconds ago, and unless you quit my rooms this instant I shall be obliged to summon the Proctors.

'Nana: Like Nietzsche, man. You know, he just turns me on . . .

Windy's eyelids droop. Peter Pan and Tinker Bell float in through the open window and land lightly on the carpet. Peter Pan is wearing rimless pebble spectacles, an afro-wig, a multi-coloured dyed vest and bleached jeans. He is 41 years old, and is carrying a cloth banner inscribed with the words "PIGS GO HOME." Tinker Bell is wearing a mauve smoking jacket, a floppy pink bow-tie, and gold lamé trousers. He is carrying a hand-bag.

Peter: The Fuzz are all over the Front Quad. I said the kids could come through this way to the Demo.

'Nana: **** off, ****! Windy and me are relating like crazy.

Tinker: Get her!

Windy: You can say that again.

Tinker: Whoops!

'Nana gives a growl and bites Tinker Bell in the leg. As they escape, Peter's banner catches on a nail on the window sill and remains hanging.

SCENE TWO

The same, twenty-four hours later. Windy is sitting cross-legged on the hearth-rug, sewing Peter's banner back on to its poles. Peter watches him, and Tinker Bell floats about the room with an aerosol air-freshener.

Windy: There.

Peter: I was wondering whether you'd like to join a direct action group I'm taking to Neverland. Distributing leaflets against the regime, that sort of thing. We could fly tonight in point of fact.

Windy: How ripping. That would be lovely!

Peter: There is just one thing. Do you believe in Fairies?

Windy: Well, I've nothing against them in principle . . .

Peter: That's a good thing. Only you may have to share a camp bed with Tinker Bell.

"Hello . . . Is that the NSPCC? Look here, they've shut me in my room again!"

Tinker: Come on, ducky! I adore your mortarboard. Where did you get the material?

They float out through the window.

SCENE THREE

A student riot in Neverland. The Lost Boys hack, kick, slash, stab and disembowel the evil Fuzz who give as good as they get. The stage is slippery with blood, explosions rock the theatre, and CS gas drifts out across the audience. Enter Peter Pan, Tinker Bell and Windy, fighting for their lives.

Windy: Oh youth! Oh joy! I'm a little bird that has broken out of the egg!

Tinker: How topping!

Peter: Keep back, Fuzz Man, nobody is going to catch me and make me a man! Oh the cleverness of me!

(He crows.)

Tinker: Hullo, someone's feeling cocky!

Peter: It's Sergeant Hook! Leave him to me! I've cut his hand off already. I call him the Short Arm of the Law.

Enter Sergeant Hook, in a policeman's helmet with an iron hook instead of a hand. They fight, and Peter Pan pushes a time-bomb down Sergeant Hook's throat. *Sergeant Hook explodes, splattering the walls of the theatre with blood. The Lost Boys cheer.*

Windy: Oh, you're so nippy at it! Couldn't you do it again very slowly? Oh I never want to grow up, I want to stay with Peter Pan for ever and ever!

Tinker: Charming!

Tinker Bell stabs him in the back with a broken pole, and the evil Fuzz Men trample him underfoot with their boots.

SCENE FOUR

As in Scene One. The Master, a crabbed figure of 97, is sleeping by the fire in a dog-kennel. Windy floats in at the open window.

Windy: Master! Not in the dog-house again? Don't tell me it's those rotten Lefties rioting! This placard round my neck? But I can explain everything, Master. As a matter of fact I was just about to write a piece for *Granta* on that very subject . . .

CURTAIN

You and Yours

KEITH WATERHOUSE pokes
inside an end-of-term satchel

FOR this composition, you have to write about Your Family if you are in Group A, and, A Day At The Zoo if you are in Group B. Even though I am in Group B, I can not write about A Day At The Zoo as, my Father will not take me. He said (Never again) when I asked him. This mean, that, even though I am not in Group A, my composition is about Your Family. My Father say, that it will not make any Blessed Difference, as it is like a Zoo in this House anyway. That my explanation.

Your Family is made up of, Yourself, Your Father, Your Mother, your brother and Sisters if, you have any, Your Grandma, Your Uncles, and also Your Aunties. Also, there is also Your Cousins, if you have any. I do not have any.

Your Father is the Leader of Your Family. He like a King in, the olden days. Sometimes he is cruel and stern, at other times, he plays with me, this is not often. His cruel tongue is feared throughout the dominion. An example of this is, if your nails have Plasticine in them, he say (Look at your fingernails lad, I could grow a vegetable marrow in them). If you do not clean them, he Show no Mercy sad to relate.

Your Mother looks After you. She does not do any Work, she just stays at home whilst, Your Father goes to Work. The reason for this is, so that she can look After you. This is done by washing your shirts, cooking, Buying cakes and biscuits, picking things up such as your Lorries, and many other reasons. If you do anything wrong she always say (Wait till Your Father get home), but, she does not tell him. She just say (Ive had a hell of a day), then My Father say (What kind of a day you think Ive had). Sometimes, Your Mother and My Father shout at each other. This is because, My Mother has had It right up to here, and, also, Your Mother gets right Up my Father's Wick. This is only

sometimes, at other times it is not, happy to relate.

As I am an orphan I do not have any Brothers or Sister, but, if you have, they can be younger than you or older than you, or, they can be your twins. If they are your Twins, and, you have spilled some red stuff on Your Mother's dressing table, you can say it was not you, it was them. You cannot do this if you are not Twins, they know it was you.

If they are Older than you, you have to wear their Clothes when they, that is, their Clothes, are too small for them. Your Brother or Sisters. But, if they are Younger than you, they can do what like and, you get the blame for it. Simon Mathieson in Group A is an example of this. Therefore, I am glad that I do not have any Brothers or Sister. Also, my Father is also glad. He say (Never again).

Your Grandma can be Your Father's Mother or Your Mother's Mother, or, she can be both. This means that you have Two. I only have One. Your Grandma was married to Your Grandfather but, he is dead. He has some medals for bravery.

My Grandma has a moustache. If you say (Grandma, why you growing a moustache), she does not give you any Money, but, if you say (Grandma, why is your hair all nice and silver) she give you 10p. She always give me 10p.

After Your Grandma, there are Your Uncles. Your Uncles are My Father's Brothers, they can be fat or thin. I have 1 fat one and 2 thin ones, as well as, my Uncle Adam. Everyone thinks that, Your Uncle has got to be older than you by law, but, this is not true, as, my Uncle Adam is younger than me. He is my Mother's Brother. Therefore, he does not give me any Money. Also, he is a Thief. I gave him some Chewing Gum, but, only to lend, but, he kept it. This make him a Thief.

My Uncle Terence give me the Most Money. He gave me 50p on My Birthday, 50p at Xmas, 10p on Feb 13, 10p on Jun 25, 10p on Sep 17, and, 50p also on Sep 17, that is, the same day. I can remember this because, it is in my diary. It is in code. The code for my Uncle Terence is Tafy, this is Fatty backwards, but, he does not know I call him that. If he did know, he would not care, for the reason that, he is always Laughing. He Laugh every time he come, as well as Singing. He always Wake me up. On Sep 17 he was singing (Good King Wencelas) at the front door, and when I opened it, he gave me 10p and say (Happy Xmas Young Man). Later on, he also gave me a drink of some Fawn Stuff and then he gave me 50p, stating (Here 10p for you). My Mother said (He has had one too many), so, she must have known he had already given me 10p. But, she did not tell him.

When my Uncle Terence goes Home, My Mother always say (Never again). This my Father's saying. She has copied it. This mean that she is a Copy-cat.

After my Uncle Terence, there is lastly, my Uncle Edwin, and, 2ndly, my Uncle Roger. They are both thin. My Uncle Edwin used to give me 5p, but, he not come anymore sad to relate. The reason for this is, My Mother said (I will not have him in house) and also, (If he come, I go) to My Father. I think My Uncle Edwin has a Disease, as My Mother say (He ought to see a Dr.) Last time he came, My Father was not In. We had cherry pie, this is my favourite. When My Father came home, my Uncle Edwin had gone home. My Mother said (What wrong with him, he cannot keep his clammy hands to himself.) Therefore, I bet he took 2 pieces of cherry Pie instead of 1 piece.

My Uncle Roger live in Australia, invented by Captain Cook. Much wool is to be had. He does not come to our house, he not send me any Money sad to relate, just a Koala Bear when I was 4. I cut it open, but, there was no Money. When Your Uncle is in Australia, it is the same as being Dead.

Some people have Uncles, but, they are not really their Uncles. Simon Mathieson in Group A is another example of this. His Father is in Africa where, much Gold is to be got, but, his Uncle Arthur has come to stay with them. I know this because he has told me this. He is not really his Uncle, his Mother met him in a Pub, she say (This your Uncle Arthur). His Uncle Arthur is always giving him Money, I wish that I had one.

After Your Uncles, there are Your Aunties. Your Aunties are married to Your Uncles, but, these do not have to be Your Father's Brothers. They can be anybody, so long as, Your Aunties are Your Mother's Sisters. But, they are still your Uncles. The people they are married to.

I have 3 Aunties, 1 of them is married to my Uncle Terence, 2 of them are not. They can be old or young,

"We've come to close the circus. Bullworth and Sons, Solicitors."

these individuals are both.

My Auntie Nellie is the one whom, she is married to my Uncle Terence. She sometimes come looking for him, when, he is Out. She say (Has Terence been round, I not seen him for 2 days). My Mother say (No). She say (It getting too much of a Good Thing). My Auntie Nellie does not give me any Money, but, this is because she has not got any, as, my Uncle Terence does not give her any Money. This is what she told My Mother. It is because, he gives it to me happy to relate.

My other 2 Aunties are both Girls. They are both at College. They always come with different Men, but, these are not My Uncles. They have long hair, the different Men. My Father always call them Mick Jagger, when they have gone he always say, (He could do with a good Wash). They never give me anything, but, one of the different Men play with my Jigsaw also my Lego bricks, he said that they were Fantastic. He made a Lego Necklace for my Auntie Caroline, but, I would not let her keep it. She call me a Little Horror.

Once my Auntie Caroline came to stay with a different Man, not the same one, but a different one. He was supposed to sleep in my bed, and, I was supposed to sleep in the truckle-bed, but, he did not. He Got Up and, upon seeing that I was Awake, he stated (I am just going for a Leak) but, he did not come back. He went to finish the Jigsaw with my Auntie Caroline, they were Doing It all night. In the morning, My Father said (Never Again).

That is all that I have found out about Your Family, so far.

95

Father of the Man

By R. G. G. PRICE

I

"WHAT are you making?"

"It's a theatre. See that trapdoor? That's where the devil comes up and takes her to hell."

"Her?"

"Portia. We're doing *The Merchant of Venice* this term."

"But she doesn't go to hell."

"It's my theatre, isn't it?"

II

"Of course, I do frightfully love Aunt Maud. It's just affectionate when I laugh at the way she pinches the tips under the plates in teashops. Sometimes when I laugh at her she gives me a share. I simply love shopping with her. I often wonder whether she won't start pinching things from the counters. I love dear old Uncle Pat, too. He's such a funny old dear, always going to meetings and sitting on the Council and standing for Parliament. He likes my friend Beryl very much. He's always tickling her. I'm his secretary now. He pays me five bob a week. When I grow up I'm going to get him to help me go into Parliament."

III

"What on earth's that?"

"Brill—he's a boy at school—drew it. He gave it to me."

"But what is it?"

"He says it's a field. It looks more like a park. I think he's good at parks. I don't think he'd feel hurt if I sold it to you. It might become quite valuable one day, if he became famous for painting parks. That dark green bit is quite good, but it would be better if it had some railings there. It would make it more park-like."

IV

"I'm the best at Singing and the best at Dancing and the best at Arith. and the best at Reading and the best at . . ."

"What are you worst at?"

"Well, actually I'm not really bad at anything. I used to be a bit bad at Cooking and Needlework, but Mummy said I could give them up. I'm going to win Beauty Competitions in the summer and do Dramatic Acting in the winter. I'm not just pretty; I've got talent, you know. I'm going to have more husbands than children, I think."

"Have you lots of friends at school?"

"No."

V

"Look, I'll teach you how to play. Do it like this and you can't lose. What about having sixpence on? Well, it's the best way to get experience. Now, look. I'll lend you a sixpence for the next game. Then you can let me have sevenpence out of your winnings."

VI

"I don't believe in impots, Mr. Frisby."

"Why not, Simon?"

"Well, I don't mean I'm exactly against them. I think if a boy is bad he ought to have them. It might make him better."

"Do you think they stop other boys' being naughty?"

"Oh, I'm sure they do. I mean if you've done something wrong you ought to be punished, oughtn't you? But what do you think?"

"I think I believe in them."

"So do I."

"What are you going to be when you grow up?"

"A clergyman."

VII

"And this dolly is a very precious dolly indeed. She's my princess and I'm her very loyallest subject. I put down everything she says and I write it in my magazine every day and when Mummy and Daddy come in I read them all about her. Daddy doesn't always have time to listen to everything I've got to tell him; but I let him buy the magazine and take it away with him to read."

VIII

"That's very kind of you, but I think I can manage to hang the paper better on my own."

"If you don't let me help you I'll kick the paste-pot over."

IX

"Brenda, you be Maid Marian and Thomas can be Friar Tuck and Billy can be Little John and Mabel, I think you could be Alan-a-Dale. Then Howard can be Sheriff of Nottingham and the rest of you can be Merrie Men. . . . Oh, yes, so I have. Well, I don't mind. I'll be Robin Hood."

Girl Guiding Yesterday

By GILLIAN REYNOLDS

BEYOND the meagre, rock fostered hedgerows were the sheep, ranks of them, on every hillside we tramped past. Blank faced, endlessly chewing, defecating with a vacant abandon, they called forth peals of mirth from our town-bred ranks. "Look at the state of that one," shrilled Georgina of the rosy cheeks and merry ringlets, "chewin', chewin', chewin' and pooin', pooin' . . ." "Georgina," warned Captain, "It may look strange to you, but that's nature."

This was the first day of our Girl Guide camp, in North Wales, in 1946. Being the time of post-war austerity meant, for some reason not entirely unconnected with the lack of tents, that we were to spend a week tramping backwards and forwards among the Youth Hostels of Snowdonia. Here we were to learn to undertake some of the challenges a Guide must be prepared for; to hike, to look for weather signs, to learn something about the out-of-doors, to get to know people and to live cheerfully with the Guide Laws.

And a merry crew we were, as we filed along the narrow lanes between the haunted rings of mountains, passing sudden crystal bursts of waterfall and balancing on our heads our assortment of tatty cardboard suitcases. "Miss, Miss," said Kathleen to Captain, "my feet are all blisters." "Remember, Kathleen," said Captain, "a Guide smiles and sings under all difficulties."

"Roll me over, in the clover . . ." began Kathleen in her pure, high treble when Captain decided it was perhaps time for us all to take a rest and see if we could spy any wild flowers among the verdant loveliness of the banks.

"One at a time, behind the hedge," said Lieutenant to the query which rose at that moment to every lip. But Sheila came back and said she wasn't pulling her knickers down in front of all them staring bloody sheep.

At dusk we reached the Youth Hostel where the stew was burnt and the bread a touch mouldy. It was instructive fun to mingle with the genuine hikers and climbers for the ten minutes it took them to sum up our ragged urban battalion and leg it back out to the nearest pub. At last, when the dishes were done, the burnt pans scoured, and the dish towels retrieved from Kathleen's suitcase by our ever vigilant Warden, we settled in the common room to write up our Patrol logs and practise a few knots. Captain said it was time for bed when Emily asked if she could go outside with the two Belgian hikers to learn the round turn and two half hitches.

As this was the first time I had ever been away from home and as I had never been in the company of this particular group of girls for more than a couple of hours every Thursday night, it came as a surprise to learn that they were such interested students of human biology. When it came to my turn to describe what my dad looked like in the bath, I was usually sound asleep although the topic seemed to have enough in it to attract more than one night's discussion.

Did I dream that night of the Brownies, where I had been so happy, singing round the mushroom, "We're the Fairies bright and gay, Helping others every day," and learning how to tie a reef knot? Admittedly, I'd only joined the Brownies in the first place for the most snobbish of reasons, because the Scouts at our church wore kilts and made our church parades much more glamorous than those of the Church of England over the road.

Was this week of foot-sore torment, of never-ending strings of Pat and Mick jokes, of echoing hunger and swamping homesickness, some kind of retribution for joining a Presbyterian Church for the wrong reasons and then having swanked so hard in front of the Church of England Guides about going to camp next *week*, not next *year*?

Each night as I turned the pillow over to the dry side, I heard the conversations in the bunks on either side hush into murmurs out of which rose repeatedly a certain new, short, word. Ever afterwards I would associate the rugged mountains of Wales with that strange word, a connection that is, indeed, popular among many English people. Was it some Welsh Georgina had learned when she was trying to "click"

*"What's with the hippies, don't they get sick like
other people? So why not go to medical school
and become a hippie **doctor**?"*

with the potato-faced lad from the farm at the bottom of the lane?

At last the week was over and as we struggled the last few miles to the bus depot, immune now to the stares of the hostile natives and their clattering tongued disapproval, our thoughts began to turn to home. "Miss," asked the irrepressible Kathleen, "can we stop in the town and get some presents to take home?" And so we did, although more than one of us operated that Guide Law about taking care of other people's possessions to such an extent that Captain was obliged to step in and mediate with the testily over-suspicious Celtic shopkeeper. On the bus, Georgina fell into whispered conversation with one of our sister Guides who was reputed years later to have followed the steps of the legendary Maggie May, our sister Liverpudlian. And once again that strange, new short word floated on the pent air between them.

"Mother," I said at dinner that first night home, "what does **** mean?" I mentioned the Georgina word with some diffidence for if it turned out not to be Welsh but Liverpudlian, I would be in trouble, since it wasn't exactly approved of in our house to talk common. "Don't ever say that again," she said. "But what does it mean?" "It means you're not going to the Girl Guides any more, that's what it means."

TIES THAT BIND

LORD MANCROFT unravels the old boy network

THE chap who used to deliver our coals in the days when we were allowed coal fires always kept his trousers up with an old Etonian tie. I was reluctant to discuss the matter with him because I felt that if he really were an old Etonian he would regret any suggestion that he might not be entitled to wear the tie, and if he weren't he would be angrier still. So I let the matter pass.

I read the other day that the chorus girls currently appearing in a Shaftesbury Avenue musical have taken to wearing old Etonian ties with white blouses whilst relaxing in their local public house, and very neat this is said to look. It is, however, contrary to current trend, for sartorially the old school tie is going out of fashion.

It is of course much worn by the numerous Senior Citizens who congregate at Bexhill, St Leonards and other towns along the Costa Geriatrica. In Whitehall's Clubland, it still jostles for pride of place with that of the Brigade. Michael Avlen went so far as to regret that a character in one of his novels was not a double-headed Imperial Hapsburg eagle so that he could have worn both ties at once.

At the Civil Service end of Whitehall however, it is now seldom to be seen. The Foreign Office Red Book which keeps tabs on the bright young men and tells the Foreign Secretary when Buggins is fit to be Our Man in Azerbaijan now contains, I believe, no reference to where Buggins went to school. I bet it was Winchester, all the same. When I last worked in Whitehall no less than seven of our loftier Ambassadors had been at Winchester when I was there myself, and most of them, even in those days, had "Azerbaijan or bust" written all over their faces.

I, personally, don't wear my old school tie all that often. It's not that I'm in any way ashamed of the place, although I must admit that I tire rather easily of people saying "Winchester? Oh, I suppose you knew all those Bolshie fellows like Cripps, Gaitskell, Crossman and Jay." No; it's simply that our particular tie doesn't really go very easily with anything. The old Etonian tie is pretty and looks especially well with a black coat and striped trousers, for which form of dress I believe it was specifically designed. But the Old Wykehamist tie is so vividly hued that it would even clash with a coalman's trousers.

Aware of this, the noble lord, Lord Shenfield designed us a quieter version which is pleasing but so closely resembles the blazon of Wolverhampton Wanderers that it has never really been accorded the acclaim it deserves. I do not, however, believe that the decline in the wearing of old school tie, even among young old Etonians, has much to do with decor. I've come to the conclusion that it's a form of inverted snobbery and a rather disturbing one at that. Let me explain.

On the door of the prefects' study in my house at Winchester there hangs a copy of a report on a boy I should like to have known. If memory serves me correctly, it reads as follows: "This boy lies, steals and does not wash. The fact that he has succeeded in seducing the gardener's wife, the under-matron and the captain of the school boxing-team would not have mattered so much had not all three of these bizarre manifestations occurred within the same week. In him, sloth and corruption are combined in repellent harmony. But he had done much better than last half." The imagination boggles at the thought of what may have happened last half.

One would also like to know how the lad fared in later life and whether his old school tie kept him out of or got him into deeper water. The Western Brothers (a musical hall turn, now alas, forgotten) once had a song on this important subject. It was fine, sardonic stuff but it muddled the prosecution's case.

An old school tie isn't, as the Brothers suggested, just something that will help you to meet the chap whose sister you will eventually marry, or even to provide you with a sort of social identity card. If, indeed, you want to use it for that purpose you can depend upon it that the man who hails you on Vancouver Airport, or in the Spotted Dog at Kuala Lumpur, will prove to be the one you most disliked at school and whom you have been anxiously avoiding for the last 30 years. Nevertheless, you will be talked into joining him and three other hearty exiles in a dinner which will be really horrible but which will eventually read well in the old school mag.

No, as I understand it, the real case against the old school tie is this. It enables you to flaunt the fact that your father could afford to send you to an expensive school.

When you want to join this regiment, that club or business, the fact that there are people of influence who wear the same tie helps you to jump the queue. If you get into any difficulties, you can always be pulled out of them by your neckwear. Worse still, there are some avenues which are actually inexplorable and some stones virtually unturnable by those who only wear the tie of Sludgeville Comprehensive.

"Mine are at terrorist training camp. Keeps them out of mischief."

There is, or used to be, an element of truth in this. But even Trade Unionists have been known to give preference to other Trade Unionists and so it is in the Inner Temple, at Barts and, though you mustn't say this, in one or two Freemasons' Lodges as well. Nevertheless, the old school tie and everything it stands for is out. If, for instance, you are trying to get a job in some trendy Advertising Agency you must now assume a bogus Cockney accent, wear a vivid magenta tie (or preferably none at all), and keep very quiet about the M.C. your Father won with the Greenjackets at Wadi Halfa. And quite right too. Away with unearned privilege! Down with undue influence! Abolish grandparents' covenants and thereby ruin the prep schools on a side win. Boo to Winchester and three cheers for Sludgeville Comprehensive.

But wait a minute. There's something which I don't understand in this line of argument. A public school education, if you want one, now costs the earth. The fees at Winchester are over a thousand a year. And yet more and more parents are still prepared to scrimp and save in order to get their sons to a good public school. Are they really prepared to go to such lengths and make such sacrifices just for the sake of some ill-defined and fast-disappearing social perk?

It is well known that Winston Churchill did not do well at Harrow. His struggles with algebra have enabled successive generations of idle little toads to call his name in aid when anxious parents seek explanations for O-level debacles. Nevertheless, I'm afraid that some parents in their perverse, old-fashioned way would still prefer their sons to do badly at a good public school than brilliantly at Sludgeville Comprehensive.

If a man wants to spend his hard-earned cash on wine, women and song, so be it. But if he prefers to spend it on a better education for his son than the one he received himself, why on earth shouldn't he? What's more, he'll also be taking a bit of the pressure off Sludgeville.

There is, I think, one small bonus still wrapped up in the old school tie. To sport the tie no longer means that the doorman at Annabel's will bow to you more deeply than to Sludgeville. It may, however, mean that there were only 20 in the maths class at your school and not the 40 that you'd have found at the Comprehensive. You may also have learnt one of the greatest lessons a public school can teach, and that is how to put up with injustice.

In view of what eventually happened to Winston, you may not think this matters. Nor, presumably does the Socialist party or they'd be founding more public schools instead of seeking to abolish them.

I do hope, however, that they stick to their guns because I'm sure this policy will lose them a lot of votes at the next General Election.

100

Child's Play
by GRAHAM

"Mickey's got him teetering on the
verge of bankruptcy."

"Well, who in hell HAS got Mr. Bunn the baker?"

"I'll see you for three."

"Sarah's put down a naughty word."

SON

By ALAN COREN

Dᴇᴀʀ ɢɪʟᴇs—

I'd like you to know that it isn't every kid that gets the chance to have a justifiable grudge against his father so early on in life. Here you are, six hours old, and about to be converted into twelve hundred words-worth of rent and rates. Instant material. Psychiatrists yet unborn may some day use this imperishable tract as the lynchpin of your diagnosis, and if you ever come up before the beak, make sure you have a copy to hand: no jury could remain unswayed at this irrefutable evidence of you old man's selfless devotion to self.

Actually, it's not that way at all. You merely made the mistake of entering the Vale of Tears via that rickety gate reserved for the sons of writers; and like any other father, I am merely addressing the situation in my own way. Had you been born a Bunting, your paterfamilias would currently be out pumping slugs at innocent rabbits in order to provide you with vest and pants, and of the two occupations, I think mine's the cleaner. Just. *Chacun à son métier*, which is French and therefore italicised to show its inferiority to English, a distinction you may not as yet be able to appreciate, since the last time I saw you you were concentrating on mastering the burp. First things first. I dropped that line in, by the way, to show that I work for a magazine of *ton* with a multilingual audience, and not for some second-rate tabloid rag. I tried the second-rate tabloid rags, because that's where the loot is, but they didn't have a vacancy, so if anyone asks you in years to come why it is your feet stick out of the ends of your boots, tell them it's because your old man is an artist.

Or was. This game being the thing of shreds and patches it is, by the time you read this I may well be flogging polythene bags from suitcase premises in Regent Street. I wouldn't have worried as much about this yesterday, when there were just two of us; but now your mother's given birth to a Responsibility, and for the first time in my life I'm telephoning in-surance agents, instead of the other way round. Or, rather, *vice-versa*: at the speed with which Latin is disappearing from the sentences of the world, I'd like to drop something in that you may not understand in five years' time, just so's you'll have a little respect for your father. God knows, it'll be hard enough to come by, with your homework consisting of such items as astro-physics and cybernetics and similar goodies calculated to leave an old Eng. Lit. artificer of the 'fifties quavering at the post. Still, I'll say this for me, no one ever translated a shapelier rune; dons talk of it yet, and weep for vanished generations.

You were born on a bizarre day, in climatic circumstances not unlike those with which novels about the Old South tend to be fraught: at the end of the hottest spell for two hundred years there was a thunderstorm which, when it departed, left the world more crowded by at least one. All extremely portentous, if a shade hammy. And don't worry about that two-hundred-years bit, and never seeing its like again; one of the things you'll discover about England is that we have the hottest (or coldest) summer for two centuries every three years, or so. Don't ask me why. Meteorology is a subject I have but skirted.

I hope you'll forgive, by the way, all this familiarity from a total stranger; but I wanted to start talking to you immediately because, oddly enough, you and I are probably closer now than we'll ever be from here on in. As of now, we shall be gradually getting to misunderstand one another; I wouldn't fret over this, since, with normal luck, we shall continue to like one another, it's simply that we'll be able to communicate less and less as you learn to communicate more and more. It's to do with generations, and fathomlessly complicated as well as being totally incurable, so there's an end. Within six months, the only response I'll glean from opening a conversation with you will be a faceful of strained apricot, in ten years I shall be failing utterly to explain sex, and in twenty you'll be chucking rocks at the American Embassy, if there's anything left of it, and telling your mates that the old man has never understood you and why doesn't someone just wheel him out into the fading sunlight and let him dribble down his bib? So let me emphasise it: don't get hung up on the understanding bag (that's contemporary argot, incidentally, or at any rate was at the time of going to press)—some of my best friends are complete mysteries to me, and if I have any sense, I'll leave it that way.

You'll possibly want to know what was gripping the newspapers at the hour of your birth, so I've expended a couple of shillings *(sorry, I mean ten new pence, if that's what it is; or, which is more likely, considering the time-lapse necessary before your finger runs along this line, one Deutschmark)* on what are laughingly called four Shades Of Informed Opinion: *The Times*, the *Guardian*, the *Mirror*, and the *Express*. At the time of reading, these will doubtless be the *Times-Guardian-Mirror-Express*, and that's if they're lucky, the way Fleet Street is shrivelling up. They don't have too much of significance to impart, packed as they are with syllables about citizens called Nixon, Kennedy, Wilson, Heath, Feather, who will pass and be forgotten like the rest. You, at least, will have the assistance of history to judge them, and be in a better position than I to yawn or snigger behind your hand. The only other gobbet to bother the front-page compositors is the Moon, which you'll certainly find hilarious, concerned as the stories are with the colour of its dirt and whether you can catch anything off it; a comical insight into the Dark Ages for a lad who'll be spending his honeymoon on the Venusian Riviera and watching a brace of Martians open the batting at Lord's.

There's just one other item, bannered only by the *Guardian*'s front page: Race Violence Renewed At Leeds. I hope this will be as out-dated an example of the pitiful ignorance of 1969 man as fear of Moonpox, but in case it isn't, I'm going to hit you with a pithy anecdote. Let me say, first off, this isn't the one about Where Would We Be Without Coloured Doctors And Nurses: of all the cheap and specious rationalisations, this comes high on the list, because tolerance has nothing at all to do with how much you're going to benefit materially from the donation of it. Discriminating between doctors and bricklayers is as sickening as discriminating between black and white. All I want to remark is that I watched you, a few minutes after you became you, being bathed and cared for and reassured by black hands; you didn't distinguish between skin colours then, so don't louse up the record. No theologian, I can't comment on whether you've been stuck with Original Sin; but as far as social sins are concerned, you don't get born with those,

they're a later contamination. That's all.

You're not, probably, in much of a position to guess what Lord Chesterfield, Al Jolson, and William Rees-Mogg have in common, and who could blame you? It's a question that would baffle someone twice your age. What marks out those three gents is their predilection for dinning into their offspring various observations concerning the world into which they have been delivered; and a decent crust they all made out of it, too. I, with few ambitions involving the *Oxford Dictionary of Quotations* or Cinema-Scope, don't intend to chance my arm. Personally, I think we can lay down the requisite codes of behaviour as we go along, pragmatism being nearer to Godliness than abstract morality in my book, which is clearly not the Authorised Version. Neither do I care to foist any potted description of the world upon you, since my view of it is essentially idiosyncratic, and I do mean essentially. No other way to look at it, and if it confuses you more and more with each unfolding orbit of the Earth, at least it'll be your own confusion, and not anyone else's. With a modicum of luck, you and I may get to swop our private confusions (which is called discussion) and gain something from the exchange (which is called laughter).

I've just glanced at my watch, to find that you're twice as old as you were when I started. Since there'll be so many better things to fritter your life on, I'll get out now and leave you to lead it. It occurs to me that I may not have mentioned how deliriously happy I am right now; but, for once in my career, that's something that goes without saying.

"It was always my ambition to smash the Portland vase till I found out it had been done."

Time, Children, Please

According to the Errol Report, in certain circumstances children should be allowed in pubs. Here are some circumstances, according to ALBERT

"He's been waiting here twenty minutes!"

105

The House the Mouse Built

By ALAN WHICKER

How can you be mad at Mickey Mouse? Don't think it's easy. To restrain enthusiasm even slightly is not only unAmerican, it's kicking Peter Rabbit's cottontail—you feel such a brute; but fresh from Florida, I'm here to say: at close quarters Disney can cloy.

Now forty-two and very rich indeed, Mickey will move his billion-dollar business to the Sunshine State on October 1st to unleash a social revolution—a project of such magnitude it stuns even a State well used to space-billions, and moon shots departing on time from Platform 2 at Cape Kennedy, just down the road from the House the Mouse built.

For the first of our new *World of Whicker* series for Yorkshire Television I watched the birth pangs of Walt Disney World, largest private building project ever known, and was suitably staggered. Not yet publicised, but about to hit, its impact will register around the world.

Seven years ago Disney quietly bought-up 27,400 acres of swamp and woodland between Kissimmee and Orlando and set his 'Imagineers' loose. Their incredible playground across 43 square miles is as big as Manchester or, for southerners, 80 times the size of Hyde Park. Against such a fibreglass fantasyland, Blackpool is Lilliput.

Cinderella's Castle alone cost £2 million, and would make Ludwig even madder. The Haunted House is almost ready—they're just moving in the ghosts—near an idealised 1890 Main Street.

Thirty-seven lifesize Presidents "authentically garbed by Californian tailors" will be in action, computers controlling 24 body movements a second. Some of these grotesque living dolls also talk. Seven-foot audio-animatronic bears in Grizzly Hall sing how Davy Crockett "killed him a b'ar when he was only three . . ." Artificial lakes heave as artificial waves pound manmade islands; and here

106

Americans are *building* Cambodian ruins (while knocking them down elsewhere . . .).

This first phase is costing £125 million; Disney calculators expect more than ten million visitors the first year and by 1980 the equivalent of half the population of the United States. The average visitor to this global village should spend between £3 and £4—though a family visit will leave Pop's pocket £40 lighter, per day.

Walt Disney bought this vast spread because at his Californian Disneyland, opened in 1955 and toured by 10 million last year, outside promoters make four times his profit out of *his* crowds. Their motels, spaghetti-heavens, gas stations press-in and cash-in along concentric circles of ugliness.

In Florida, determined to contain his captive audience while they have any cash left, Disney decreed they should stay, as well as play. Phase 1 has five giant resort hotels—the first so big that express monorail trains run right through a lobby big as a football field, silently disgorging passengers at Reception. Its 1,057 modular rooms, prefabricated down to wallpaper and bathroom mirrors, were just slotted in. Conventions already booked through to 1977 include the Catfish Farmers of America and the South-Eastern Peanut Association. Soon, another four motels, camping and trailer parks, hotel for pets, 200 ships on five lakes, a submarine fleet, two railways, park for 12,000 cars, golf courses, and eventually a Community of Tomorrow for twenty thousand people, living-in.

Though kept at a distance, developers fly towards Disney's honey: hot-dog-and-motel strips already surround his phantasmagoria. In satellite new-towns for 80,000 inhabitants, eighteen-storey motor inns are abuilding.

The gentle countryfolk of these ravished counties are still unaware, I suspect, of the magnitude of the coming blow. Kissimmee, once a trading post and the State's Cow Capital, had a gallop-in bar: "Bovine-orientated Kissimmee", said one magazine. There, and at the senior-citizens community of Windermere, residents are discovering Disneyland brings profit to promoters and real-estate men, but to others, just increased taxes, Cup Final traffic every day, roads jammed solid for twenty-five miles, crime, drugs and general disruption imported by the onrushing millions. "We'll be overwhelmed by people problems", said an official. "If everyone only drops a gum wrapper, we'll be knee-deep in gum wrappers."

So central Florida has had greatness, of a sort, thrust upon it. Now the fastest-growing part of the United States, Disney World brings the wildest statistics since

"He's terribly proud of having won the School Parents' Day Egg and Spoon race . . ."

107

space flight: to the Florida domain it will add £3,000,000,000; at least 1,000 hotels, restaurants and service stations; 80,000 jobs. A frantic landrush has sent promising one-acre sites up to £125,000.

Disney's take in the first year should be more than £40 million—much of it from concessions: the Florida Citrus Commission is paying £1½ million for the ten-year right to sponsor a pavilion selling orange drinks; Gulf Oil is putting up £7 million, Eastern Airlines £4 million. Big Business hopes some of Disney's wholesome mystique will rub off, that under his childish spell visitors will be in the right mood "to accept the Corporate message." Could be, for this international institution peddles instant happiness to a passive public which empties its mind and queues to buy.

Those 'imagineers' are chillingly efficient; they improve-upon and tidy-up nature. On Swiss Family Isle the giant tree spreads magnificently; only when you touch do you find branches are fibreglass on steel, leaves vinyl. It's creepy. Clouds of pigeons will wheel-around sunset ceremonies, their primary feathers pulled-out until they learn to straighten up, fly right and *love* that place! Dissatisfied with available pansies, they bred a longer-lived strain that's *faceless*. There's Disney for you.

My reaction to his original Californian operation was, I think, typical: I went to smile tolerantly, stayed to be enchanted. Florida will be the same, only more so; impossible not to succumb to such homespun charm, however phoney and over-sweet. Not a child's world, but a middle-aged view of what a child's world might have been . . .

The man himself spun fantasies and relished an innocence that did not mix with the times. Walt Disney, a sort of genius, ignored the difference between children and adults; his sweet and harmless vision—mawkish, sugar-coated—reconciled generations and awakened old, warm dreams. The man-child who never tired of toys died of cancer five years ago, aged 65; he will not go short of memorials.

He escaped criticism by being resolutely cleancut and against sin; but his patriotic nursery whimsy is also waxen predigested nostalgia and a caricature of American history. The individuality of man and nature lies smothered by plastic, controlled by computers. Man dehumanised, nature defiled—but there I go again, being rude to cute mice.

At close quarters the insufferably sugary front displayed by this pushy industrial complex leaves me a trifle queasy. A sharp sense of double-entry book-keeping pervades, and all is artificial—even those inescapable white smiles, switched on and off with chill discipline. Over the whole dollar-hungry scene hangs a Jehovah's Witness sense of mission.

At the Disney 'University' in California Hosts and Hostesses (in Euphemism-land customers are Guests, uniforms Costumes, crowds Audiences) are indoctrinated and taught how to be "people specialists", which seems to mean frozen grins and canned answers. Simple mass psychology is aimed at keeping Audiences in a spending mood.

One of the Hostesses explained "When you work for Disney the glory falls upon you and you start to glow—it's pixie dust!" She didn't smile when she said that, unfortunately.

Meanwhile back in Paradiseland Walt Disney seems about to be canonized. Though far from popular in his lifetime, employees' eyes now light up at his name. Legends grow more loving as years go by and good works proliferate. In discreet corners throughout his growing empire, small portraits await their candles.

Our pilgrimage into his world was suitably humble, but we emerged perplexed; this was not only due to an alarmingly inept Public Relations department. We had driven five hundred miles to Orlando and received a guarded welcome from Disney's Marketing man Sandy ("This is a first-name operation, Alan"). They had their own television film to sell, he said, so although my thirty million audience around the world was acceptable, they preferred to control publicity. Indeed they

"Melvin here is one of our founder members."

do. Chosen groups are brought in for an organised tour, lecture, brief word with selected personnel—and away, clutching handouts. What they can't control, they fear. And there was this unchosen Englishman; when you wish upon Disney's star, it makes a *lot* of difference who you are . . .

After much charming hesitation they allowed we might film, provided not more than ten minutes of Disney World appeared in the final programme. (We actually used seven minutes). We started carefully, to do the place justice.

Next morning a gritty PR man called Charles ("Now lissen here, Alan . . .") abruptly ordered us to leave the site by midday. I had mixed emotions: it was almost a relief to meet someone being thoroughly nasty—at least there was nothing bogus about *his* attitude.

He didn't say "These 27,400 acres are too small for both of us" but he *did* imply, with a stern stare over my left shoulder, that if we were still there, come sundown, we should be run out of town. It was High Noon in Fantasyland, and the pixie dust was coming down sour. We departed, meek but sorrowful. Our white hard-hats were taken away, symbolically. Disney's private army of cops gave us brief automatic smiles as we drove into the sunset. Up music, run titles, fade.

Let not such curious incompetence, the unsure organisation man's fear of the committee above, cloud our reaction to a staggering achievement. Disney's earnest army is making the world's major bid to solve problems of expanding leisure-time—and incidentally, problems of surplus cash.

Their organisation is wholesome, well disciplined and (usually) friendly. Within it the outsider will find no alcohol, no long hair, no drugs, no litter, no sex, no moustaches, no violence. Instead, a reassuringly bland blend of whimsy, brilliance of imagination, cunning crowd control; a sentimental spread of antiseptic entertainment to delight those millions who love to get their teeth into a marshmallow-covered cream puff, artificially sweetened.

So—sorry to be out of step, but this Prole (one ten-millionth of the first year's throughput) can do without such manipulation, however innocent. I'll glow my own way, thanks, if it's all the same to St. Walt. Let's face it, there's something positively *inhuman* about Mickey Mouse.

****

TERRY JONES and MICHAEL PALIN (straight from Monty Python) present

THE LITTLE RED CHRISTMAS BOOK

THE LIVING GUIDE TO CHRISTMAS FOR THE RADICAL NIPPER

"Children unite! Parental dynasticism is a paper tiger! The power lies in the pupilage, and th juvenescent syndicalism of the status pupillaris will gravel the toothless lackeys of gerontocrat parentalism, that have coerced our nonage throughout past history to be recipients of such fairings a matching ballpoint pen and pencil sets, Tootal ties, books on How To Keep Warm, woolly jumpe and gloves."

(—San-Ta Clau

Yes kiddies! Here's what you can do now—Don't just talk! Don't just write lists! ORGANISE YOURSELVES!

AGIT-PROP

Here are some of the already existing Direct Action Groups you may like to be affiliated to:

N.B.L.F.*
P.F.P.**
H.N.C.***
M.K.N.F.P.A.G.****
C.F.G.O.O.T.J.H.K.L.D.V.H.G.*****

THE LAW

And remember! The law is there for you to USE! Don't be afraid to *sue* if you get: matching ballpoint pen and pencil sets, ties or more than 6 diaries. Try:

Breach of Promise (younger brothers cannot be used as witnesses) or sue parents under Trade Descriptions Act. Court action is not recommended for real Tinies, as they may wilt under cross-examination (viz. Crown v. Ba-ba Wilkins 1968, Mr. & Mrs. Potter v. Little Willie 1964 *et al*). They are advised to accept the gift and stick to Civil Disobedience.

CIVIL DISOBEDIENCE

This method accounts for some 90% of our success rate. Recommended tactics:

a) First thing Christmas morning get up early and get your head stuck in the banisters.
b) Contrive to be sick over the sofa before lunch.
c) Tell Uncle Jack what all his presents are before he opens them.
d) Be sick round the back of the television.
e) Put a couple of Uncle Jack's prophylactics in the Christmas pudding.
f) Make the dog sick.

*New Bike Liberation Front.
**Presents for Profit.
***Helicopter now! Committee.
****Meccano Kit Number Four Please Action Group.
*****Committee For Getting One Of Those Junior
Hospital Kits Like Deirdre Vickers Has Got.

CONSUMERS' CORNER

The following toys break on Christmas Day:

i) The Whizzo Super Ace Strongbeam Torch (With Inte Galactic Signalling Attachment).
ii) The Little Wonder Two-Way Walkie-Talkie—(As Us By The U.S. Army).
iii) The Grantham "Staybrite" Video Recorder.

The following toys break on Boxing Day:

i) The Young Wizards' "Saw Your Granny In Half" Kit.
ii) The Little Wonder Self-Loading Automatic Rifle—(Used By The U.S. Army).
iii) The Leonardo Da Vinci Icing Set.

The following toys last the whole year:

i) Matching ballpoint and pencil sets.
ii) Tootal ties.
iii) New plimsolls.
iv) Any Norman St. John Stevas book.

The following toys get lost:

i) The "Mercury" Radio-Controlled Glider.
ii) The Rod Laver "Flingandbring" Boomerang.
iii) The "Mariner IV" Mars Probe—(As Used By The U. Army).

THE PSYCHOLOGICAL APPROACH

If you still find Christmas presents a disturbing factor your home life, you would do well to read a new book th has just been published under the title: "Human Yuletic Inadequacies". It is the result of 11 years of painstakir research and laboratory observations at the University Illinois.

Here is a typical extract:

"PRESENTAL DYSFUNCTION

CASE HISTORY: Child A was 7 years of age and ha shown considerable interest in each several desire-objects: a) A clockwo tram, b) A Football, c) A Jetto Se

****

Elevating Missile Launcher & Camping Stool, d) A Junior Rodeo Suit, etc., etc. During the months preceding Christmas, he indicated to his parents his preference for a), b), c), & d) in turn. In the event he was presented on the 25th with a matching ballpoint pen and pencil set.

ANALYSIS: Obviously the parent had become disorientated during the gift-arousal stage, by the disparity of desire-objects indicated by the child. This resulted in blind panic followed by loss of identification of the child with the present in the parent's mind. This condition is known as Presental Dysfunction.

TREATMENT: On or around noon on November 15th the child should make the first mention of the article or articles required for Christmas. At first the mentions should be only 2 or 3 times daily. If by November 30th there has been no apparent reaction (e.g. slap on the head, refusal to allow staying-up for 'Man Alive', running-down drugs and pop music) then begin to mention the article in selected high-embarrassment situations (e.g. during brief but angelic post-bath appearance at dinner parties, in shops or in front of bank managers).

If by December 24th there has still been no manifestation of parental perception of the desire-object indicated, be sick over the sofa."
(from "Human Yuletide Inadequacies"
Masters & Johnson 1971)

BOOKS TO AVOID

The Young Capitalist's Christmas Annual. No revolutionary nipper should let himself be given this. This is the sort of thing it contains:

"Hallo Young Capitalists!

Well, last year we showed you how to make box girder bridges, but this year we're concentrating on the thing which more and more kiddies are looking for at this Christmas Tide; a really well-managed, Equity-based, High Yield Growth Fund with maximum tax-free profit expectancy.

OTHER BOOKS FOR REVOLUTIONARY YOUNGSTERS TO AVOID:

a) *My Life*—by Sir Lew Grade
b) *His Life*—by Bernard Delfont

111

"Carnegie Hall is nibbling."

"I see that this first volume of autobiography only takes you to the age of four."

Infant Prodigy

by ffolkes

"Sometimes I almost hate him."

"I'm afraid this is goodbye. You've taught me all you know."

Fair Play for Fathers

By P. G. WODEHOUSE

THE advent of Father's Day in America has inspired the advertisement pages of the magazines to suggestions for brightening the life of this poor underprivileged peon. "Buy him an outboard runabout speedboat 14 long with a 62 beam," say the magazines. "Buy him a synchromatic wrist watch, water and shock resistant. Buy him a fishing-rod 7 long with reinforced ferrules and large-capacity spinning Beachcomber reel," say the magazines, knowing perfectly well that if he gets anything, it will be a tie with pink horseshoes on a blue background.

What he really wants, of course, is a square deal from the hellhounds of Television.

It is difficult to say when the thing started, but little by little the American Father has become established on the Television screen as Nature's last word in saps, boobs and total losses, the man with two left feet who can't make a move in any direction without falling over himself. Picture a rather exceptionally I.Q.-less village idiot and you will have the idea. Father, as he appears in what is known in Television circles as heart-warming domestic comedy, is a bohunkus who could walk straight into any establishment for the care of the feeble-minded and no questions asked.

There are two sorts of heart-warming domestic comedy on American Television. One deals with the daily doings of the young husband and the young wife who converse for thirty minutes without exchanging a civil word. The other features Father, showing him, to quote a recent writer, as "a miserable chinless half wit with barely enough mechanical skill to tie his own shoes." Almost any domestic crisis will do to make him a mockery and a scorn to twenty million viewers. The one the writer selects is Operation Refrigerator. Mom finds that the refrigerator won't work, and Pop says leave it to him, he'll fix it.

Now Pop, says the writer, may be a mechanic during his working hours—he may even be a refrigerator repair man—but in the home he reverts to the Stone Age. He strews the floor with more parts than there are in six refrigerators and a cyclotron. Then, baffled, he *(a)* goes berserk, *(b)* collapses or *(c)* so assembles the parts that the refrigerator spouts boiling water.

It is at this point that Junior steps forward. Junior is an insufferably bumptious stripling of ten or eleven with a freckled face and a voice like a cement-mixer. He straightens everything out with effortless efficiency, speaking patronizing words to Pop over his shoulder. It is obvious that he regards the author of his being as something that ought not lightly to be allowed at large.

I suppose the dim-witted American Father will some day go into the discard like the comic Frenchman with the beard and top-hat and the comic Englishman with the front teeth and whiskers, but it is going to be a grim struggle to get him out of Television. Those Television boys don't often get an idea, but when they do they cling to it. But where they got this idea of the American Child as a mechanical genius it is hard to say.

In the village to which I retire in the summer months the trouble shooters who come round to me when anything goes wrong are grave elderly men in overalls who are obviously experts at their job. I cannot believe that in their homes they have to rely on a freckled child to fix the leaking washer in the scullery tap. I have never come across any mechanically-minded children. Fred Garcia, one of our younger set, has "souped up" his car so that it will do a hundred and thirty m.p.h. and recently covered the fourteen hundred miles between Miami, Fla., and New York, N.Y., in thirty hours, which is unquestionably good going; but Fred is eighteen and training to be a jet pilot. Junior in those heart-warming domestic comedies is never more than twelve at the outside. Often he is nearer six, with curls and an all-day sucker.

What the American child *is* good at is dialogue. There he definitely shines. One specimen of the breed in knickerbockers and a Brigade of Guards tie (to which I am almost sure he was not entitled) looked in on me the other day as I worked in the garden and fixed me with an unwinking stare.

"Hi!" he said.

"Hi to you," I responded civilly.

A pause.

"Wotcher doin'?"

"Gardening."

"Oops."

Another pause.

"Have you got a father?" he said.

I said I had not.

"Have you got a mother?"

"No."

"Have you got a sister?"

"No."

"Have you got a brother?"

"No."

"Have you got any candy?"

Crisp. That is the word I was trying to think of. The American child's dialogue is crisp.

Coming back to the American Father, there was the other day just a gleam of light in his darkness. On the Kraft Theatre programme a family was shown having all sorts of family problems, and who should the wise, kindly person who solved them be but Father. It seems incredible, and several people have told me that I must have imagined it or that I switched the thing off before the big scene at the end showing Father trying to fix the electric light. It may be so.

Meanwhile, I think it only right to warn the Television authorities that if they allow things to continue as they are, they are in grave peril. There has been a good deal of angry muttering of late in the Amalgamated Union of American Fathers, and if you ask me, I think the men are about ready to march.

I am watching the situation very closely.

"Setting 'em a bad example? On the contrary—it's a sound preparation for the world they'll grow up in."

Suffer Little Children

The way the law stands, says FENTON BRESLER, you haven't got much choice

THE law has always believed in shutting its eyes to reality. And so it is with children.

Everyone knows that the modern child is not merely, in Wordsworthian terms, the father of the man: he is his ruler. The case last year at Nottingham juvenile court, when a father admitted to the Bench that he had left home because he was frightened of his eleven-year-old son—"and I am not going back until he has gone"—was only an extreme example of a general trend.

Children are our bosses today. In many homes, they rule the roost. In many schools, it is they who command the teachers. "Pupil power" is not just a cant phrase.

But, in the eyes of the law, Victoria is still on the throne. Piano legs are still hidden by demure frills, children "know their place" and the maxim "spare the rod spoil the child" remains an essential truth.

Every parent has the legal right of "reasonable chastisement" of his children. This can—indeed, according to the older judges, *should*—take a physical form. The same applies to school staff. As Lord Chief Justice Cockburn said in 1865, "The authority of the school master is the same as that of the parent. A parent when he places his child with a school master delegates to him all his own authority so far as it is necessary for the welfare of the child."

Yet what is "reasonable" chastisement?

All decent public school men will be glad to know that the cane is completely legal. Its "moderate use"—

four strokes on the hand—was upheld as long ago as 1889. Even in 1960, two strokes on the buttocks were held to be "not excessive."

Other forms of corporal punishment are, however, legally dangerous. School teachers should find other methods of combining business with pleasure. Leather straps, hair-brushes, clothes-brushes, belts have all been used—of course, only in the stern line of duty—but regrettably ended in fines.

Women's Lib may care to take notice of the unsatisfactory state of the law with regard to girl pupils. There is discrimination. The use of the cane on schoolgirls is, almost certainly, unlawful. The leading authority in a case in Scotland in 1883 when the Court of Session, although unable to bring itself to rule that inflicting corporal punishment on girls was *necessarily* illegal, yet said it was "strongly to be deprecated."

Perhaps they are tougher North of the Border. In another Scottish case some years ago, when a woman head teacher was found guilty of assaulting seven little girls "by administering with a leather strap punishment which was excessive and unreasonable," her lawyer told the judge: "It is consistently clear that she sincerely believed she was doing her duty to the children. The evidence does not suggest premeditated cruelty or reckless abandon."

Children have legal rights against parents, and other representatives of the adult world: but we have few legal rights against *them*. The Swedes say, "Children are certain sorrow but only uncertain joy." Jewish parents have known, for centuries, "Small children, small worries. Big children, big worries."

But the law has always taken the view that *they* are the ones who need to be protected against *us*.

All parents owe a legal duty to protect, both physically and morally, their children and to maintain them. All youngsters under sixteen have a specific legal right not to be ill-treated. All children under twelve have the right not to be left alone in a room with an unguarded fire.

No child under five can be given intoxicating liquor—to quote the 1933 Children and Young Persons Act—"except upon the order of a duly qualified medical practitioner, or in case of sickness, apprehended sickness or other urgent cause." What does "urgent cause" mean? I haven't got the foggiest idea. I suspect it would not be enough to plead as a defence that the child told you it was "dying for a drink."

"Form 1B lost six-nil to Form 2A . . ."

"They call themselves communists and we call them communists. They call us capitalists, but we don't. Why?"

Schoolchildren have all sorts of specific legal rights with regard to the premises where they are given instruction; and the need, for instance, for classes there not to be more than thirty pupils in a class "unless this is unavoidable."

A comforting thought for parents, however, is that we are not responsible for our children's acts. As I recently assured a friend, he could not be made to pay for the damage to his neighbour's car caused by his eleven-year-old son's scratching it with his cycle.

Another good thing is that the only fare legally demandable for a child under fourteen on a train or bus is a half-fare. Furthermore, on London's buses you can insist on having one child under three with you completely free of charge—and on British Rail's trains, you can claim the same privilege for *any* number of children under three.

Kids, of course, are much brighter these days. Yet even that can cause legal problems. Like the divorce case last April when a thirty-five-year-old Romford husband's infidelities were only discovered when his girl friend's young son spotted him travelling on a bus with his wife, and cried out to his mother: "Look, there's Uncle Ronnie!"

So far as the criminal law is concerned, it is conclusively presumed that no child under ten has the necessary mental capacity to commit a crime. The legal fiction persists even into the nineteen seventies, that they are too young to be villains.

But in civil law there is no such lower-age limit. In one case, a boy of eight has been validly held to be a company director. A child model has to pay income tax. And, as Mr. Justice Latey's 1967 Committee on the Age of Minority reported: "No statute imposes a minimum age for trade. There is nothing except the commonsense of his customers to prevent a six-year-old setting up in business."

The same tolerant attitude applies to children as witnesses. The law obviously agrees with the psalmist that out of the mouths of babes and sucklings can come truth. No child is too young to be a witness. A three-year-old girl was allowed to give evidence by Acton magistrates in a case against a drug addict last year; and the testimony of a five-year-old child has recently been accepted in a case at Sheffield.

But both these children gave unsworn evidence, and in such cases a conviction is only possible if there is corroboration.

In a murder case at Leeds Assizes in January, the prosecution wanted to call a nine-year-old boy to give *sworn* evidence of what he saw when his mother was, in his presence, stabbed to death. Mr. Justice Forbes refused to accept the testimony. The boy had received no religious instruction at school and had never read the Bible. So ruled the judge: "Unless the child knows something about Almighty God it is useless swearing him.

"He was there all the time, but we cannot have the evidence because we cannot have it sworn."

Mr. Justice Forbes was only following the established legal policy with regard to children: that in 1971 the law is still administered as if it were 1871.

"Nothing much, mum—we're in between educational experiments at the moment."

117

Northumberland Education Authority has asked teachers to prepare reports on parents as well as children. This end-of-term sheet has been circulated as a guide.

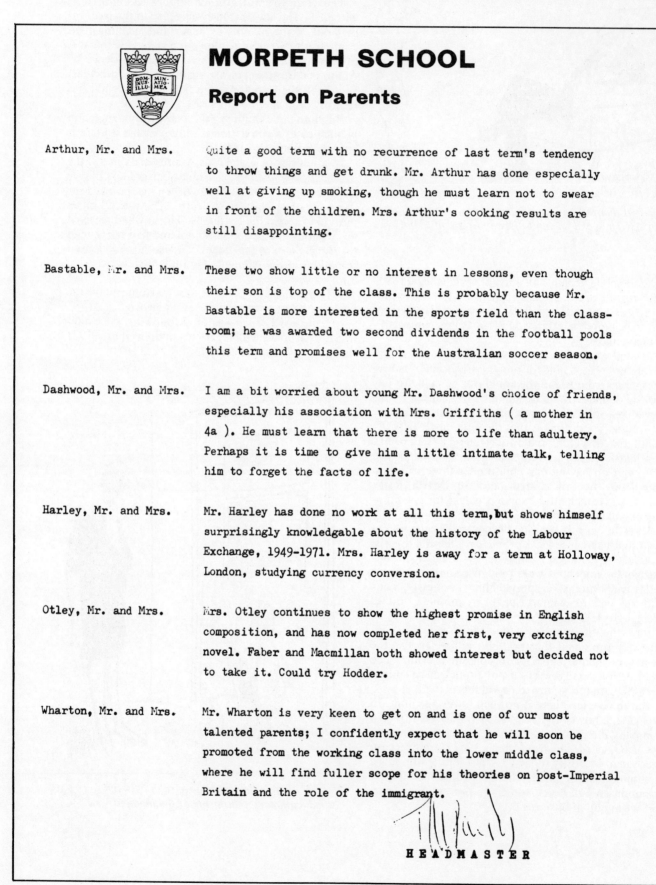

MORPETH SCHOOL
Report on Parents

Arthur, Mr. and Mrs. — Quite a good term with no recurrence of last term's tendency to throw things and get drunk. Mr. Arthur has done especially well at giving up smoking, though he must learn not to swear in front of the children. Mrs. Arthur's cooking results are still disappointing.

Bastable, Mr. and Mrs. — These two show little or no interest in lessons, even though their son is top of the class. This is probably because Mr. Bastable is more interested in the sports field than the class-room; he was awarded two second dividends in the football pools this term and promises well for the Australian soccer season.

Dashwood, Mr. and Mrs. — I am a bit worried about young Mr. Dashwood's choice of friends, especially his association with Mrs. Griffiths (a mother in 4a). He must learn that there is more to life than adultery. Perhaps it is time to give him a little intimate talk, telling him to forget the facts of life.

Harley, Mr. and Mrs. — Mr. Harley has done no work at all this term, but shows himself surprisingly knowledgable about the history of the Labour Exchange, 1949-1971. Mrs. Harley is away for a term at Holloway, London, studying currency conversion.

Otley, Mr. and Mrs. — Mrs. Otley continues to show the highest promise in English composition, and has now completed her first, very exciting novel. Faber and Macmillan both showed interest but decided not to take it. Could try Hodder.

Wharton, Mr. and Mrs. — Mr. Wharton is very keen to get on and is one of our most talented parents; I confidently expect that he will soon be promoted from the working class into the lower middle class, where he will find fuller scope for his theories on post-Imperial Britain and the role of the immigrant.

HEADMASTER

"They do grow up so fast!"

Other People's Babies

PETER PRESTON probes the crib crisis

I'VE been queasy on the whole population problem ever since (in Dacca) I shared a mutton curry with the Director of the International Planned Parenthood Federation. He was out there arranging abortions for raped ladies. I was out there watching. And how many children—inevitable conversation cruncher—do you actually have? Well. Four. But—my equally inevitable justification—we'd got two and the national average was 2.5 so we decided on being up market and the .50 per cent excess turned out twins. Truly, I'm a small-family man and dedicated parenthood planner who just happens to have four kids. Silently he passed the mango chutney.

Thus the guilt has gathered, a compendium of long pauses and snooty looks. In Stringalong society we sleep with the Club of Rome report under our pillow; we know that the earth will burst at the seams; we stagger from statistics which calculate that each year Britain inflicts an extra city the size of Nottingham upon its groaning fabric (why Nottingham? why not Brighton or York or Salisbury or somewhere appetising?); we know that the Government is concerned, that Mr. Robert Carr is Minister in charge of curbing

119

procreation, that the Inner Ring Motorway and Maplin and Mrs. Thatcher's teeny problems are really our baby.

Only last November, I recall, projections still set UK populace for 2000 AD at 63 million, all our green and pleasant land a teeming Croydon. Westminster Select Committees sought for instant action from Downing Street think-tanks. In America, population control was a regular, if not potent, election issue, the kind of thing McGovern was eager beaver for once he had the boys home from Saigon.

And now? Now the figures speak for themselves and spin an altogether different yarn. A yarn which reminds me irresistibly of the London computer which tried to prophesy the Irish election results. On first declaration it forecast a Lynch landslide; ten hours later it was swallowing its own tape in embarrassment.

Britain's population growth, we are suddenly and currently informed, is ZPG (zero population growth) —the lowest in the country's recorded history. Abruptly our Nottinghams of the future have shrivelled to mingy hamlets. There are, and will continue to be, 56 million people on this island. Births are down 4.8 per cent since March last year. The average family size is 2.1 kids (as opposed to 2.4 fourteen months ago). And a cold snap, plus concomitant bronchitis, might in fact soon produce net losses. Official quote: "There is some concern in Whitehall that a continuing slump in birth-rate could lead to a positively dwindling population by next year."

And in positively dynamic America? Birth and fertility rates, it is freshly recorded, are the poorest in history. Last year's total of babies was the lousiest crop for 27 years. The average family size is 2.03 children. The birth ratio was down nine per cent on 1971. Zero population growth stands at 2.3 infants a time, so the situation is zero minus. They call it, predictably enough, a "birth dearth", a "baby bust".

Perhaps a "numbers bumble" might be better. Anyone who has anything to do with social science predictions (and not just Irish elections) proliferates terrible tales of limitless bungles. To be serious: bizarre birth oscillations demonstrate a triumph, a human caprice over computerised certainties. Birth rates, on past form, have always wavered wildly. They are doing so again, and no seer can tell how wide the wavers may run. But still the Doomwatch teams seize isolated examples and puff them to horrendous visions of Earth as a Japanese railway station in rush hour.

At root, the variations mean nothing much until they're soberly worked out over a decade or more. But sober workouts aren't a Stringalong forte. Already (and not pure imagination) I find my quadrupal brood a mild source of strength, the entire acceptance pattern changing.

At least three random acquaintances who swore that two was enough, have, in the past couple of weeks, begun chatting wistfully of the grand old days when a family of under a dozen wasn't a family at all. November's wisdom—rising prices plus ecological restraint equals slow starts, quick finishes and twenty years on the Pill—has already turned to a more fructifying Spring. It seems mind-curdling that such decisions flit by fashion, but the pressures are there, are real and will soon have a flow of little Tristrams and Samanthas as yowling evidence.

More discomforting still, ancestral voices who latterly preached abstinence are beginning to shift pulpits. America has wide open spaces, continuing demands for manpower—and deeper worries. Whilst Negro, Mexican and Puerto Rican birth rates follow general trends, they follow at a distance. The baby bust—in net terms—means a minor ethnic explosion; and that isn't anything your friendly Statehouse politician applauds. Already, my American friends tell me, there's a note of anxious virility creeping into public pronouncements. Nobody has quite urged Homer to have another for Uncle Sam's sake—but it won't be long and it can easily come about: France is well accustomed to such entreaties, particularly the official advice that two litres of rouge a day makes Jacques a dozy, impotent boy.

All of which makes one rather grateful for Robert Carr. He is responsible, but careful scanning of the published records shows only responsibility without activity. A "low profile", the Select Committee called it. Lord Avebury, who wants Britain's population actively reduced to 40 million, would doubtless have another phrase ready. Yet Mr. Carr is steadfast in doing nothing. A cautious fellow, he clearly wonders how in the sacred name of Marie Stopes one engineers the non-mechanical, and bafflingly human, the capricious coupling.

"Certainly," said Mr. Airey Neave MP last August the tenth, "certainly we expect to see ministers here before the Select Committee answering questions during the next twelve months." But just as certainly the answers they are giving will be as out of date as last night's scorecards. Power strikes, European Cup-ties, *Last Tango*, mortgage rates, the long walk home thanks to ASLEF—they're all factors; and factors, on present reckonings, that none of the prophets fully comprehends.

I know about our overpopulated world. I've lived through the zenith of the Enoch apocalypse. And maybe the next set of statistics will send Lord Avebury into orbit. But meanwhile I'm off to Dacca again with courage refortified, hoping to see the splendid IPPF toilers again, prepared to praise their sterling efforts—and pass back the chutney without a blush.

"Gerald, think of the children."

Speak Roughly to Your Little Boy or Try Ignoring Him

By STANLEY REYNOLDS

THERE is weeping in Hampstead this day and down in Gloucester Crescent, N.W.1, clouds darken the brow of each advanced Mom and Pop. All over Britain, wherever concerned parents fret about their kiddiwinkles' minds, Doubt, that dark monster robber of sleep, is at work. No longer, it seems, will parents feel they are doing absolutely the best thing for their child when the place wishy washy liberal thoughts into their tiny minds. When jolly dads wink and nudge an elbow into little Che's rib cage and say, "Okay, son, let's work out these logarithms together, we're pals aren't we, eh? And chums should do things together," they will now pause to wonder. Perhaps after all the snivelling little rats should not be locked up in their rooms and refused dinner until those

121

nouns are parsed or stuffed or garnished or whatever it is they do to nouns nowadays. Perhaps the little rats should be left alone.

Last week, just in fact as my third male entry to life's grim game was getting himself born, my fatherly eye caught hold of an amazing item in the *Guardian*. According to a Dr. Gordon Miller, research officer of the department of education at London University, the children who gained least from educational opportunities tended to come from homes where their thoughts were dominated by their parents. On the other hand, children who were allowed to think for themselves untended by concerned parents got the most out of education. Dr. Miller did a survey. He apparently felt there might be something wrong in the old middle class liberal idea that the best little performers in the classroom came from the best little homes where the walls were lined with books and Henry James and T. S. Eliot are always popping in for tea and where Mum and Dad and little Tom or Jake or Daisy sit round discussing things just as if the kid had the sort of mind you could actually bother yourself with when you are actually sober.

Not so says Doc Miller! He studied 489 kids; (why is it always a number like 489 in these surveys? I mean, if I were going to survey Dr. Millers I wouldn't get 489 Dr. Millers, I'd get an even number, say, 400 or 500 Dr. Millers to survey, wouldn't I?). Anyway, these children, from ten schools, and "all social classes," showed that the ones from terrible homes—in the great liberal Hampstead use of the word "terrible"—didn't do too good. The best results came from children who had to think for themselves because their fathers didn't sit around puffing on a pipe like Fred MacMurray, as the friendly prof in some lousy movie, being really keen about the younger generation, but from homes where the dad didn't tell the kids anything or just told them, "Leave your mind alone and go take a cold shower."

I paraphrase the doctor's philosophy of course, but the real thing can be got in *Educational Opportunities and the Home* which was published by Longman's last week. And what will come of this new theory I wonder? Will the *Guardian's* own Woman's Page suddenly blossom with columns by ladies who have found the secret of getting little Dan off the works of Kant and Alan Brien and out into a snooker parlour where it is each kid for himself and no turning to Mummy? Will Borstal replace Holland Park Comprehensive as the *in* school? The future looks troubled.

But I am all for Dr. Miller. I have often woken in a sweat, frightened by a nightmare in which my old father had been a pal to me, had prodded me in the chest with his cigar butt and had carried out long man-to-man chats like Mickey Rooney's dad in the *Andy Hardy* movies. Worse still are the night dreads when

my sons in my dreams seek my advice. Often nowadays I touch them for money, even when I don't need it, just to keep them away.

Luckily enough when I was a boy most fathers were away at the war or, being too old for service, came from a generation that believed a good clout on the ear was parental guidance. I guess I had to use my own mind back there in my childhood in New England on the green banks of that meandering river that wound her way from the white granite mountains of New Hampshire picking up garbage and sewage and industrial waste from every lousy mill town along the way until it bubbled brown into the Atlantic at scenic old Mystic, Connecticut. But just what sort of stuff fills a child's mind that the Dad who is a Pal could have straightened out? Your correspondent has been casting his mind back to the things that really "filled his thoughts in childhood.

For one thing I remember believing that the hunchback of Notre Dame was a poor crippled lad who had somehow managed to master his disability and became a star full back for Notre Dame University in South Bend, Indiana. I thought about this sporting Hunchback of Notre Dame University quite a lot of the time and used to wonder if he played any other sport. This was not a particularly rare thought of mine. Any football game could suddenly be brightened by one of the boys grabbing the ball, tilting one shoulder higher than the other and shouting, "Look at me, I'm the Hunchback of Notre Dame," which we pronounced "Noter" and Dame as in "there is nothing like a . . ." I also believed all ships were made of wood because iron would not float and we proved this by making a raft out of corrugated iron and sinking. I believed that the newspapers were written by a pack of lying dogs because they reported that Tom Mix had been killed in a car crash when it stood to reason that he must have been shot in the back by some sneaky rat. The newspapers really showed themselves up when they reported Buck Jones dying in a fire in a night club, not even a saloon in Texas, but a nightclub in Boston, Massachusetts of all places.

I believed that all Japanese had thick glasses and buck teeth and were, any morning now, going to appear on the Willmansett Bridge marching on us from Chicopee Falls with the sun shining on their bayonets, teeth, and eye glasses; that if you stuck a metal toothpick or some thin piece of iron between your front teeth and stuck your head out of the window of a very tall building and at the same time you rubbed your shoes on a rug causing electricity you could get radio station WHYN.

I, at one point of course, saw the Charles Laughton movie of the Hunchback of Notre Dame, but when I told Jack Long that the Hunchback was not an athlete, a fabled member of Notre Dame U's "Fighting

Irish" football team but some kind of looney who rang bells in a church in Europe somewhere in the old days, he was so broken up with this destruction of our dream of the brave crippled lad that he beat me up. Later we agreed there must have been two Hunchbacks but Laughton's screen role took over in our imitations of the sporting Hunchback.

Was there anything here that needed the kindly Dad to step in, saying, "Now, now, boys, what seems to be the problem, maybe I can help you?" The thought never entered our heads to ask our fathers for anything but money. I mean, what did they know? Were they fabled hunchbacked football players? Did they have jobs in which they pondered the dark secrets of the universe seeking the route to Mars?

This was in the space of six or seven years, from the time I was about five until I was eleven or twelve. I am sure my father must have spoken directly to me but I cannot remember anything he ever said to me about any particular subject. As for my mother, I can only remember her saying, "Wait until your father comes home."

When my father did come home he'd ask me about my day. I did not say, "I have been standing on top of Tuck Brook's garage roof with a wire in between my front teeth trying to get WHYN." Instead he would say, "Where have you been?" "Out." "And what did you do?" "Nothing."

You were either "in" or "out" or "at school" and that took care of everything. Is this the sort of ideal home Dr. Miller has in mind? I certainly have followed the same lines with my own sons, although often when I am lounging in the grass wondering just why you cannot turn the human body into a radio receiver—I mean, we've got all this electricity inside us—and I see the boys in their tree house trying to entice wasps into an empty Tizer bottle, I wonder what little problems may be on their little minds that Dad could perhaps set right. Actually I know what is on the eldest one's little mind because I've just seen a flash of young blonde legs climbing up the holly tree and disappearing inside the tree house. No need to worry about the kids of today, Dr. Miller, you can rest assured they will be the fathers of tomorrow.

Chorus : ' 'ERE—LEGGO THE BAT ; YOU'RE AHT ! '
Batsman : ' NO I AIN'T—NOT AFORE THE UMPIRES IS AGREED ABAHT IT.' [1923]

123

God Rest Ye Merry Parents

ALAN BRIEN sounds a sour note in the Yuletide symphony of carols

Is there a journalist in the Western world for whom Christmas does not loom on the horizon of the year, like some aboriginal calamity, immutably forecast in all the calendars and almanacs? A mind-bending planet curdling the milk of human kindness as it comes more near the earth that it was wont; a tidal flood of good cheer threatening to asphyxiate us in its detergent foam; a landslip which has been known to shake the topless towers of department stores and quelch last-minute shoppers with acceptable gifts dropped from a great height.

The galley-slaves sweat at the massed banks of typewriters, quinquiremes adrift on a seasonal sea of purple prose. But after 1900 years, who can steer a new course? Christmas among the rich, among the starving, under the Antipodean sun, under the midnight sun, with the oldsters or the orphans, amid unbelievers and nun-believers, in Ulster, Vietnam, Moscow, in Rome, Canterbury, Bethlehem, in a sewer, in prison, on the moon. Christmas will not be ignored as it retreats ever more slowly before our eyes—a pillar of smoked turkey excreting stuffing by day, a pillar of flaming puddings by night.

It is, so everyone says, especially the children (looking at their watches) the time for children. As if children, all the year round (rising unnaturally early, obscenely cheerful, even singing, each morning before dawn, resisting the lure of sweet, mindless oblivion each night after dusk, coming home each afternoon at what seems to be the middle of lunch, taking longer weekends than company directors, longer holidays than MPs or judges), were not already monopolists of our time. We have trained them to be Stakhanovites of conspicuous consumption, experts in the art of inducing premature absolescence. And at Christmas, they achieve apotheosis, the chief guests at the Feast of St. Francis de Sales-Manager in whose honour bank accounts are printed in cheery red. Christmas is the continuation of capitalism by other means, when every director of the family firm better have other means.

Their holy places are not churches but toy departments. The pilgrims converge on the West Ends of a thousand big cities. The children's crusade is under way again. The very names of shops become sacred words to be intoned by a Nanny-Priestess in giant effigy as she looks down upon the annual Battle of the Parcels staged nightly during December in Oxford Street.

I invented a version once when jammed for an eternity in a Hamley's lift with two amorous six foot pandas and a dwarfish uncle breathing whiskey into my armpit: "Now Master Fortnum, don't be Harrod to your little sister. It's very Selfridge not to share a Gorringe. No, Ponting is rude, and don't you take Libertys with me. You'll do yourself a Gamage unless you do a C & A on the Derry and Tom."

It must amaze my friends on Alpha Centaurus to see Christmas celebrated as a kind of Guy Fawkes night of the population explosion. After all, it is the birthday of the man who was born to be King, yet not born to be a husband or father; the confinement of a mother whose marriage was never consummated. And for most of its history, Christmas was under the protection and aegis of a succession of Popes (whose title means "father") who denied themselves, with some exceptions, the privilege of matrimony and parenthood. And their representatives too also adopted the name without the duty. Is not celibacy after all a form of birth control? If King Herod had been able to make the Pill compulsory throughout his domain, around March in the last year of B.C., he would have been spared having to institute the Massacre of the Innocents.

To be around at Christmas without a child is like midnight on New Year's Eve without a glass. Bachelors and spinsters, married couples without offspring, unmarried couples whose children are former spouses—these are the real waifs and strays, reduced to cruising the bars and soliciting outside hospitals, booking cruises or going to bed with a good bad book, to conceal their shameful lack of progeny. They quarrel over nephews and nieces, lay spurious claims to godchildren, whose names they misspell and whose ages they can no longer even estimate approximately. (Other people's children are always older than you think.)

Why not a rival festival for the sterile, the unparents, the homosexual, all those who by necessity or choice have omitted to people an overcrowded planet with replicas of themselves? Instead of hiding away, or sidling about on the fringe, why not boldly proclaim their determination to enjoy themselves in their own way with a massive grown-up 'X' certificate

orgy of peace and goodwill—Gay Lib with a difference?

If it is thought to be tasteless or sacriligious to hold this on December 25, perhaps the middle of the school summer holidays would be a more enviably spectacular moment for a week-long Saturnalia (Saturn ate his children, remember) of parties and outings—without babies, but also without babysitters; sofas but no highchairs; nobody to cry in the night, except with pleasure; nobody to leave outside the pub; nobody to be told to finish up their nice caviar. The selfishness of Christmas is often hidden under wrappings of religiosity, tied up with charitable ribbons. In my celebration, the ego, and anything else you care to mention, would be naked and unashamed. Our motto would be—O Come All Ye Unfaithful . . . to Acapulco, Venice, Ibiza, Tangier. With no half-fares.

"Chocolate cigarettes, yes; chocolate joints, no."

125

Bad Day at Generation Gap

Jail was too good for Doctor Spock, screams American father ARNOLD ROTH!

Some kids just can't handle positions of command.

In America every daughter is a princess, every son a prince and everybody else is everybody else.

WHO ARE THE MASTERS NOW?

The kids allow us to be inspired and altruistic towards them.

Many of our children encourage meaningful dialogue and the ability to communicate.

When To Tell The Kiddies What

By ALEX ATKINSON

CORRECT timing is as important in this matter as in the planting of begonias out of doors anywhere north of a line drawn roughly between say, Trenton in New Jersey and Tientsin. It might not have occurred to you (we can't all be expected to keep abreast of everything in the hectic rush of modern living) but in fact a child can be warped just as easily as a begonia plant, and will make a good deal more fuss about it, irrespective of latitude. You can draw lines roughly between Trenton and Tientsin until you're black in the face: the fact remains that a child can get warped as thoroughly in, say, Brisbane as in Reykjavik. And whoever planted a begonia out of doors in, say, Reykjavik? It's no good your insisting that some of your best friends are warped. You know very well that if their mothers and fathers had only timed their sex instruction a little more carefully they would be far more responsible members of society today, and better fun at parties.

I have no wish to pontificate, but there was an urgent need for clarity and plain speaking here, and I think I may say I am not shirking my responsibilities.

Take Christmas. Christmas is not a good time. It can be a pretty traumatic experience for you in itself if you're a child, what with the adults going around being crazy cornucopias one minute and dyspeptic misanthropes the next, and new clothes to get used to, that make you look a complete dope, and nobody knowing how to stop the lights on the tree exploding, and doubts existing as to whether it will snow or not, and stark misery setting in when it is discovered that not another single parcel in the whole house remains unopened, and hysterical joy taking its place when the

flames from the brandy over the pudding set fire to all the Japanese lanterns, and remote leather-skinned aunts with beards kissing you twice if you don't find somewhere to hide after the first time, and uncles with heady smells throwing you up to the ceiling where all the cigar smoke is and tickling you under the arms until you want to be sick, and the manic uncertainty about which new thing to play with next, and the wonder of seeing grown-ups clobbering one another with rolled-up newspapers or arguing about the rules of musical chairs, and the bleak despair that accompanies the realisation that the insides of mince pies don't taste any less like families of boiled insects this year than they did last. To introduce a brisk initiation into the art of love at such a time would be to invite complete psychological disintegration, and that's not going to mix very well with the severe stomach-ache the kid's going to have tomorrow anyway.

I don't care if you illustrate your talk with the jolliest, most colourful biological charts obtainable, and lighten the thing with simple puns and brief selections from *The Rape of Lucrece*, you're asking for trouble if you choose Christmas for your well-meant interference with the healthy growth of your offspring. You have to remember that if they're at a certain age they are already coping at this season with the mysteries surrounding the existence and mode of life of Santa Claus, and they're going to be in no fit condition to take in a lot of stuff about the courtship habits of vertebrate bipeds while they're still trying to figure out how reindeer, although demonstrably wingless, manage to lug a sledgeful of toy trains and plastic space-suits through the sky, having in mind already the very plausible theories put forward by Isaac Newton. They are quite liable to get mixed up. Indeed I once knew of a child who, having been indoctrinated at this unsuitable time of year, went through her whole life (up to the age of thirty-three, anyhow: I don't know what became of her after that) under the firm impression that babies come down the chimney on Christmas Eve, wearing little red suits trimmed with white fur. What her notion of Santa Claus was I have no way of telling, but I do know that she would rush home and lock all the doors if she caught so much as a glimpse of a man in wellington boots; and she once caused quite a commotion in Selfridge's in late December by striking the incumbent Father Christmas with her wet umbrella and crying out "What did you do to all those bees?"

I have no doubt she led an interesting life, but she missed an awful lot, and I put the blame squarely on the shoulders of her parents.

Half-past four in the afternoon is not a good time either. Children get drowsy around half-past four in the afternoon. Half-past seven is even worse, because around that time you're liable to get drowsy yourself, and there are few things more maddening than to have your story-teller fall asleep just as he's getting to the exciting part. If you're not drowsy at half-past seven you're all excited about rushing off to a dinner party, and far more interested in seeing that the baby-sitter has everything she wants than in settling down to a sacred chat about sex with a couple of kids who don't think they know anything about it. All you want to do is go and have a *profane* chat about it over the pheasant, with a crowd of people more your own age, who think they *do*.

Do not attempt it in the dark. Have a good strong light burning, or make sure there's plenty of sunshine available. If you just go droning on in pitch blackness (because you're embarrassed, or because you don't want them to be distracted by external influences like the deer little bunny rabbits with scarves around their necks on the wall of the nursery) you will leave them with a morbid impression of the whole business, when as a matter of fact, as everybody knows, it is really terribly gay and light-hearted. Besides, unexpected things can happen in the dark. I knew a father who lectured his son for a solid three quarters of an hour on the subject one night, and when he switched on the light to ask if there were any questions he found he had been talking to his wife, who was lying on the settee with her feet up and her eyebrows raised. His son was out at the flicks, watching *The Blue Angel*.

His wife had some very *good* questions as it happened, but the episode left him nervous for days.

"I tell you I thought you were Harold!" he would shout.

"You ought to be ashamed," his wife would say.

"*. . . and this is Prince Kong.*"

129

She gave young Harold the lecture herself the next morning—very chirpily, while he polished his shoes. He never turned a hair. When she'd finished he said, "I see. And precisely what am *I* expected to do about it, may I ask?"

He wore glasses, and grew up to be a chartered accountant.

Another good tip is not to leave it until the kids are twenty-one. That's a very bad time. A twenty-first birthday is supposed to be a day of carefree jollity. You may argue that on their twenty-first birthdays kids should begin to assume some of the solemn responsibilities that are going to make their lives tedious for the next forty-four years or so, such as being careful to help females on with their coats if they're male, and being particular to keep their mouths shut at breakfast if they're not; but by the time he reaches twenty-one a kid is inclined to be impressionable, and it's downright dangerous to pump new notions into his head. Indeed, he may be so impressionable that he already has a wife, two children and a broad-minded mistress, and if you start explaining to him how he should have gone about it you're going to make him insecure and moody. Far better let him muddle along in his fool's paradise, making up his own sex instruction as he goes.

Six months has been found to be an ideal age from several points of view. For one thing, at six months a youngster has no preconceived ideas on the subject at all, except that he's liable to be rather fond of his mother. For another thing he can't answer back, or confound you with any of the snide comments you're apt to get from ten-year-olds.* For best results you should make sure that the child is not only six months old, but fast alseep.

Do not be tempted to tell the kiddies about it more than once, or they will get the mistaken idea that the subject is more important in life than arithmetic or clay modelling. They will fall behind at school, and spend their study periods day-dreaming gloomily about honeymoon etiquette or the pros and cons of twilight sleep. To conduct recapitulation sessions every week, adding new facts as they come to mind and keeping the kids up to date in the latest techniques and fashionable trends, is to run the risk of making them surly and unresponsive. Kids get bored with a subject if its theory is being rammed down their throats regularly and they see no chance of ever getting into the lab and starting on some practical work.

Above all do not assume, as so many parents do, that the kids know all about it anyway. In the majority of cases their ignorance on the subject, especially between the ages of two and nine, will astonish you. It has been known, certainly, for a boy of eight to fall hopelessly in love with Jayne Mansfield; but the farthest extent of his ambition has been to buy her more ice-cream sodas than anyone else ever did, to carry very heavy parcels for her, or to rescue her from a gang of three-headed Martians by alertly manipulating a death-ray powered by two elastic bands set in an electro-magnetic field. This plainly has very little to do with sex,† and it is typical of the state of mind of the youngsters of today. They don't know, they don't care, and when you tell them they don't believe you. ("I know what it is," they say. "It's just another trick to make me eat my porridge.")

Those who learn about it at school, of course, are different. In a calm scholastic atmosphere, with chalk dust in the air and population-explosion charts on the wall, the subtleties of the subject enter their little minds as naturally as Euclid's theorems or the events leading up to the Thirty Years' War. Their clip-boards are stuffed with arid notes about fertilisation, and in their diaries you come across entries like this:

Tues. Memo. Take in Scripture homework to Miss D. Trig, French (elementary), Sex (intermediate), Gym. See Mavis at lunch re borrowing answers to Birth Control test paper and notes on character of Lady Macbeth. See dentist 3 p.m. re having band taken off teeth. Evening, prepare essay on The Birth Of A Rat.

They approach the whole business with such clinical aloofness that when the time comes for them to go out into the world, they tend to whisk their chosen partners through the motions of dalliance, courtship and scientific procreation with an efficiency that removes all the uncertainty and most of the pleasurable skylarking. Moreover, if their chosen partner happens to have had the same sort of instruction, the first weeks of marriage will contain all the colour and excitement of a game of noughts and crosses and a nice cup of cocoa.

If you must tell them anything at all, the question of

---

* Typical snide comments from ten-year-olds, selected at random from surveys carried out simultaneously in Cheshire, South Dakota, Provence, North Wales and San Francisco:

"This mingling of emotion with biology strikes me as being slipshod and impractical."

"Huh. Big deal."

"What you say sounds reasonably fascinating, but surely in this day and age we should be more concerned about getting a man on the moon?"

"Plus ça change, plus c'est la même chose."

"If you had your life to live over again, ma, would you rather be a frog?"

"Okay, fine. And can I start smoking as well?"

† Let us forget about S. Freud for the moment, shall we? His turn will come.

what to tell the kids is simply answered. Tell them all you know, and about half of what you suspect. And don't assume that you're entirely familiar with the subject yourself. With all due respect, in fact, far, very likely, from it. When you come to prepare for the great day your lack of precise knowledge in certain areas may come as something of a shock. You will discover a number of gaps in your experience—pools of ignorance so profound that you may wonder how you ever managed to get beyond the hand-holding stage as you went on your way through life. To give you some idea of just how backward you probably are, I have taken the trouble to prepare a short quiz. It is included here at no extra charge. The answers will be found at the bottom of the page, and a score of two right has been found to be par for the course, including lucky guesses.

1. Hops are bisexual. True or false?

2. Is petting necking?

3. What is the difference, if any, between a bovine freemartin and an XY-chromosome?

4. Supply the missing words in the following sentence:

When a European male ——— ——— is crossed with a female, normal males and females result in the first generation; but if the individuals thus obtained are interbred, they produce a proportion of males with female characters.

5. What was it that a girl in Bohemia used to in-troduce a few drops of into a man's beer if she wanted to make him hers?

6. Did it work?

7. Why not?

8. Are female butterflies digametic?

9. What are the chief distinguishing marks and/or characteristics of the lateral gynandromorph?

It only remains now for me to wish you the very best of luck, to assure you that worrying about this crisis in your life will get you nowhere, to assure you that any questions or complaints that are sent to me on the subject marked Confidential will be sympathetically ignored, and to warn you, if you happen to be satisfied with the results of your own cosy chat, and are tempted in your crusading enthusiasm to try it on anybody else's kids, I shall stubbornly refuse to be responsible for the consequences.

Answers to Quiz

1. True.

2. No.

3. I have no idea.

4. Gypsy moth.

5. Bat's blood.

6. No.

7. Because it made him throw up.

8. Yes, they are. So what else is new?

9. A slight squint and a hesitant manner.

"The Educational Psychologist says he has the viewing age of twelve."

GENERAL CERTIFICATE OF EDUCATION

Ordinary Level

ENGLISH LITERATURE

Answer FIVE questions, or stare out of the WINDOW, or fold this sheet into a paper DART

Three hours are allowed, unless you have
another engagement, or think of one

1. Write an essay on ONE of the following subjects:
   (*a*) Milton's debt to Ariosto
   (*b*) "Othello's reputation's gone!"
   (*c*) Jane Austen's male characters

   OR: (*a*) Play *Annie Laurie* on the edge of your desk with a nail-file
   (*b*) Write down all the words ending in -bum you can think of
   (*c*) Fill in all the o's and a's on this paper.

2. Compare and contrast the use of the sonnet form by Keats and Wordsworth OR Go for a pee.

3. "Swift was, above all else, a humorist." Discuss with particular reference to the set texts OR Empty your jacket pockets onto the desk and attempt any THREE of the following:
   (*a*) Stand the acorn on the whistle
   (*b*) Hold the 10p piece in your left eye for twenty seconds
   (*c*) Suck the Polo without biting until it dissolves
   (*d*) Wind the rubber band around your thumb until it goes white
   (*e*) Carve your initial on the desk with the key
   (*f*) Straighten the cigarette out.

4. Give a brief account of the effect of the Restoration on the English theatre OR See what's in your ear.

5. Read the following passage carefully, and answer the questions below it:
   "Farewell! Thou art too dear for my possessing,
   And like enough thou know'st thy estimate:
   The charter of thy worth gives thee releasing;
   My bonds in thee are all determinate.
   For how do I hold thee but by thy granting?
   And for that riches where is my deserving?"

   Attempt not more than THREE of the following:
   (*a*) From which sphere does the author draw his imagery?
   (*b*) Can you balance a pencil on your nose?
   (*c*) How does the language typify its period?
   (*d*) How loud can you belch?
   (*e*) Is it possible to blow a ball of pocket fluff into an inkwell?
   (*f*) Can you complete the sonnet?

6. Write on ONE of the following:
   (*a*) Marlowe's debt to Kyd
   (*b*) The future of allegory
   (*c*) The neck of the candidate in front (*pencil only*).

7. EITHER (*a*) "The Romantic critics are more concerned with the artist than with the work of art." Discuss this statement in relation to some of the essays in your selection
   OR (*b*) See how many swastikas you can draw in the margins of this paper.

8. EITHER (*a*) Discuss and illustrate Scott's power of creating memorable personalities in *Redgauntlet*
   OR (*b*) Stop doing that IMMEDIATELY.

Down at the Pond

By ALEXANDER FRATER

THE first aspects of spring were appearing on the trees and in the park people paused to note the crocuses. Sam Grindl noted them too, but he was ambitious and preoccupied with his place in the world and they qualified only for a brisk, snapping glance. He drove the pram round the corner at speed, the rear wheels drifting somewhat, and waited for Mrs. Grindl to catch up.

"Boy," she panted. "What's got into you today?"

"I'm breaking in my Hush Puppies," he said.

"I wish you wouldn't wisecrack so much, Sammy. The neighbours are commenting. Old Dr. Firkin next door calls you Laugh-A-Minute Grindl and says it's a cover-up for insecurity and lack of small talk. And he should know, Sammy; he's *qualified*." She squeezed his arm affectionately, listening to the bones click. "Or is it just the spring?"

"I hate the goddam spring," said Sam. "All these buds and pinched faces and this lousy thin sunshine. It's like watered beer."

She smiled. "What about the young lovers?" she said, softly.

"Goddam lust," said Sam, marching on. "You wanna go to the pond?"

"What a nice idea," she said. "And how our little Barney will love it. Look! I do believe he understands!"

The child, seven months and balding, raised himself on his elbows and, face puce with effort, fixed his black eyes firmly on his father. It was, reflected Sam, an unremarkable face. But for the pendulous ear lobes and the domineering jut of the lower lip it was as anonymous as a wave at sea. The child drooped abruptly and sank his toothless gums into a spotted bambi.

"Look at his little barrel chest," said Sam, proud despite himself. "Very robust and strong. I guess it'll look even better with a neck. When does the neck come?"

"About the eighth month," said Mrs. Grindl. "My, isn't this nice? Being out among people? I can feel the life flowing back into me like sap; I been shut away for a long time now, tending to the child, and I've so often yearned for the great outdoors." She skipped girlishly and crooned "We'll ride all daay, on top of a load of haay . . . You know what I heard, Sammy? That a baby in a pram is a social advantage; you *meet* people when you tote a pram, people with other prams or just people. You know, who want to chuck the kiddie's chin."

"I don't want to meet people," said Sam. "I hate to be obligated, Mrs. Grindl. You know that. I think we ought to leave people well alone. You wanna go home now?"

"We're going to the pond," she said firmly. "Like you promised."

"Provided I am granted immunity, Father, I cannot tell a lie."

133

He shrugged. The shrug was Sam's favourite and most habitual gesture and he used it to convey a thousand subtle shades of meaning. His shoulders were positively Gallic and far more articulate than his tongue. They braked at the water's edge and stood watching a mallard preening itself randily on the islet in the centre of the pond.

"Pardon me," said a deep, hesitant voice behind them, "but is that a boy or a girl?"

"It's a duck," said Sam. He turned and saw, right behind him, a tall, thick-set man in torn tweeds and chukka boots. The man frowned. "I meant the child, sir. The one in your pram."

"Yes," said Sam, shaken and unable for the moment, to remember.

"It's a boy," supplied Mrs. Grindl. "Seven months old and potty trained."

"Right," said Sam. "A boy. Right."

"Well, no matter," said the man urgently. "Would you mind if I borrowed it for a few moments?"

"I certainly would," said Sam. "What are you, some kinda nut? I don't hire my kid out to strangers."

The man glanced about him—looking, Sam reflected, nonplussed. "This is urgent," he said. "I need cover. I'm on the run."

"From what?" asked Sam, feeling spurred wings brush his suburban cheek. "The law?"

There may be a reward in this, Mrs. Grindl thought to herself, smiling tautly at the water. The mallard finished preening itself and, with a squawk, leapt upon its mate. Mrs. Grindle smiled tautly up at the treetops.

"The Foreign Legion," said the man.

"The *French* Foreign Legion?" murmured Sam.

"What others did you have in mind?" said the stranger roughly. He wiped his forehead with a sleeve and Sam felt a momentary pang of pity for him; perhaps he too liked subgum fried noodles and Humphrey Bogart and Billy the Bee. "Sorry, folks, but I'm a bit keyed up. I deserted and crossed the Channel two days ago and I have this feeling they're on to me. The Legion always get their man, you know; right now I'm worried about that nun feeding the swans over there who looks like Akim Tamiroff and keeps glancing over his shoulder at me. Listen, just let me wheel the pram with you for a few hundred yards and I'll be eternally grateful."

He grabbed the pram and swung off down the path, the Grindls swinging with him. "You appear to be in earnest," observed Sam.

"Boy."

"Why did you abscond?" asked Sam. "Were you savaged by your camel?" He grinned and glanced at Mrs. Grindl, wishing to share the joke. She stared dead ahead, thinking analytically about her husband, the knight who went off to the Crusades so loudly on the 8.50 train each morning. She pursed her lips, looking a little surprised. "Or didn't you have a camel?" said Sam.

The Legionnaire glanced over his shoulder. "No camel," he said. "Just dunes and bleached bones, I was going to be a prophet walking in the desert, drinking from the wells and eating wild honey. Just my burp gun and me." He laughed bitterly and, with the air of one putting something from his mind, bent down to Little Barney. "How's the gout?" he said.

Mrs. Grindl nudged her man. "I honestly think he's *mad*," she hissed. "He's got that pink light in his eye."

"I shoulda joined the Swiss Guard or some outfit like that," muttered the stranger. "I could have mixed with Roman Society in my codpiece and slashed doublet and had myself——"

"Are you French?" asked Sam.

"Me?" said the stranger. "Do I look French? I'm just . . ."

They turned a corner and came face to face with a uniformed park attendant. The Legionnaire gave a yell and disappeared into a grove of seasoned yews. "Good gracious," murmured the attendant in astonishment. He glanced at the Grindls and raised an eyebrow. Sam kicked at the brake and they moved off, silently. "Well, he said at length. "What do you make of that?"

"Perhaps he should be locked up," volunteered Mrs. Grindl. "Put behind bars."

"It could have been genuine," said Sam. "I mean, people do run away from the Legion and they are hounded. I once read about it on the back of a coco pops packet."

"I believe you," said Mrs. Grindl, "but what would an escaped Legionnaire be doing in this part of the world?"

"Whaddya mean, *this* part of the world?" barked Sam. "Karl Marx once skated upon the pond, remember. It was on that pond that he was reputed to have hit on the idea of an alternative to democracy, remember. This neck of the woods isn't entirely cut off from——"

"That isn't what I meant," said Mrs. Grindl. "Nevertheless, we did meet someone, didn't we?" She smiled to herself. "That was nice."

"What was nice about it?"

"I don't know," she said. She started to hum softly. The stranger had had a good profile, she recalled and, should it ever come to the pinch, she would certainly forgive him his madness. She glanced at Sam, who was conscientiously grimacing at the product of their union, and thought he looked shrunken, a trifle blurred. He, in turn, glanced at her and realised, instinctively and with a mild sense of shock, that he wasn't the only man in the world.

THE MARK OF CANE

As Baroness Wootton moves a bill to outlaw corporal punishment in schools,
ALAN BRIEN lashes out

As every foreign schoolboy knows, perverts begin at Dover. The English, in their own eyes so cool and kindly, so restrained and self-controlled, are in international folklore a cruel and bestial people, practising on wet Sundays every bent aberration and painful paraphilia known to Krafft-Ebing. (Two ffs and one b, please—those neatly representing the proportion of effing to b-ing in the pages of that famous anthology of tales of mystery and imagination.)

In every *lycée* and *Gymnasium*, in finishing schools and military academies, the European young hear whispered after lights out, behind cupped hands, the fearful stories of English debauchery—brothels at Newnham and Girton, whores in the Cabinet, transvestites on the bench of bishops in the Lords, drug pushers queuing at Piccadilly Circus Underground every display case in Soho bulging with flesh and hair, the bridegroom's gift to the bride a set of handcuffs and fetters, entire regiments of homosexual guardsmen on duty nightly in Hyde Park, beery vandals wrecking coaches and trains to the tune of "For he's a jolly good fellatio and so say all of us," incest a local sport in the countryside when the roads are impas-

"We decided to give him the money this year!"

135

sable, while hell-raising clubmen stagger St. James's in the early hours in search of wine, women and thong.

When Englishmen protest the difficulty of finding a warm light ale in mid-afternoon, a cup of coffee and a sausage roll after 11.28 in the evening, the overseas visitor simply adds a new crime, hypocrisy, to the charge sheet. As Leslie Hale, MP, once observed in the Commons, thus no doubt securing an entry in every Continental Dictionary of Aphorisms, the real *vice anglais* is humbuggery. But most unnatural of all our supposed perversions is the infliction of pain for the production of pleasure—this delights you more than it does me. Though the two partners have French and German names, it is assumed that it is in this other Eden that Master Sade and Miss Masoch will spend their honeymoon.

Recent newspaper reports of the film star who beat his wife and the prefect who bashed up his fag must have added a new lustre to the old legend.

Corporal Punishment once again is hoisted aloft as the symbol among the English that General Winter is among the Russians. If the English, as they boast, prefer to stand on their own two feet, it must be because this royal throne of kings, this seat of Mars, is usually too tender on the inflamed backside.

As an Englishman, I would like to argue that this Breughelesque picture is no more than a fantasy landscape dreamed up in the fevered imagination of those who lack the stomach to cross the Channel. But I fear there is a tendency among us to believe that the best explanation to a child is a cuff round the ear. The cane is an unknown instrument in continental classrooms. But it was only on January 1 this year that it was abolished in London in primary schools—that is, to keep order among small creatures of under eight years of age—while the state-subsidised church schools may retain it at their discretion.

It is an illusion that only the fee-paying boarder is subject to physical pain as an encouragement to learning. In my elementary school, there was a year in which I sometimes had my hands swished, until the knuckles were swollen, a dozen times a day. And by comparison with most of my fellow pupils, bullet-headed indestructible young warriors, their pates shaven except for a forelock, their faces decorated with Maori masks of dirt and snot, I was Little Lord Fauntleroy. I was caned for asking questions, and for not answering questions, for talking and for not speaking up, for being in the playground when I should have been at my desk and for being at my desk when I should be in the playground. All it taught me was the survival value of conformity. Whatever was happening, the safest course was to join the majority. The master had only a finite amount of muscle power and it was the minority who felt the impact of his stick.

But, at least, I never regarded the experience as building anything except callouses. And I am glad that I have been saved the impulse to pass on the habit to my children, mainly because of my cowardice. I was taught early by my father (perhaps the most accident-prone member of the Amalgamated Engineering Union on the North-East Coast) that it was always better to cry *before* you were hurt. It was a motto that had often saved his life, and often saved my fingers. I never grew a stiff upper lip, but I avoided some stiff lower limbs.

It may be the English cult of suffering in silence which encourages the continuation of suffering as an educational aid. As Sir Walter Raleigh observed at dinner once, having been thumped by his father and instantly thumping the man next to him—"Box it about, it will come to my father anon." The English admiration for the hierarchy leads them to believe that every pain must be passed down the chain of being, often with accrued interest, until it arrives at the base of the pyramid, among the women and children.

In almost all European communities, domestic quarrels begin and end in public, accompanied by a noisy, lengthy, and operatic abuse and counter-abuse. The English squabble in mutters, and grow ever more furious at each silence. "Wait till I get you home," is the most potent of threats from the stronger to the weaker. Violence is the repartee of the inarticulate. The Englishman's home is his castle and he makes sure it has its 3 b/rms, 2 l/rms, k & b, and dungeon.

It is the nature of duties to become pleasures. Once the pattern is established that one person has the right to chastise the body of another, the unconscious assumption is made, as with traffic wardens and public hangmen, that it might as well be enjoyable. Somehow I have never been able to convince myself that the victim may not one day hit back. None of us, once we are old enough to marry and have children, is getting any stronger. And I do not relish the thought of offspring who measure their height each morning, waiting for the day when they overtop me, or the idea of a wife who might even now be baking a powdered-glass cake or sharpening a knitting needle while I doze over the paper. Like many honourable decisions, the determination to deny myself the power and joy of corporal punishment is rooted in a healthy concern for my own skin.

Both sadism and masochism seem to be means of expressing unacted aggressions, turned hatred of yourself against others and hatred of others against yourself. The most healthy signs of a decay in the English wish to punish and be punished are the noisy refusals of women and children to accept this as part of our way of life any more. The English vice is probably at last on its way out, cured by the decision at last to raise the English voice.

Mothers of AMERICA

Recent events having proved that any red-blooded American kid can get to be President, it didn't seem a bad time to take a look at how the other 199,999,999 got brought up. Here RALPH SCHOENSTEIN casts a Mother's Day eye over the ladies who do the upbringing.

IT is said that when a Chinese mother is due to have her baby, she excuses herself to the field hands, trots indoors, offhandedly delivers, and then returns to the rice, just another automatic Asiatic who was able to multiply on the fly. But if an American mother ever attempted such a coffee break delivery, it would only be for the purpose of setting a new world's record, for the chance to tell all the other mothers in town, "I took fifteen seconds off the fastest known time of the Cantonese communes."

Dr. Francis Bauer, a noted psychiatrist, has said, "Since the usual symbols of status—money and goods—are so accessible, mothers have turned to the only things left to manipulate, their children." And so the moment that an American child is born, it is entered in a kind of infant Olympics, in a desperate competition against the progeny of mommy's friends. The issue is simply issue: which woman has most grandly reproduced. Although she has performed an act that is not beyond the skill of a backward chimpanzee, the American mother takes supreme satisfaction in the

"He reads too many comics."

137

fruit of her womb, no matter how big a lemon it may be.

The first cause for boasting is the baby's looks. I have passed many insincere hours in New York maternity wards, where I have yet to hear a mother say, "You know, he really looks like a nondescript prune, but at least I think he's honest." Never insult an American mother by telling her that her baby looks like a baby, for she knows in her swollen chest (an Everest of milk and pride) that this particular child is a living piece of the Sistine Ceiling, a feeling that would be true if the Ceiling bore diapered Eisenhowers. Some of the dreariest moments of my life have been spent hovering over cradles, solemnly intoning my catalogue of superlatives, but still unable to summon the rhapsody being requested for the pink chicken beneath me.

"Did you ever see anything so *gorgeous*!" the mother will hint. "And you can easily see that he's going to be a great man."

"I'm sure of it," I reply. "He already looks like Beethoven."

Once the American mother has made it clear that she has produced a six-pound Mona Lisa, she moves on to establish the child's earthshaking superiority in all other departments. The next achievement is to triumph in toilet training, a triumph that brings enormous prestige to the mother of the first rump to control its pump. In a kind of urethral one-upmanship, each child is grimly driven to become the captain of his kidneys, for nothing so warms a mother's heart than to be able to take a drier-than-thou tone towards the mother of the soggy little chap next door.

The new world's record for toilet training has been claimed by Mrs. Henrietta Windish of Akron, Ohio, who succeeded in putting her son on automatic at the age of nine months. This record, however, has not yet been verified by the Official Elimination Committee, which is now checking if Mrs. Windish cheated by making the boy sleep uphill.

Once an American child is both uniquely gorgeous and splendidly dry, it can then go on to conquer its peers with mental and social feats. There are, of course, the routinely fierce contests to see which children can be the first to kiss, to walk, and to talk; but since kissing and walking are also the achievements of baboons, most mothers concentrate on talking. In America, it is all right to have nothing to say just as long as you start saying it sooner than your peers. In fact, the reason for the impressive number of mature American bores is that they were forced to hit conversational peaks much too soon. They were driven by their mothers to achieve oral parity with the glibbest babies on the block.

The talking contests are hard to sustain once all the contestants have reached three or four and even the dumbest have learned to play back an adorable blend of TV commercials and domestic obscenities. Then the mother has to score points by inspiring the development of less common skills.

"Grace, you'll never guess what a *brilliant* thing little Myron did," says a mother to one of her frilly foes. "He stuck his finger in a fan and then pulled it *right out*!"

"*All* of it?" says Grace.

"Yes, *all* of it! Isn't that *amazing*? *You* know how fast those fans go around."

"Jane, that's really *something*. I mean, my Harvey can walk between raindrops, but to have the kind of timing that you need for a *fan* . . . I wonder what Myron's IQ is?"

"About five points below Nietzsche's, but he has *much* better manners."

"Well, Harvey's is only a hundred and eighty-three, but he's already got two little hairs on his cheek. He may be the first five-year-old to reach puberty."

"Oh, Grace, you must be so proud. I mean, if you can't have the highest IQ, a gland case is still a wonderful thing."

By the time that the American child has reached the age of three, he is known as a sub pre-teener. He is also known as a big baby, but only in those unenlightened circles which refuse to realise that his childhood is over. At the age of three, the average American child, whether or not his bladder has been tamed, is set to enter both scholarship and society, the next campaigns in mommy's war games.

Studies start in nursery school, but not just any one that will keep him off the streets; for the kitchen commando called mother fights to put him in the very best of schools, in one that will lead to a prestige kindergarten, where only well scrubbed thumbs are sucked. This kindergarten, in turn, will be the gateway to a golden grammer school, whose sole function is to launch the child into a college that can place him in a medical school. In short, therefore, that oversized foetus chewing his blanket in the admissions office is about to begin his introduction to surgery.

The best nursery schools have long waiting lists, for the mothers so love their children that they can't wait to throw them out of the house and into academic orbit. The competition, therefore, to enter these schools has been known to drive tots to suck toes as well as thumbs. Those three-year-olds who've been wasting their time with non-accredited play are made to stop their dissolute ways and take the cram courses necessary for storming the hallowed halls of lower education.

"George, we've got to start tutoring Debbie," says the mother to the father. "Her interview for Nugget Nursery is only a year away."

"You're right," he says. "There are one or two

subjects we could work on. For example, I think I'll teach her to stop setting fires. The whole problem may be that Bunsen burner she got for her birthday. I mean, I know that we're insured, but . . . ."

"Well, I'm still glad we got it. So we've lost a couple of rooms; but meanwhile we've given Debbie the fundamentals of chemistry; and since all the *other* kids already know math, it's a way for her to impress the interviewing committee. Yes, she's strong in chemistry, all right."

"But she's weak on elephants: she keeps calling them whales."

"Well, they may give her credit for imagination."

"She also keeps forgetting her name."

"Well, *that's* the kind of thing you can look *up*; it has nothing to do with wisdom. By the way, we could use more recommendations. Is there still a chance to get one from the Cardinal?"

"I'm afraid not. My friend at the archdiocese was transferred to Kenya. But I just met a guy who knows the Secretary of Agriculture, and that's as good as the Cardinal, especially if Debbie's going to major in sandbox."

Once the sub pre-teener is established in an institution of maximum maternal prestige, he can then make mommy's life a total triumph by letting her give him the sophistication that has turned many American children into pocket-sized adults.

If the mother's weapon in the struggle for status is a little girl, she can buy her a "beginner bra," whose official size is 28AAA. This particular piece of anticipatory lingerie is not as pointless as it sounds, for it can also be used as a tourniquet. If the mother wants to make the child a definitive siren, she can also buy her one of the children's wigs whose ads announce, "Now your daughter can be as glamorous as you." All over America, small boys are huddling at gum machines and whispering, "Does she or doesn't she?" a question that once referred only to sleeping with a night light.

My nine-year-old niece not only has been sporting both a beginner bra and lipstick, but since she was six she has also been attending catered birthday parties, where the tails aren't pinned on a donkey but worn by the maitre d'. Other elegant frolics are held in private homes, where little sirens in nylons and hairdos beckon to runty Romeos, where blind man's bluff has given way to a sport that's considerably funnier, for two ten-year-olds necking is like two turtles having a debate. And hovering over it all is that fluttery field marshal, Mother, wondering how many points she'd get for the first bastard on the block.

*"That's one thing about your father.
He's certainly a good provider."*

139

More Equal Than Others

. . . As education-snobbery grows ever more complicated, HOLLAND tours the trendy comprehensive circuit . . .

"That's the only bit of the school we don't like the looks of, headmaster!"

"It was a poor turnout for the Parents' Association meeting—there was a three-line Opposition Whip in the Commons."

"We were determined that William should have a more egalitarian start in life than we ever had."

"It prepares boys for entry to the better comprehensives."

"Unfortunately there was a Preservation Order on the old grammar school building."

. . . while BILL TIDY follows Sam Hinchcliffe Jnr. to Eton

"Good, good. Now we form a union."

"Gosh, you're for it, Hinchcliffe. Only the 1st team rugger and cricket chaps are allowed turned-up collars and Rita Pegley!"

"I usually turn a blind eye to dorm. feasts, matron, but—dammit—send Hinchcliffe and that tripe to my study!"

"Don't be hard on him, Headmaster. Our turnover was pathetic till he suggested splitting the business."

"Don't move, you two! Parents drinking team."

*"Can't you toss a coin or something? One of you has **got** to have custody of him."*

Five go off to Smuggler's Grope

Today's kids have clearly outgrown Enid Blyton.
Unless, of course, ALAN COREN steps in for a bit of swift rewriting

"GOSH, just imagine! Two whole weeks!"

It was the first day of the holidays, and Robin had come home from Snickett, Snickett and Tombs with the glorious prospect of fifteen days of fun in front of him. He stretched luxuriously in bed! No more grinding away at a desk with old Snotty Snickett ticking him off, no more awful lunches of stodge, no more moaning from old Tiger Tombs, who was always dumping extra work on him for something or other, no more shivering in the freezing lavs to get away from Snickett Senior, the firm's bully and a rotten tick, to boot! Not that being a chartered surveyor wasn't fun *sometimes*—Robin liked games most of all, and the Weybridge and District Surveyors XI had a jolly good side that summer (they'd thrashed the Surrey Minor Accountants by six wickets, *and* had the best jam tea he could remember!)—but it didn't begin to compare with the hols. He stretched again, and wiggled his toes.

"It's going to be absolutely *super!*" cried Susan, who had pulled off her nightie and was doing a war dance on Robin's tum. Susan was Robin's best friend, and a brick. She was married to a Mister Eric Bowles, who was something very important in the City and had to be abroad a lot of the time.

"Arf! Arf!" barked Timmy the dog, leaping round the bedroom after imaginary rabbits. Timmy loved nothing so much in the world as chasing rabbits! He never bit any, though, because he was a nice old thing and loved everybody. He was a mongrel, of course, because they're the best kind; he slept at the foot of Robin and Susan's bed. For most of the night, anyway.

"What shall we do today?" cried Robin, yelling as Susan grabbed him playfully—she was jolly strong for a girl, and her stamina surprised everyone. She looked so slim, but she could do more than most boys, and was always thinking up new and super things.

"Wouldn't you like to know?" she replied, after a minute or two. "I'll just bet you can't guess what I've got!" She looked at him impishly. "*Mummy and Daddy's cottage!*"

"*NO!*" shouted Robin, jumping up and racing round the room, closely followed by Timmy the dog, who knew something was up. "Not Mummy and Daddy's super fifteenth-century cottage in Cornwall near that hidden cove where smugglers used to come ashore at night with their vast hoard of brandy in olden times?"

"Yes!" cried Susan.

"The one which is supposed to have a priest's hole and a secret passage and a library full of old musty books that might have strange parchment maps in them?"

"That's the one!" cried Susan. "And Jimmy and Jane are going to join us there for the whole fortnight!"

"Hurrah!" shouted Robin.

"Come on!" exclaimed Susan, taking his hand and pulling him after her, "let's get under that shower!"

Hiss, hiss, went the cold water! Shriek, shriek, went Robin and Susan!

"Arf! Arf!" barked Timmy the dog.

Tickety-tack, tickety-clack, tickety-tack, tickety-clack, the train wheels sang as they carried the fortunate five down to Cornwall. Robin lay in his bunk, exhausted but happy, listening to the song of the wheels and gripping the handrail tightly to stop himself from falling out. It was only a single berth, and what with Susan and Timmy the dog, who had his paw in Robin's mouth, things were a bit cramped. And Susan kept giggling as she listened to Jimmy and Jane in the bunk below, and wriggling.

Robin liked Jimmy and Jane, who, next to Susan, were his best chums. Jane had the reputation of being a bit of a tomboy (she had left her husband and gone off with Ingrid, their au pair), but she could tie knots, and climb things faster than any boy, and break bricks with her hand, and was a jolly good person to have around in a crisis. She and Jimmy got on famously, too, and always went about together when Ingrid wasn't around. Everybody liked Jimmy, who was very much a boy's boy and had been something very high up in the Scouts and had all sorts of badges; until he suddenly left. He was married, too, or had been for a week or so, until his wife went to Australia and became a nun. They all felt a bit protective towards Jimmy, because he had very slim hips and cried a lot if his cigarette went out or a button came off his kaftan and people were always teasing him about his eye-shadow, and sometimes Robin would let him climb into his bed when they were on hols together if there was a thunderstorm, and although it was a bit crowded with them and Susan and Timmy the dog and Nijinsky the Persian cat, who went everywhere with Jimmy, that was all right, because they were firm friends.

And that's what friends are for.

"It's *lovely!*" cried Jimmy, clapping his hands in delight, and that was what they all felt. The little cottage nestled in the hillside, overlooking the sparkling sea, and little pink roses rambled round its door, and there was a white picket fence and a brown thatched roof with swallows' nests under the eaves, and a sheep in the front garden.

Everyone looked at the sheep for a bit.

"Gosh!" bellowed Jane, "Isn't it absolutely *ripping* being on holiday? We can do anything we like!"

Without further ado, they all rushed inside, and began exploring. After that, they took a look round the cottage, and it was everything they'd hoped, all creaky old floors and big black beams and lots of ingle-nooks and brass fire-irons shining in the hearth and a great big black stove and a funny old tin bath that only held one person at a time. It was then that they suddenly realised that, with all the excitement, they hadn't had anything since breakfast! So Jane rooted around for a bit, and found the pot; and they all sat about smoking it, and were happier than they could ever remember having been in their whole lives before!

It was some time before they noticed that little Jimmy was missing, and when they did, they ran all over the house, giggling and bumping into things and falling down and singing and trying, from time to time, to fly, but not finding Jimmy. That had to be left to Timmy the dog, of course!

"Arf! Arf!" barked Timmy the dog, and they all managed to crawl to where he was and they found him sniffing at the skirting board in the little dining-room and pawing at a Welsh dresser frantically.

"It must be the secret passage!" whispered Susan.

"I wonder where the knob is," enquired Robin, running his hands carefully all over her, "how shall we find it?"

"Give it a jolly good thwack!" cried Jane, and she did just that, and lo! and behold, the Welsh dresser fell to pieces, revealing a solid wall behind.

"Quick, over here!" shouted Susan. Accidentally, she and Robin had rolled against a piece of skirting, which suddenly gave, and the secret panel slid open with a soft sigh, and a blast of cold, musty air! It was jolly dark inside.

"Come on!" cried Jane.

"We'd better take his dress," said Robin, "he'll freeze to death in there!"

They rushed in, through the cobwebs and the dust, and the narrow passage went this way and that, and at last it opened out and became a little room, and in that room sat Jimmy, surrounded by old leather-bound books!

"It's the secret library!" cried Susan.

"Yeth!" shrieked Jimmy. "And look at thith!"

He held up an old, old book, its pages yellow and dog-eared. Eagerly, Susan grabbed it.

"Why, this is the book that locals have searched for for years!" she exclaimed. "It's the private journal of Blackbeard the Pirate, who died without ever telling where he left a fortune in gold and precious gems such as rubies etcetera!"

"*That* book!" cried Robin. "Can it really be . . .?"

"Yes!" shouted Susan, holding it up so they could all read the flyleaf: YE DEVIOUS PRACKTICES AMONGE YE MELANESIAN ILANDERS AS OBSERVED BY E. F. BLACKBEARD, ESQR. As she waved it aloft, something dislodged itself from the pages, and fluttered down! They leapt upon it.

"It appears to be some kind of chart or diagram," said Robin. He peered at it in the dim light. "Yes! It's a plan of how you can get to the long-lost pleasure of the South-Sea natives!"

Everyone gasped!

"Do you think we can find it?" breathed Susan.

"We'll have a jolly good try!" shouted Robin.

NEXT WEEK: *Who is the man in the fawn raincoat lurking near the cottage? Why is the local bobby nonplussed? What is Mister Eric Bowles's solicitor doing in a frogman's suit with a pair of powerful German binoculars?*

Snobbery in Schools

By DAVID DIMBLEBY

MY adolescence was spent at an expensive but unpretentious school whose social standing eases the path to membership of many golf clubs. Since these are now more concerned with whether their members have any Jewish blood than with what school they went to, this is only a minor benefit. Anyway I do not play golf. No other advantage has come to me from going to a public school. At Charterhouse we had little chance of becoming snobs. Our self-esteem was kept at a low ebb by our being dressed in shapeless brown tweed and being forbidden, or finding it impossible, to speak to girls.

The school, founded by a coal merchant several hundred years ago, was devoted to the not unworthy task of educating six hundred sons of the middle classes. Its ambition had once been to find its pupils posts in the British Empire. Now it aimed at Boards of Industry and Chairmanships of Corporations. We were given a grounding in a wide range of subjects by our masters, and spent our free hours revealing to each other the mysteries of sex. These two activities took up most of our days and nights. There was no time left to teach us to be gentlemen.

It is true that from time to time we were called on to admire the somewhat hazy traditions of the school. We performed a masque which commemorated our past, in which I rode a horse of indeterminate breed and lazy nature. From its height I watched a procession of our famous old boys crossing the courtyard. Richard Lovelace was pursued by Judge Jeffreys, Addison, Steele, and John Wesley. There followed a brief pause as we passed in silence over the sad career of our only Prime Minister—a man chiefly distinguished for the tears he shed in Cabinet. The procession ended dully with Baden Powell. Max Beerbohm, to my irritation, was excluded.

Our claims to fame, you see, were modest. Among the living we numbered only a handful of titles and most of those the sons of barons of recent creation. None of us was anything in his own right. But people thought of us as snobbish or rather we brought out the snobbishness in them. There are still people who think it a superior person who can say "I went to Charterhouse." If this were not so the school's order books, now full, would be empty.

The only school I would accept as a snob school is Eton. Etonians themselves are commonly thought unsnobbish. This is an exaggeration. They are, however, less snobbish about being Etonians than people who are not Etonians, like earls who do not have to defend their earldoms. I did not meet any Etonians until I went to Oxford. I soon thought I could tell them at a glance. I was wrong. One turned out to be a Harrovian. Another, though he claimed to be an Old Etonian, was the product of an exotic school run by the Roman Catholic Church. So unnerved was he by his failure to go to Eton that he invented a fantasy Etonian career for himself, which fooled all outsiders and many Etonians too. He knew the geography and details of the house he claimed to have been to, and could reel off the names not only of the masters, but of the boys, and the dates they came and went as well. He even knew the dates of famous canings (a minor Eton obsession). Etonian snobbery is different from other snobberies. To have been to a public school other than Eton is now a disadvantage. At Redbrick Universities mere Marlburians or Carthusians take great pains to disguise their past. Grammar schools, being the norm, are acceptable. Public schools are not. But revolutionaries, full of good sense, seem determined to allow the best of the old order to remain intact. This is not least because they themselves spring from it.

The New Left in Britain was conceived in the Lower Fourth at Eton. These scions of a noble breed now publish the papers and spread the word that would change and destroy all, one suspects, but Eton. Eton is the haven of the revolutionary, the Labour Minister, the New Rich, the Faded Aristocracy, and the Tory Party. It combines both the destroyer and the to be destroyed.

Teachers, of course, are snobs. There are still said to be a few who care about teaching, but they get fewer every year. The majority are too busy winning scholarships for their pupils and promotion for themselves. It suits them to teach in a school whose pupils come from a class a fraction higher than their own. It gives them an easily acquired sense of superiority and a chance to enjoy, vicariously, the life that their own low income forbids.

Teachers will always move from a less smart school to a smarter if the chance

"I don't know what we'd have done if I hadn't been given this for passing my 11-plus."

arises. At Charterhouse we occasionally had masters who had been educated at Eton. We knew we could not keep them. We were always right. The masters who stayed longest came from humbler schools or from abroad. To them our gothic towers were a healing balm and it was rumoured that they were given special dinners once a week off silver plate to maintain the illusion of grandeur.

But the worst snobs are parents. They are total snobs. They justify this by saying that they are worldly wise, that they must do their best for their children, that an expensive education is an investment (though not for them presumably, unless they are thinking of support in their old age). Parents resent and dislike children who are cleverer or better mannered than they. Yet they persist in sending their sons to the most expensive school they can afford. I have known families to scrape together their last pennies and pool all their savings to prevent their children going to the local grammar school. Instead they send him to a small, unknown, private school, in the depths of the country, which provides neither an education nor the style for which the parent was paying in the first place. After four years these children emerge into a world which treats their social and scholarly pretensions with scorn and usually refuses them work. Their parents are then heard grumbling that "things are not what they were" and that "once a public school education was a guarantee of a good job." They forget that four years in the care of these avaricious exploiters of their snobbery never fitted anyone for anything grander than a minor clerical post in the Colonial Service. The wickedness of this kind of snobbery about education is that so many people still *choose* to be badly educated, allowing these racketeers in the minor public schools to make a profit from their foibles.

The world, alas for them, is getting wiser. Perhaps in the Foreign Office or the Stock Exchange it still helps to speak Home County and have a public school tie to wear, but in other places change is coming fast. The BBC, for instance, once a firm believer in the dinner jacket and the Surrey voice, has left that obsession for the daring ground of talent and ability. It can still be difficult to get in, but is better than it was. A few years ago a young graduate from Oxford, which helped (to be precise from Christ Church, which helped even more) was applying to join the sparse ranks of BBC trainees. He felt himself at a disadvantage throughout the interviews because he had been to a North Country grammar school and spoke with the unmistakable cadences of his home town. At Christ Church this had been something of a success. He had even discovered his tutor, a part-time novelist, including a parody of his accent in one of his books. But at the BBC he was nervous and thought he had failed, until a formidable and senior woman bore down on him and asked him to have a drink. "Well young man," she said, "what qualifications do you think *you* have for joining us? And what would you do if we accepted you?" In despair, and knowing all was already lost, the young man said, "I would make a film about how Bingo has liberated the working women of Britain." This unconventional reply, at a time when intelligent people thought Bingo only slightly less wicked than going on unofficial strike so startled the lady that she gave him the job on the spot.

Snobs prefer the bad which people think good to the good which is thought bad. This is a shame, but understandable in a country that cares so little for education and so greatly for wealth and position. But business and industry is being forced to discard its snobberies about schools, as the demand for skill rises. School snobbery however will last a long time. Fifty years from now there will still be middle aged men solemnly donning their blue striped ties before going on train journeys so that no one but another Old Etonian will dare address them. There will still be guarded discussions between parents and teachers about what school will be "best" for their sons (i.e. what is the snobbiest they can afford). And generations of the middle classes will burble on about public schools being "a suitable training for life" while the working classes win hands down, which, as the middle classes will be quick to tell you, was not the point of the exercise.

*"How can Mummy suddenly start calling you
Jennifer after all these years, Button?"*

*It Seems
Like Yesterday...*

By GRAHAM

148

*"Of **course** he's not a man now—he's just
pretending to be a man!"*

"Start with the camping ones, when they were
running around with no clothes on."

"Let's face it, old girl . . . time to fill
in the sand-pit."

"But Daddy's booked the seats! We **always**
have a family outing to the Pantomime!"

"It seems no time since you were
teaching him to roller skate."

Dear Kate

My boyfriend wants me to come off the pill because he says it takes the Russian roulette thrill out of sex. I suppose if I have a kid I'll have to marry; but one gets attached to the old pill. Norma P., Ely.

Don't let a man talk you round. The pill is a girl's best friend. But marriage is a good way of life and you can have so much fun furnishing a nice home. Look through the ads in this issue and pick up some ideas. Marrying means setting up home with somebody; but no house stays nice for long with children about. Why not tell your boyfriend you'll marry him but keep on with the pill?

I am expecting my first soon and can't decide on nursery decor — pastel blues and pinks, of course, but would a baby recognise characters from children's classics? Would cows be better? Sanya H., Chester.

Talk about idealising kids! You're going to learn the facts of life soon, Sanya, and I can't feel much sympathy. What nurseries need are indestructible fittings, vomit-resistant furniture and good soundproofing.

How comes it there are so many delinquents around? My five boys and I are real chums. There is nothing they like more than giving Mum a day in bed while they cook the dinner and clean the house. I hope it's alright to send my question in. I do not usually see your paper but was lent one. Mrs. P., Corby.

You are certainly making a rod for your own back. Where delinquency is repressed, the ultimate condition tends to be more severe. Are you sure that you are not letting your children come

between you and your husband? Many marriages break down because children prevent the man of the family getting his share of attention. How certain are you that your son's methods of food-preparation are safe?

Can you suggest any unusual food or games for an under-fives' party? Marion Sibyl T., W.1.

The guests will snivel, squabble and be sick so trouble is wasted. Left-overs are quite good enough. Make them hard to get at — e.g. really *tough* pastry cases — and some of the afternoon will be filled. There is no need to organise games. There's always one child to start a fight and you can use up some more time by leisurely First Aid. If they stay till the last minute, you have only yourself to blame. Have an attractive meal with plenty of drinks ready for when the last mother drags the last child out of the door.

Why are the girls on supermarket cash-desks so rude? Pearl, Ealing.

Try to look at things from their point of view. How would you like being stuck there all day, being grumbled at because the queue is moving so slowly? What reduces this modern shopping system to something that makes a glacier seem like *Concorde* is the children. They chase round the displays, get in the way of the trollies and jam up the exits. Not merely prams and carry-cots ought to be banned from all self-service stores, but minors. Then the relationship of customer and cashier could become a worthwhile experience.

Can you tell me anything about insuring for parenthood? Lady T., Hull.

The premium for insuring against parenthood would be prohibitive, also

for insuring against damage done to your health and property, also for insuring against damage done by your children to other people. Why not insure against something else, say fire?

My husband believes in letting our ten-month-old scream himself to sleep; I believe in picking up and cuddling. Whose side are you on? Mrs. de Q., Exmoor.

Children mean sleepless nights and yawning days. Whether you are kept awake by yells or by having to drag yourself out of bed to pick up a squalling brat, you are not getting your full ration of sleep and in time your husband will find you less attractive. He married a girl, not a mother. Now you know what you are in for, don't repeat the experience and lose another year or two's rest. Anyhow, the problem's been pointless since the invention of the earplug.

I have been brought up not to believe in contraception but I don't care to say "No" to a boy who's done me no harm. I can see I'll end up with a huge family. Viv L., Brighton.

Not a bit of it! There are all sorts of enjoyable things you can do with a boy and never need contraceptives. Send me a stamped addressed envelope for some ideas. My list includes a special appendix on including your girlfriends in your love-life and thus greatly enriching it.

Are there any snags to adoption? Professor Mary C., Australia.

The same as for volunteering to have your appendix out without having appendicitis.

I must have been a beautiful baby

ROBERT MORLEY remembers his first role

ANYONE who has ever been stowed away in an ambulance will, while the operation is actually being carried out, have glimpsed on the faces of the spectators a look of shocked enjoyment. It is the same look as I experienced in my pram during the first few months of life. People peered at me as though I had been the victim of an accident, and so I had—the accident of birth.

I had a difficult birth, and after an anxious eight hours for all concerned, mistook the doctor for my father. I remember lying perfectly still with my eyes closed in a chill of terror. "My God!" I told myself, "I've landed right in the middle of it." My mother lay in a euphoric trance at having produced so splendid an infant, and I could not, even if I had wanted to, disturb her complacency and exhaustion. I could only lie there and shudder.

The doctor was not my idea of a father. I remember I particularly disliked his hands. I was not introduced to my real parent for some hours. It was not the fashion in those days for fathers to attend the birth of their children, and I approve of the modern attitude in this matter. The least a father can do is to welcome his offspring in person. I am all for coming out into the drive to greet my guests. I do not expect them to find their own way into my study.

In point of fact I was a singularly beautiful baby— all ten and a half pounds of me. They don't come that size any more, and it was with justifiable pride that my mother handed me over to the nursery staff. Nineteen hundred and eight was a good year for my father, and we could afford a nursemaid as well as a nanny. I remember them both perfectly, although neither stayed with us for very long, my father's affairs calling, as they did so frequently, for sudden retrenchment. In those days we were always moving house, which was perhaps fortunate, as the farm where I was born was burnt to the ground soon after we left it. It had, after all, perfectly fulfilled its function. My father at the time dabbled in and dreamt of champion saddlebacks. How amply I was to compensate him for his early failures in that field, although he was not to discover until some years later that he had produced the greatest ham of all.

My father was the sort of father who upset treacle on the tablecloth to amuse his brood. Quite early in my life he had the disconcerting habit of lifting me high in the air. Babies do not on the whole like being lifted,

and none of them cares to be dropped. I don't say my father ever dropped me, but he came damned close to it. He lived until I was over thirty, a life of extraordinary crisis and financial adventure, full of alarums and excursions. He never understood money, but believed, like his son, that this was because he could never get his hands on enough of the stuff. He was in turn soldier, cafe proprietor, night-club impresario, club secretary, farmer and postal poet. He was often a bankrupt, always a gambler, and of all the excitement, happiness and occasional despair he brought me, I remember him best sitting pretending to be asleep, a handkerchief over his face, and four, sometimes even five chocolates arranged on his lap, while I, choking with pleasure and the effort of restraining my giggles, tiptoed towards him to seize a sweet while he feigned unconsciousness. Then he would wake, remove the handkerchief, look down with astonishment, count the remaining chocolates, and express bewilderment, rage or resignation before once more replacing the handkerchief and pretending to nod off. If there has ever been a better game, I certainly have never played it, and if I was honest I should say that the only acting I ever learnt was at my parent's knee.

But back to the nursery, the boredom of starting tea with bread and butter, and the constant delight of Keplers, a patent medicine much favoured by my parents, which along with Parrish's Food, kept me and my sister fighting fit, or at any rate fighting. We fought with each other, with nanny, and later with a selection of governesses. We were apt to boast, the two of us, that we could get rid of any governess within a fortnight of her setting foot in our nursery. Later, my parents despairing, or possibly unable to afford the redundancy settlements, sent us to a Dame School at the end of the road. It was a long road, and halfway along it a dog barked menacingly at my approach. It was my ever-present terror that one day he would detach himself from the chain to which he was shackled, and tear into my ample and defenceless rump. I did everything I could to avoid alerting him. I walked in the ditch, I tiptoed along the road, I stooped beneath the hedge, I played truant. My mother poo-hooed, my sister chiiked, my teacher scolded, and I grew up terrified of man's four-footed alleged friend. Looking back on my first few years, I realise now they were ones of continuing anxiety. At six I craved chestnuts

151

"I think he means it this time."

to bore through and thread on string. I hurled a stick one afternoon at a chestnut tree and brought down a couple attached to a small branch. Instantly at my elbow a lout appeared, threatening to tell the owner of the tree. He bluffed me out of sixpence and made me promise to meet him the next Saturday for a further contribution. I have forgotten now whether I did or not, but I remember the terror of my first experience with guilt and blackmail. As usual I overstate the case. What I experienced, I suppose, was being found out.

Nobody found out much about me when I was a child. There wasn't perhaps a great deal to learn. I survived to tell the tale, to hold my own grand-children on my lap and to try and remember how my father looked when I played the chocolate game. I resisted lifting them high in the air. I never tickle them. (God, how I hated being tickled!) On the rare occasions when I preside at teatime, I give them cake first. There is no logical reason not to do so. When my granddaughter is older I shall try and persuade her never to curtsy when shaking hands. I dislike "manners." I avoid finding things for them to do. I lived in an age when children were always being given simple tasks. I have never forgiven Mrs. Boddam Whettam who, when I was a child, once gave me seventeen invitations to a bridge tea, to be delivered personally by one who was frightened of dogs, who was shy of strangers, and who loathed exercise. Fortunately we were living in Folkestone at the time, and I climbed to a rocky pinnacle of The Leas and let the wind carry each invitation separately over the cliff and out to sea, and when Mrs. Boddam Whettam waited disconsolately at her bridge parlour, the cards set out on the green baize tables, a marker and a pencil arranged in every place, bravely blinking back her tears, I never gave her a thought. I was sitting in the Electric Cinema watching Charlie Chaplin playing the same scene far better on celluloid.

Ruth Rivers' winning cover

How the Young Saw Europe

. . . On the day that Punch took our Young Europe Competition prizewinners to 10 Downing Street for their certificates and then on to Brussels, accompanied by Editor WILLIAM DAVIS

MR. HEATH showed them his sailing trophies and said we had to stop being insular. "We mustn't go around thinking everything foreign is worse," he told Ruth Rivers, the eleven-year-old Derby girl who had painted the winning cover in our "Young Europe" competition. Ruth remained silent. If she had any such thoughts about foreigners she failed to communicate them to the Prime Minister. The others were no more forthcoming: 10 Downing Street left them speechless. Mr. Heath, who had spent several hours with far from silent trade union leaders earlier on, seemed grateful. "Give my regards to Sir Christopher," he said as he handed each of the six winners a special *Punch* certificate. "Say I congratulate him on his elevation to such an important post."

In Brussels, Sir Christopher Soames, the Common Market's new "foreign secretary," looked harassed but pleased. He and the children posed for press and television cameramen in his office on the thirteenth floor of the vast glass palace which serves as the headquarters of the EEC. Nicholas Johns, who came first in

the essay competition, took in the drinks tray, the bevy of aides, the photographers, and the smiling Sir Christopher and made what the Italian guide later called "a most perceptive comment." "Does anyone," he asked, "ever do any work around here?"

Sir Christopher assured him that he and his colleagues didn't spend all their time meeting children. Indeed, this was something of an occasion: it was the first time a group of children from Britain had come to see for themselves what went on in the glass palace. "We are doing all this for you, you know," he added. "We are merely laying the foundation." If he expected thanks he didn't get them: none of the children seemed greatly impressed.

Some hours before, they had been taken on a tour of the European school, and swapped information with a Dutchman whose main job is teaching English. "What time do you start here?" asked Chris Wade, one of the other prizewinners. "Eight-fifteen," said the Dutchman. "Well," Chris replied, "I'm glad I live in England." Jacqueline Main, from Scotland, wanted to know about dis-

153

cipline. He explained that there was very little punishment, but that his approach varied according to nationality: some were more difficult than others. She told him that, in Scotland, one was "belted." He looked surprised. "Belted?" he said. "For being cheeky," she added.

At the Common Market headquarters, a voluble Italian official handed them a fat portfolio of documents with titles like *The Urban Phenomenon in Europe*, *Industrial Policy and the EEC*, and *Curbing Pollution*. He also explained that, in order to be a good European, you had to learn to live with other people. In his own department there were Italians, Belgians and Germans working together. It was not compulsory to eat spaghetti on Mondays, or sauerkraut on Tuesdays, but it was important to try. One also had to make some attempt to learn languages: it was bad form to stick to one's own. The British, he went on, were welcome because they were "so practical." Continentals tended to spend too much time arguing, and getting bogged down in details. "When we first signed the Treaty," he said, "we made sure it covered everything, but paid too little attention to the immediate problems. We built a fine casserole, but no one was ready to put anything inside."

The children listened attentively, but were more taken by a highly irreverent film made specially for the EEC. Narrated by Peter Ustinov, it is meant to be a fierce attack on prejudice—which, Ustinov explained, is "a major obstacle to European unity." The film mocks familiar cliches like "Italians are lecherous cowards" and "all Germans are militaristic."

Ustinov blames history lessons. "On the playground," he says "we re-enacted the old wars, repeated how we loathed foreigners, and played the parts we had heard about in class. Our enemies were always people who spoke a different language or had a different colour of skin." The film ends with a modern European family looking at all the old stereotypes in a zoo. The children laughed but claimed to have little prejudice themselves: it was, they felt, much more common among older people, including their parents. Nicholas Johns went on to say, however, that the endless war films on BBC television were doing a pretty good job in passing on bad feelings towards Germans and Italians.

The six prize-winners with the Prime Minister, who presented them with Punch certificates. "Mr. Heath's place", said Ruth Rivers (far left) afterwards, "is a bit like Dr. Who's Tardis, small on the outside and large inside."

Lunch in the Common Market canteen was, well, a canteen lunch. The staple diet of EEC officials, it seems, consists of spaghetti, steak and chips. When you have to cater for 6,000 people you can't go in for Cordon Bleu cooking.

The EEC headquarters are too large to encourage intimacy: people frequently get lost in its long corridors and tend to keep close to their own kind. One can work there for years and still be challenged by security guards. Officials complain that, because of its size, the machinery is dreadfully inefficient. This certainly seems to be true of the telephone service: it took more than half an hour to make a call from the Soames office to London.

The children were taken on a tour of Brussels before flying back to London, and said they liked it. Nicholas Johns bought himself a book—in French. Yes, he said, he might well try to get a job on the Continent when he left school. The others were more cautious, but there was general agreement that Europe wasn't really such a bad place after all. We have passed the good news on to Mr. Heath; he will no doubt be glad to hear it.

Ruth Rivers shows her prize-winning cover to Sir Christopher Soames.

YOUNG EUROPE

The Winning Article

by Nicholas JOHNS
aged 15

THE PRIME MINISTER sits nervously on the edge of his Parliamentary seat. He wonders if his pet project will come to a satisfying conclusion. Sssh! The voting—a Government majority—I am sorry, Britain is in the Common Market! Hurrah! He rushes out to play the national anthem on his portable harmonium, or perhaps to weep a crocodile tear of emotion in the Commons' cloakroom.

We are the people that will suffer the consequences of a unification with Europe. Ted and Harold will be dead (sigh of relief). We will bear the responsibilities of governing the new superstate—Europe. Yes, us—the people who try to drink in pubs under age, the race apart that hurls cricket balls at your greenhouses: today's sub-sixteen-year-olds, who will rule in 2002.

Whether we like it or not, we are in Europe for good. I am not in a position to voice the opinion of the people, simply because I don't know what it is; but I tend to think that it is economically a good thing for Britain. We cannot match the industrial output of America and Japan with our pig-headed unions and decrepit machinery. Britain needs to join an economic community—the E.E.C. As an organ of the body of Europe, we will once more have a vital part to play in the world. Our technical "know-how" far exceeds anything which present day Europe can offer: we need Europe badly, but Europe needs us even more.

Industrial considerations apart, we know little or nothing of the effects of forthcoming unification. Will we still despise the "Hun" and spurn the "Frog"? Will an old age pensioner from Scunthorpe ever become accustomed to eating real Italian spaghetti for lunch, instead of Heinz? There are many questions, but few answers.

To lead a happy life in the year 2002 (when we teenagers will be middle-aged men-in-the-street), we must strive to find the things we have in common with our Continental cousins. Unfortunately, this will demand a loss of national identity; an Englishman's kibbutz will have to serve as his castle and city gents will be forced to leave their pinstripes at home and don cheap, lightweight Italian suits. Of course, the other eight Common Market countries will gradually lose their national identity

C. R. Wade, 15, joint winner with Ruth Rivers, 11

too—this is something adamant anti-Marketeers seldom think about. (What is Luxembourg's national identity like anyway?) But I am sure we will all get along famously together: after all, we have more in common with European Young'uns (no pun intended) than we do with our parents. We all look alike, dress alike and generally "dig the same scene, man". Our friendship will no doubt flourish as it has never flourished before, greatly assisted by an inevitable common language (perhaps a revived form of Esperanto), no frontiers, a common currency, common eating, drinking and recreational habits, in short, a common way of life.

Of course, the greatest thing we will have in common with our community members is that we shall one day be ruled by a European Parliament. Let us hope that our generation will find the means to form a peaceful, unified Europe. The solution (not the *final* solution) will mean a slackening of racial tension. There will be no room for any aspiring Enoch Powells or Adolf Hitlers, who hum "If I Ruled the World" to themselves in the bath;

or on the other side of the coin any Lenins from Nuremberg, Wapping or Lille. No, Europe must strike a balance between all political forces and must remain a centre of democracy.

If we all put our minds to it, our Young Europe will be a wonderful place—a dream of heads of state come true. Europeans will live together happily and healthily, with a hitherto unequalled standard of living.

Industry will thrive, and there will be wealth for anyone willing to work for it. The environment will not be neglected either, there will still be plenty of green fields for our Euro-crats to relax in—the Alps will not turn into a creamy yellow, they will stay white. We will no doubt look back on the "bad old days" and wonder why on earth we nearly elected to go it alone: to allow Britain to die an ignominious national death.

Perhaps our new Young Europe will serve as an example to the other nations of the world. In fifty years time you may be living next door to a Mongolian!

"*I asked him what he wanted for Christmas and he said a syringe.*"

The Generation Gap

by MICHAEL HEATH

"*But you must want something else for Christmas besides peace in Vietnam.*"

"Just because our daughter's on the Pill, does it mean she doesn't believe in Santa?"

"It seems like only yesterday that you were only knee high . . . wait a sec, it was yesterday."

"Pop fans and groups are getting younger and younger."

"No Dad, you were quite right to come and see me—we all have problems from time to time— feel free to pop in any time."

"He's wonderful with children . . ."

Bully
for
Who?

ALAN BRIEN
measures up as
a father-figure

HE'S bigger than you. Even worse, he's not bigger than you. He may not even be stronger than you. He's almost certainly stupider than you. Your feelings towards him, ordinarily, would be at strongest contempt, at weakest boredom. Yet he frightens you, all the time.

He's that knot, like a cat's hair ball, just beyond the depth of your deepest swallow, as you wake in the morning. He's that constriction in your throat as you eat your mid-day meal, that commotion in the rib cage as the heart beats against its bars like a wild budgie. The mote in your eye is the beam in his. He's literally a pain in the arse, a clot on the brain. For he's your own personal predator, your self-appointed, made-to-measure Nemesis—not a word he would understand, but one, not understood, which would goad him to greater malevolence, to an even more motiveless malignity which makes Iago seem like Jeeves.

How can such things be? Surely, you can complain to the authorities? But they have other problems on their minds. Anyway, they can only act after the event, when you can produce a medically-attested broken finger, or torn ear, or scraped eyeball, the very evidence you are trying to avoid. You don't fancy being a witness

158

on a stretcher. Be brave, they say, heroes are always afraid. Yes, but are they ashamed of being afraid?

In books and films and TV series, the villain, once down, stays down. Yours is renewed by opposition, given a fresh charge to his batteries by your defence. If you beat him off, or even up, today, he would still be there tomorrow. You fantasy about force fields and ray guns, cloaks of invisibility and death traps, Mafia revenge and appeals to International Rescue, becoming overnight an expert at Judo, karate and Kung Fu. But nobody will take the threat seriously, except you.

After all, your bully looks a nice boy, with a pleasant if simple-minded smile, the kind your mother likes the look of on the form photograph, and he can't be more than eleven.

The problem is one familiar to all fans of the American thriller writer, John D. McDonald. (Not to be onfused with Ross Macdonald, the egghead's favourite pet, whose private eye with a poetic iris, seems a metamapsychosis of Philip Marlowe, and like Chandler's hero invariably discovers a woman did it on the last page.) But the pacific, law-abiding citizen threatened by the indestructible, violent cannonball of an enemy who will stop at nothing seems fortunately a trans-Atlantic horror which so far cannot be imagined here. Except in the playground.

Wandering around London last week, during the half-term holiday, with my ten-year-old son, I realised what adults secretly know but conveniently suppress—that a child's world is much more extreme, emotional, erratic and baffling than ours. So the worst that can happen to him is probably a bleeding nose or a black eye. But hiding in the lavatory, skulking in the dining hall, taking cover in a crowd, peering out of the window to make sure the street is empty, the whole Hitchcockian routine, seems inside him as real and dangerous as it would to us.

Children exist in an enclave of barbarism, a society with rituals and initiations and dictatorships and tortures and taboos and totems, which exists just a few feet away from our own civilised, domesticated domain. We push them towards each other while we have our drinks, lock them up in schools while we go to work, drop them off at summer camps, leave them alone all night in dormitories, as if they possessed instincts for democracy, freedom and justice which three-quarters of our grown-up world has not yet evolved.

The years rush by for us, while the days crawl for them, forgetting that no child can grasp the concept of a fortnight. We assume that all members of their age group are more or less interchangeable without considering how choosy we are about our friends and colleagues. We deny them the right to have moods, obsessions, inexplicable likes and dislikes, fads and fancies, which make us so interesting and complex personalities.

We deprive them of the solace of sex and drink, money and responsibility. We sort through their possessions, throwing out what we regard as broken or useless. We dress them to suit our tastes and illustrate our style. We betray them in public by reproving them for behaviour we practise in private.

And yet we are surprised when, at adolescence, we discover that, after a lifetime of waiting, they seem to want all our pleasures and privileges and vices *now*.

Our mistake is not that we fail to treat children as adults, but that we fail to realise how childish adults are. They feel everything we feel and we should not be surprised or shocked to learn that our cowardice, greed, vanity, envy and ambition is already there among them. If it were not, where did it spring from? The best I can do for my offspring is to assume that they are as fallible and vulnerable as I am.

When I discuss bullying with my son, I should not try to travel backwards in time and imagine what I would have done in his place. I have to ask myself what I would do here and now. The exercise may not help him but it teaches me a few truths.

You've got to face such people, son, take a risk, hit back. Should I speak to the boy from my immense superior strength and size? What's that, speak to his father? His father's a boxer? Well now, let's not be hasty. We don't want to descend to his level, do we?

159

Stokowski and Emma

By EAMONN ANDREWS

THE word culture and I reach for the ear-muffs. Hating the highbrows more than I do the hippies, I experience a great sense of shame, hoping that my seven-year-old, Emma, will turn out to *be* a highbrow.

Drying the Sunday night dishes, getting that familiar ache in the neck trying to watch the television set from the sink, I heard the announcer on BBC-2 say that Stokowski was going to conduct the London Philharmonic in Beethoven's Fifth. Hell, even I know the opening bars of Beethoven's Fifth. When the famous conductor made his appearance, he looked so frail—the colour, in fact, made him almost translucent—I suddenly felt I might never see this man doing this again. Not that I'd ever seen him before. I suppose I was swept by the same kind of greedy emotion that makes shops that claim to be going out of business tomorrow do such tremendous trade today.

Whatever it was, I yelled upstairs.

"Emma. Emma. Come down quickly."

She must have thought the house was on fire or that *Tom and Jerry* were on.

"You must watch this. But you're late. You're late. You've missed the opening."

She began to panic.

"Must watch what? Missed what?"

"Ssh. Just listen. You must hear this. It might be the last chance. That's Stokowski. You might never see him again."

"Is he going to die?"

"Of course he's going to die. We're all going to die. Just listen."

"When is he going to die?"

"Darling, I don't know when he's going to die. He's a very old man and you might not get the chance of watching him again. Just watch and listen. He's a great composer and this is a great piece of music."

Silence for a few minutes, and I could only assume, since they'd said so, that all that was following really was Beethoven's Fifth. They'd long since passed my familiar tum-ti-ti-tum, tum-ti-ti-tum.

"Is he good at whistling, too?"

"I'm sure he is."

"How do you know?"

I wriggled out of that one somehow.

"Why did you want me to hear the beginning?"

"Because it's famous. The beginning of Beethoven's Fifth Symphony is very famous."

"Why do they call it Symphony?"

I felt defeated and frustrated as the music swept on that she hadn't asked me why they called it the Fifth. Why do they call it Symphony? How do I know why they call it Symphony. They just do.

By now I was sitting down on the kitchen stool and she had drifted over to the cutlery drawer.

160

"Yeah, they're all right, I'll take 'em."

"Try to remember to put the spoons in there. Not here."

"Will there soon all be colour on television?"

"Yes."

"That'll be a pity. I like to see the black and white."

Defeated again, I said, "Why don't you sit down and listen to this famous music and this famous conductor and this famous orchestra?"

She sat down.

"How did he become famous?"

"By becoming a great musician. By becoming a great conductor. Everybody got to know about him and listen to him."

"And if he doesn't do it right, he won't be famous any more."

"No. You can't stop being famous if you're famous once. At least, you might be forgotten but you wouldn't stop being famous in that time. So, even if he did it wrong, he'd still be famous. But he won't do it wrong, and why don't you listen?"

I was shouting.

"You know who should be famous? The orchestra. They're the ones who are doing it all."

"They are famous—in a way. In a different kind of way. There are a whole lot of them, as you can see, and a whole lot of different instruments."

A softer piece of music and the maestro barely moved his tapering hands.

"What's he doing now?"

"Concentrating."

The movement came to an end before I had to deal with that one.

"Why don't they clap?"

"They don't clap between movements."

"Why?"

"I think it's because it might disturb the mood."

That one got by.

"Have you ever been clapped?"

"Yes."

"What did you do?"

"Nothing."

"Nothing?"

She pranced around the kitchen, bowing to an imaginary audience, with a look of unbelievable smugness on her face, and then sat down again.

Somehow we reached the end. The climax. The applause. Emma came to life again.

"You see he gives himself the great reward at the end."

"How?"

"Zoomp. Zoomp."

"What on earth do you mean?"

"That last bit of music with his hands. Zoomp. Zoomp."

I think I'll settle for a hippy.

FATHER
(OF SIX)
CHRISTMAS

By PAUL JENNINGS

WHEN ONE HAS SIX CHILDREN there's such a row going on all the time that one can't even hear the deafening roar of Advice, Hints and Suggestions for Living that is responsible for so much of today's restlessness, insecurity, moist palms, juvenile delinquency, inferiority feelings, sleeplessness, indigestion, blushing, divorce, and nervous breakdowns in wallpaper shops. Hints reach a climax at Christmas for people who haven't got six children. (Surely it can't be long before the Hints industry hives off completely from journalism, the parent it has so monstrously outgrown. "What's Jennifer doing when she's finished at Wessex?" "Oh, she's going into Hints. She was doing a TPD [Tiny Personnel Diploma] but now she's switched, she's reading Central Heating with Tot Advice as subsid.")

Naturally, even without the Hints for all those complicated punches or A Christmas Caravan Holiday or those Japanese paper decorations—what is it again, *noguchi*, *fujiyama*, *cocacola*, no, of course, *origami* (I think)—it's perfectly obvious that planning begins way back for people who live on the completely different time-scale of life with four, or less, or no children. This may mean anything from the purchase of two stalls for some such Christmas treat, in London's magic theatre wonderland, as that play about the homosexual barbers, to careful saving up of £7 10*s*. for something I saw at the beginning of October. In a stationery shop that was like a last statement of England before the blank sea, a defiant brightly lit place full of jars of salty commercial fudge, knitting magazines, cigarettes, beach balls, wire display stands of pornographic paperbacks facing the slow tide creeping over the Essex mud, they had cleared a space for a proud exhibit, with a card saying ORDER NOW FOR XMAS. It was a Missile Projector, made with loving verisimilitude and detail, encrusted with handles and triggers, mounted on a tripod, painted official dark green. It was about three feet long, and beside

162

it was a smaller case on which it said WARHEADS in that stencilled lettering. It cost £7 10*s*., and it's gone now, so *some* Essex carol-singers had better look out.

Well, no doubt the Hint boys and girls would say, *have* said, in God knows how many column-inches, that this kind of toy is harmful and develops aggressive tendencies and should not be encouraged; and OK, I'm not encouraging it. On the other hand we are almost certainly buying for one of our children a Captain Morgan Siege Gun, "a beautifully moulded large size cannon which fires harmless plastic cannon balls" (surely there's no such thing as a dangerous plastic cannon ball), "the loading is effected by the ramrod. Elevation is adjustable and wheels will turn." More important, the illustration in the catalogue shows the barrel to be black, the body bright red, the wheels yellow and their rims blue. None of that functional olive green stuff.

It's no use the Hints people saying that's aggressive too, and I'm well aware that Henry Morgan was one of history's nastiest thugs. The Hints people can't possibly know that its recipient, probably the least aggressive of the six, leapt into our minds the moment we saw it; it's *him*, if it's got a ramrod and the wheels will turn. Maybe aggression is OK if it's far enough back in history, maybe the perfect toy would be a prehistoric man trap, harmless plastic spikes set in a plastic pit. But we're out of earshot for Hints about that already, it's time to settle which day is the best for the pantomime (we stay with our ex-neighbours in London each time, we fill up a whole row. Last year it was *The Curse of the Daleks*, all human dialogue had to rise above a constant babbling of toddlers, who were only silent when those idiotic pepper-pots trundled on; this was a pity, since one of the lines really was, I swear, "I've been a blind fool!").

Giving Hints to people with six children is like telling a swimmer to rise when a wave comes. All you can do is just go on swimming (in our case, slightly against the tide) and the wave will lift you anyway. Mind you, I'm not suggesting we don't do *anything*. Of course we do. Last Christmas Eve I had to go out, just when we thought we'd got everything, to buy a spade, since the old one was broken and there was nothing to fill the old bread bin with old wet mud (it always rains on Christmas Eve, in Suffolk at any rate) to pack round the roots of the Christmas tree (had to borrow a saw to do that, could have borrowed a spade too, but had vague ideas of gardening on Boxing Day, or at least of getting the bean-poles out, in time to dry them for next year's beans).

The fact that everything has to be done at the last minute often means an un-expected bonus (just as it did when we bought fireworks on the morning of November 5 and all they had left was sparklers and three tremendous rockets costing 7*s*. 6*d*. each—the kind that go bang on the ground, then climb to about three thousand feet where they go bang again and ten different-coloured globules fall from them and then *they* all go bang—a much more satisfying and clear-cut evening than all that messing about with 4*d*. Snow Fountains). It's just the same on Christmas Eve; the shops are almost empty, the floors are littered with paper and old balloons as if after a dance in the parish hall, there is a sound of staff parties behind screens and partitions, from which smiling assistants emerge to serve us. Very often only the biggest dolls and steam engines are left; but very often they are reduced, already.

Actually we are one of the few families that has a bonfire on Christmas Day, as well as November 5. We are a family of eight, and everybody gives everybody something, even if it's only a packet of Smarties (sometimes, after a giver has been saving it for a few days, half a packet of Smarties), so that's fifty-six for a start. With godparent's presents, another twelve, that's sixty-eight, before one counts friends. Nearly all these things come in vast cocoons of cardboard and paper, and watching those splendid fifteen-foot flames in the December dusk gives one an appetite for tea. This year I'm thinking of putting the bean poles on (they've really had it this time) and I saved one of those great rockets. You don't get ideas like *that* from the Hint columns.

No such trees in Bethlehem. Wrong climate!
But not pagan custom. Slaughter of trees
represents Massacre of Innocents.

Far out.

The Greatest Story that Ever Fell on Deaf Ears

This Christmas,
give the kids
a tirade

by HANDELSMAN

Tasteless and vain? Yes!
Pagan custom? No!
Symbolizes tawdry glitter
of inn contrasted with
austerity of manger.

Groovy.

Not pagan. Lovely old Disney favourites. Rudolph comes to terms with his red nose. Good tidings of great joy which shall be to all people.

Too much.

Shopping and shoving pagan customs? Unlikely. Pagans had fun. More in keeping with "a man of sorrow and acquainted with grief."

Heavy.

Father Christmas—modern equivalent of Magi, or Joseph if you prefer. Nothing pagan about him!

Cool.

Drunken revelry. Why not? Nothing in gospels about shepherds guarding flocks by night being sober. Must have had a few. Temperance is recent pagan invention.

Like, blasphemy.

CAUTION: CHILDREN AT WORK

The TUC wants the Government to stop children taking part-time jobs. We sent little PETER PRESTON to find how children are hitting back.

MR.VICTOR FEATHER and his entire Trades Union Congress were described as "rotten beasts" and "jolly stinkers" today by Sir William Bunter, incoming President of the Boys Own Union (writes our Kindergarten and allied practices correspondent). "We must all be prepared to bounce the stinking old fogies," he warned hot-panted delegates at the Dreamland Marina and What-the-Butler-Saw emporium, Collywobbles-on-Sea.

Sir William was moving the emergency censure motion "that this body demands its slice of the national cake and boo to Big Daddy." "I say you chaps," he declared. "I say Ouch and Yaroo. Ouch to middle-aged repression. Yaroo to the killjoy yahoos of the Lower Fifth." The BOU had known the national cake since it was a cream bun in the first form at St. Hilda's, he said. "Anyone who tries to take our cream bun away from us at this stage in history can stuff it."

Seconding, Lady Bessie Bunter put it on record that she was solidly behind girls' liberation—"indeed, nobody has a solid behind more needful of liberation than me." Just because girls lacked pockets did not mean they should lack pocket money. "I am quite prepared to find a pocket for my share of the cake any day." (Derisory cries of 'Share my Doughnut' off.)

Comrade Mowgli (Jungle BOU branch chairman) called conference's attention to the difficulties of good scouts already fallen upon hard times. "Once we could charge a bob a job; now there are no bobs and no jobs." How would Lord Baden-Powell have taken to five new pence per domestic chore? "We say no new p. for B-P. We say dib, dib, dib to the TUC. Not to mention, dob, dob, dob."

There was widespread groaning and cries of 'Greww' as Comrade J. Hawkins (Treasure Island branch secretary) insisted at this stage upon "adding his fifty doubloons". The newspaper round, he affirmed, was a vital right. "There be no crocks of gold no longer me hearties. And what there be some damned gubbimint steals." Old Long John Silver himself had often pulled legs on this subject. "X bain't be marking no more spots, shipmates. It be only indicating the follies of our ways putting yellow bellied tax lubbers in that there office."

Comrade P. Pan (Never-Neverland branch) interposed to state he thought it was about time Comrade Hawkins grew up. "I am the only one here under no compunction to grow up." Comrade Hawkins complained to the chair about "this scoffing at me sentiments." Sir William ruled hastily that he had not scoffed anything all afternoon.

Speaking in support of the motion, Comrade O. Twist (Dickens and BBC classic serials branch) said that he had personal experience of the alternative to honestly earned pocket money. "You gotta pick a pocket or two." A General Council ban on car cleaning, path sweeping and other legitimate tasks might open the floodgates once again to teenage larceny on the grand scale. "Such a reversal would be denuded even of the literary overtones the nineteenth century brought it," he added. "We in this isle may be swamped by a tide of pornographic Fagins sweeping in from the orgiastic back alleys of Naples under the so-called free entry terms of the Common Market, with only Lionel Bart between us and utter exploitation." Conference passed a subsidiary motion expressing the hope that this phrase—"particularly commended"—might be woven into a forthcoming edition of Mr. Harold Wilson's memoirs.

On the question of sanctions, Comrade ("Just") William Brown (of the Interminably Twee sagas branch) said he didn' spose it'd reelly work but how would it be if e'vry boy unner twelve what spoke like he did and thought simil'r told his mum that he was gonna run away and not go to bed on skedool, not ever, until his mum told his dad that at their proper uni'un meetin's they had to tell this Feather where he got off? "Othe'wise they won' have sexooal relashuns with 'em." A kind of "Lysistrata at one remove" interjected Comrade T. Brown (Classical Schooldays branch). Sir William said that he was the Owl of the Remove and that this Lysistrata was out of order, unless edible.

Comrade T. Brown went on to claim that, since it was still in order for junior youths in the great schools of our land to perform menial duties for senior boys, it seemed extraordinary for the TUC to dictate on the employment of minors by adults. "I am a fag and proud of it," he said. (Cries of "Meet me in the dorm after dinner, darling".) Comrade C. Brown (of the 'How to make a Million out of Peanuts' branch) said that we must all love each other. "Everyone at this conference is quite welcome to share my blanket."

Comrade R. Bear (of the Express Aggrandisement and Rothermere ruination branch) said in this time of self-restraint he did not wish to make complaint. But Oh cried Rupert in alarm. There is one thing that gives me qualm. Ted asks us not have a bash, but Vic would strip us of our cash. And getting on without much money has no pretence to being funny. I know I'm just a little bear but I do know it's most unfair.

He said he could go on and on and even sing a little song about the Chancellor's exhortation and the interests of the nation, but on the whole he thought he'd cease and let others say their piece. "Though some do like a rhyming lad I understand it turns some mad."

Herr H. C. Andersen, an elderly Danish observer, craved conference's attention to compare Whitehall policies, upon which the TUC's actions were doubtless based, to an emperor without clothes. "If I may be startlingly derivative for the moment, Mr. Barber is naked of policies: but until one small boy shouts out that the Chancellor is nude all of Britain will be deluded." Comrade William Brown said he'd seen 'is mum in the barfroom an' didun see where all this strippin' stuff was gettin' us. Lord Fauntleroy denounced Scandinavia's permissive society and its sapping effect upon English metaphors. "I am prepared to swear upon my mater's marriage bed that Mister Barber wears a nightshirt at all times."

At this point Comrade E. Paminondas (of the Piccaninis Incorporated branch) declared urgently that several bars of butter under his hat would melt if this jawing went on much longer, and a smattering of railway children left in protest against "aspersions cast upon an old gentleman." A vote was called and unanimously passed, when Sir William announced: "I say you fellows I do believe I was just tasting the cake to see what it was like and now it's absolutely gone."

Comrade R. Cherry: "Bounce the fat fraud." Amid cries of "Ouch leggo you beasts," the President was wrapped in C. Brown's blanket and cast palpitating to the winds. Closing the meeting to a disorderly hall, C. Brown himself observed that where children were concerned his psychiatrist always felt anarchy a step away. "Perhaps, instead of making recommendations to Departments of Social Security, unionists who are also fathers should simply give us more money so we kept pace with inflation and didn't have to work," he said. "Or perhaps there are some things that even Jack Jones and Hugh Scanlon can't fix. But don't thank me for telling them: I'm precocious."

"I SAY, YOU FE
LETTING THI

Mrs Thatcher gave permission for 350 independent schools to raise their fees—with shattering results at Greyfriars. Another rattling yarn from E. S. TURNER

MRS. THATCHER was waxy. Mrs. Thatcher had not wanted to come to Greyfriars to give away the prizes. Mrs. Thatcher had no wish to figure in a topping long complete story by Frank Richards.

Nor had Greyfriars wanted Mrs. Thatcher. Dr. Locke, the Headmaster, would have preferred even a bishop to a woman. Besides, he had a bone to pick with Mrs. Thatcher. By giving permission to the Governors to raise the fees, she had closed Greyfriars to all but the most vulgar rich. And the vulgar rich would debase the manly ideals of Greyfriars.

Already the trustees of Lord Mauleverer had written to say that they might as well send him to Holland Park Comprehensive.

But Greyfriars, unknown to Dr. Locke, was preparing its own reception for Mrs. Thatcher. The boys were organising another grand barring out! They had barricaded themselves in their classrooms, with fifty tons of tuck, and were preparing to defy, not only Mrs. Thatcher, but the whole world.

"Go home, Mrs. Thatcher!" cried the banners. As her motor car entered the drive, the ventriloquists of the Remove had the chauffeur driving in all directions at once. Then soot bags and stink bombs began to rain on the car. A well-aimed arrow removed Mrs. Thatcher's pink hat and pinned it to an elm.

"Yarooh!" exclaimed Mrs. Thatcher. "Gurrrrrgh! Stop it, you cads! Play the game!"

"Ha! Ha! Ha!"

"Pluck and tuck! Greyfriars for ever!"

"All right, you rotters!" cried Mrs. Thatcher. "You have won the first battle, but I shall raise your fees by a thousand per cent."

LOWS, THEY'RE BOUNDERS IN"

Harry Wharton and Co. led the cheers as the car headed back for London.
Next week : On a holiday cruise by airship, the boys of Greyfriars are forced down at Wounded Knee and fight a terrific battle with Redskins. Billy Bunter loses his scalp!

*

"OH, crumbs!"

Oh, haddocks!"

The Famous Five fell swooning into each other's arms.

"What is it?" asked Bob Cherry. "It has two legs and it looks almost human. But it has an old and fish-like smell."

"The face is like a rat's," said Frank Nugent.

"The ratfulness is terriffic," agreed Hurree Jamset Ram Singh.

The object of their mirth wore trousers tighter even than those of William Bunter. His jacket was composed mainly of zip-fasteners. If he had had any shoulders, his long golden hair would have reached them. He wore beads.

"It is the offspring of a Labour M.P.," suggested Bob Cherry. "It has ideas above its station. Let us strew the hungry churchyard with its bones."

Harry Wharton looked at the tight trousers. He did not like what he saw. Tight trousers on Bunter were one thing. But these faded blue trousers bulged where they should not have bulged. The blood rose to Harry Wharton's cheeks.

"I say, you fellows," he exclaimed, "have you seen those bags?"

"The tightfulness is terrific."

Lord Mauleverer strolled up and surveyed the stranger.

"It really is extraordinary," he drawled. "Why is it wearing its grandmother's glasses?"

The stranger looked at them coolly.

"Is this Greyfriars?" he asked. "If so, you steaming twits must be the Famous Five. Say, who makes with the hash around here?"

"What is it talking about?" asked Johnny Bull.

The Famous Five were amused no longer. "Steaming twits" was not the language of Greyfriars. It did not sound like a compliment. As for hash, Cook would see that they got more than their share.

Harry Wharton was peeling off his jacket when there was a loud cry of "Siggy!"

It was Vernon-Smith, the Bounder of Greyfriars. He rushed up to the new-comer and embraced him, as if he were a centre-forward.

"Tell your prehistoric friends who I am," said the newcomer.

Smithy explained that Siggy was the son of Cindy Lou Rumbuck, singer with a group called the Kidney Disease.

"The diseasefulness is terrific," said the dusky Nabob.

"Shut up, you illegal immigrant!" said Vernon-Smith, "or I'll see that you catch the next flight to Bhanipur. Mrs. Gandhi will have your guts for garters."

At mention of Mrs. Gandhi's garters the Famous Five paled.

"My advice to you fellows," said Smithy, "is that you begin to read the news-papers, starting with January 1, 1910. The fees of Greyfriars have been put up. Only stinking rich parents can afford them. Not that Siggy has any parents—only a stinking rich mother."

"Is she—er, married," asked Johnny Bull.

Vernon-Smith and Siggy clutched each other helplessly.

"She's an unmarried millionaire," said Smithy. "That should be good enough for Greyfrairs."

The furious blood rose again to Harry Wharton's cheeks. It was time to teach these rotters a lesson.

"Come on, Siggy," said Vernon-Smith. "The muffins are going cold in Study Four. I suppose you brought some books?"

Siggy took a specimen volume from one of his many pockets. It was not a Latin primer. It was not *Robinson Crusoe*.

The chums took one look and gasped.

"Oh, crumbs!"

"Oh, haddocks?"

"I say, you chaps, Wharton has snuffed it. We're now the Famous Four."

*

William George Bunter could not believe what he saw through the keyhole.

Not in his greediest dreams had the Fat Owl drooled over such a spread of cream buns, such quivering masses of jelly. And the cads devouring this tuck were Foskett and Cramp, two of the new fellows from St. Judas.

Foskett drove Mr. Quelch nearly insane by ending every sentence with "then" or "and that." But his father had forecast eight draws and Foskett was now a fixture in the Remove.

Cramp's father worked for Vernon-Smith's father. While the one made millions by opening factories, the other made millions by closing them

"Oh, my sainted aunt!" exclaimed the Fat Owl. Unable to bear the sight, he put his ear to the keyhole instead.

"What's the matter with your old man, then?" Foskett said. "Why doesn't he buy up Greyfriars, then?"

Bunter gasped. Buy up Greyfriars, his home for more than sixty years!

"It's on his list," said Cramp, his mouth full of cream. "The site should be worth eight million smackers."

"Let me in on it, then," said Foskett.

Horror strove with greed in the Fat Owl. In his excitement he fell through the door into the study. A bucket of water spilled over his head.

"Ha! Ha! Ha!"

"I say, you fellows," exclaimed Bunter, picking himself up. "I just happened to be passing and I heard you talking about selling Greyfriars."

"Get lost!"

Bunter used a phrase he had picked up from Vernon-Smith.

"I did eighteen months National Service for the likes of you!"

"I want some of the action," he said.

"You've just had it," sneered Cramp.

"Have you any assets, then?"

"I am expecting a postal order," said the Owl. "It came last week. I mean it should come this week."

"Come back when you've half a million in cash," ordered Cramp. "And get your paws off those cream buns."

They booted him out just as Mr. Quelch arrived.

"Ah, Foskett and Cramp. About that little—ah, enterprise we were talking about. I have here about £100,000 in nine per cent convertible unsecured loan stock . . . thank you, dear boy, what a splendid cream bun!"

Bunter slunk away. Greyfriars was not what it used to be. That was putting it mildly. Even Quelchy was in the plot to sell the old grey pile. But take-overs could wait, whereas Bunter's stomach could not.

That Christmas and Elsie

By HARRY SECOMBE

IT was Christmas Day and I was fourteen and suffering from a severe attack of puberty.

"Silent Night . . ." I sang, head held slightly forward to catch the ray of winter sunlight coming through the stained-glass window above the altar. Elsie Thomas was in the front pew with her mother and I wanted to catch her eye. "Aaa-meen," I intoned loudly, trying to catch her ear as well.

The choirmaster glared at me in the mirror over the organ keyboard. My voice was breaking and the previous Sunday it had cracked in the seven-fold Amen.

"If I want yodelling I'll ask for it," he had said. "This is Swansea, not the Swiss Alps."

Now I blushed back at him in the mirror and knelt piously on my hassock, wearing my "Mickey Rooney as Andy Hardy being told off by his father" expression.

Elsie Thomas tittered and nudged her mother. The rest of the choir were sitting back comfortably waiting for the sermon to start, hard-boiled sweets already bulging in cheeks. I dropped my head and pretended a prayer while the Vicar said, "In the name of the Father and of the Son and of the Holy Ghost. Amen." I then rose gracefully and sat back in Arthur Williams's lap.

"Gerroff," he bleated, loudly enough to earn me another glare from the mirror and a further titter from Elsie.

I resumed my own seat and fumbled sweatily for a pear drop in my cassock pocket. Things weren't going as I had planned. I did a mental dissolve into the Church Social the week before when Elsie Thomas had swept into my life.

She was a new arrival in our midst, her family only recently coming down from one of the valleys north of the town. She was blonde and pretty and had the lads at the Social swarming around her in no time at all.

I kept aloof, though. Mildred Rogers had caught hold of my jacket.

"You go and join that lot around Elsie Thomas, and I'll tell my Mam you wanted to play 'Doctors and Nurses' in the coal house last Saturday." That stopped me. Mildred's mother used to carry her husband home under her arm from the pub on pay nights.

"I have no intention of going. Anyway I'm doing my impressions later on and I've got to go and rehearse."

I walked away towards the unheeded plates of sandwiches and stuffed myself. I listened to the boastful chatter of the boys surrounding Elsie. Wait until I do my impressions, I thought.

The Vicar clapped his hands. "Take your seats please, our concert is about to begin."

There was a clattering of chairs and faces all turned towards the little stage. I took up my position behind the two draped blankets which acted as curtains.

"First we have Master Harry Secombe who is going to give us a comedy turn. Master Harry Secombe." The Vicar waved a plump hand and the blankets jerked slowly back.

"Hello folks," I said nervously, my lips cleaving to my gums, revealing my teeth in a macabre grin. Laughter immediately rang out. Tinkling laughter from Elsie Thomas. "Ooh, there's funny."

I went into my impression routine. Stainless Stephen, Sandy Powell, Lionel Barrymore could hardly be heard for Elsie's continuous laughter. The others joined in, not really knowing why, because after all I had done the same turn at Church Socials dozens of times. But Elsie's laughter was infectious. I was so elated by my reception that I even gave an impression of our milkman, which was a mistake as he was sitting in the third row.

Then I swaggered back down into the audience.

"There's funny you are," said Elsie giggling.

"Hush!" said Mildred Rogers, "the Curate's tap-dancing." She looked furious.

I turned to Elsie and did my "Mickey Rooney meets Anne Rutherford for the first time" look.

"I'm Harry Secombe."

She burst out laughing again. Someone hit me heavily behind the left ear.

"A bit of order for the Curate," said our milkman, smirking.

Elsie was now stuffing a handkerchief in her mouth, and tears were running down her face. I could see Mildred's mother making her way stealthily towards us.

"I'll see you tomorrow night at the top of Morris Lane after choir practice. Half-past seven." She nodded, gurgling away into her hanky.

I reached the door of the hall just before Mildred's Mam did.

"What's this about you operating on our Mildred?" was all I heard before I shut the door.

All next day in school I was in a happy daze, although no one noticed. My attitude towards learning was one of perpetual bewilderment only paralleled by the despair of those who had the task of teaching me. I took three years to make a wire dish mop in metal-work class. When I took it home my mother thought it was a clothes brush.

As soon as I saw Elsie that night she started to laugh. I hadn't even spoken a word, but she was off. She didn't even notice I was wearing my father's grey trilby and my brother's off-white mac with only two buttons missing and a slightly torn pocket.

I walked alongside her in silence until she had settled down a bit.

"Will you be my girl friend?" I was wasting no time in asking her. That set her off again.

"Ooh dear, stop it," she gasped, clutching a lamp-post for support. "I've got a stitch, take me home."

We had only been together about five minutes, but there was nothing else to do. As we passed Mildred's house her mother was at the gate. Elsie was still laughing and holding herself.

"Oh yes," said Mrs. Rogers, "using laughing gas to operate now, are you doctor?"

I pulled my hat further over my eyes and took the helpless Elsie to her front door.

"See you in Church on Christmas Day, I'm singing a solo in the Carol Service. You won't laugh then." I left her and walked home determined to show her the more serious side of my nature. After all laughter is not the only thing in life.

"Amen." I came back to the present quickly. The sermon was over and my big chance to impress Elsie was coming up fast . . . my solo. After this, and the pink sugar mouse I'd bought for her waiting in my overcoat in the vestry, she'd have the sort of adoring respect for me that Judy Garland had for Mickey Rooney in *Babes In Arms*.

The face in the mirror was glaring again. I gripped my carol book tightly and opened my mouth.

"Noel, Noel Noel, No . . ." On the fourth "Noel" my voice disintegrated. It splintered into a thousand fragments. With it went my boyhood and before me lay a wilderness of pimples, spots and slow-growing hairs to be crossed before I could call myself a man.

I stopped and turned to the choirmaster pointing at my throat.

From the front pew Elsie's smothered laughs came in waves. Someone else took over the solo and all eyes went back to the books. Except Elsie's. Her mother was guiding her swiftly up the aisle towards the door, giving her little thumps on the back to try to stop her laughing.

That's it. Voice gone, girl gone. Then I thought of that pink sugar mouse in my overcoat pocket and my face began to stop burning. I wondered if Mildred was doing anything that night.

"On long journeys you can keep the kids quiet by playing hide-and-seek."

Daughter's Wedding
by GRAHAM

*"I can't go into all that now, dear!
Didn't you read that book I gave you?"*

"Marvellous! Absolutely marvellous!"

"Dad, this is Robert."

*"Am I right in thinking I have the
honour of addressing the bride's
Aunt Harriet?"*

174

"Hire department? I want to report a
nasty accident with a meringue."

"At roughly four pounds a head, say,
I can't see old Charlie getting much
change out of a thousand."

"Few words . . . not going to bore you with long
speech . . . known Jennifer since she was a baby
. . . watched her bloom into womanhood . . .
prettiest bride ever seen . . . congratulate Robert
on his choice . . . long life and happiness
together . . . am reminded of story . . . ask you
to raise your glasses . . ."

". . . And thanks for everything, Mr. Burton
. . . er, Dad . . . er, Pop."

EXCLUSIVE— FOUR UNPUBLISHED EARLY MASTERPIECES

Now thats it's becoming the fashion to dig out the juvenile works of famous writers, MILES KINGTON jumps on the bandwagon with a quartet of previously unknown works of genius

THE CASE OF THE MISSING NAVY

Conan Doyle's first story (age thirteen)

"What do you make of this, Watson?" said Holmes, throwing a paper dart at me across the room. I unfolded it and saw that it was a letter.

"It has a message of some sort written on it," I said. "Gosh! Is this a new case?"

"Read it and find out," said Holmes, filling his mouth full of the liquorice all-sorts which he always stuffed himself with when he was hot on the scent of another villain.

"WATSON IS GETTING TOO BIG FOR HIS BOOTS," it said. "WE SHALL GET HIM."

"Well," I said, "I would deduce that it has been written by someone who thinks that I am getting too big for my boots and they are going to get . . ."

At that moment the door burst open and in came Queen Victoria, the Prime Minister, the First Lord of the Admiralty and several crowned heads of Europe. They were all disguised.

"Please sit down . . . Your Majesty," said Holmes. "Have an all-sort."

The Queen gasped.

"You recognised me!"

Holmes smiled.

"I could not help noticing the little marks on your forehead, which can only be caused by a crown. Perhaps you have read my essay on 'Marks made by Hats'. You are not the Kaiser, therefore . . ."

They all gasped.

"Wow, you certainly have an incredible gift for deduction," said the Prime Minister. "But let us get on with the story. We are in great trouble, Mr. Holmes. The First Lord of the Admiralty has reported that the British Navy has vanished. If some German spy sneaks on us to the Kaiser, it could mean the end of civilisation as we know it, or at least it could mean the German Navy coming and shooting our holidaymakers."

"Have *all* the ships gone?" said Holmes to the First Lord of the Admiralty, his keen eyes (Holmes's eyes, I mean) looking out from under his keen eyebrows. "Even the Zeus class destroyers with twin fourteen-inch turrets?"

"Unfortunately are they all disappeared," said the First Lord. With one stride, and then another one, Holmes leapt forward and pulled the moustache, beard, spectacles, hat and false nose from his face.

"Gentlemen," said Holmes. "Otto von Krempel, the German spy!"

*　　*　　*

"But how did you know?" I asked Holmes later.

"Jolly easy," said Holmes. "Any

chap knows that Zeus class destroyers have a sixteen-inch turret, also he spoke in a German accent. I am writing an essay on German accents. They only have one, the Umlaut. I thought of that joke this morning."

"One thing more."

"Yes?"

"Who wrote that threatening letter to me?"

"Who do you think?" said Holmes, throwing a cushion at my head.

DEATH AT TEA TIME

Ernest Hemingway's first story (14 years old)

Haley went out into the school yard. The first leaves of autumn were falling and it was chilly. The teacher told Haley to get his coat on or he would freeze to death. Haley went and got his coat. Then he went out into the school yard. It was a school yard much like other school yards, or I suppose so as I have not seen other school yards yet. Even if I had I would say it was much like other school yards as I have just discovered the expression "much like" and I like it.

"Hello, Haley," said Andersen.

Andersen was a huge Swede, standing well over five feet. He had blood on his chin where he had tried to shave himself. His shoulders were much like big shoulders.

"Hello, Andersen."

"I am going hunting in the woods. Are you coming?"

Haley knew what he meant. They were going to look for rabbits. They had never caught one yet and Haley was glad inside himself because they said that when you cornered a rabbit it was much like a mountain lion and tried to bite you, only lower down, about the knees.

When they were in the woods, Andersen stopped and shivered.

"It is a funny feeling, hunting rabbits. It is like the feeling of the thing between a man and a woman."

"What is the thing between a man and a woman?"

"I am not sure. I thought you knew."

"No, I do not know. But I thought you knew."

"No."

They went on a way further and they watched the leaves fall from the trees and hit the ground, which is the way of

leaves when they fall off the trees. Haley shivered and said it was cold. Andersen said nothing. Haley said it again. Andersen said that it was not too cold to hunt rabbits. Haley said he did not mean he was trying to get out of hunting rabbits, he only thought it was cold and that was all he thought.

"Look!" said Andersen. "A rabbit!"

"Where?" said Haley.

"Over there."

"I cannot see it."

"It has gone now. It does not matter. Perhaps it was not a rabbit at all. It is very cold."

"Shall we go back to school now?" said Haley.

They went back to school and did some more lessons and then Haley went home but he did not tell his parents of what had happened.

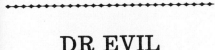

DR EVIL

The first James Bond story
(Ian Fleming, 14½)

James Bond strode into the hallway of Dr. Evil's house, wearing an immaculate school blazer which had been made for him by Jacob Schneider of Lucerne, which I think is in Switzerland, and asked the receptionist to tell Dr. Evil that James Bond had come to see him.

"Dr. Evil?" she said into the phone. 'There is a boy called Bond to see you."

"Who is almost 17," said James.

"Who is only 17," she said. "Yes, sir. Will you take the lift to the third floor?"

When Bond left the lift at the third floor he found himself face to face with Dr. Evil, a squat, ugly, horrible little man who was uncannily like a certain schoolmaster.

"What can I do for you, Master Bond?" he said leering.

Bond felt in his pocket casually to check that his 2½lb catapult, made of choice elm wood by a master craftsman in Bond Street, which is a very important street near Piccadilly, was loaded. He only used the very best conkers, imported from his aunt in Ireland, which was better than most aunts who only sent you book tokens.

"I think you know what I have come for," he said coolly, no, icily. "You have my replica authentic Japanese destroyer which fires real hara-kiri aeroplanes, which you confiscated for your own devilish ends. Sir."

The face of Dr. Evil went pale and he reached for his poison gun, but before he could pull it out Bond had pounced. At lightning speed he fastened the evil man in a half-Nelson, gave him a Chinese burn, did a quick knuckle-crusher and punched him in the nose. Dr. Evil sank lifeless to the ground, only he wasn't really dead. Like a flash, Bond entered the nearest room. There, on the bed, was the most fantastic blonde, really smashing, with no clothes on at all, if you know what I mean, like in books. There, on the table was his authentic Japanese destroyer.

"Who are you?" she gasped huskily gazing at the handsome stranger.

"I am James Bond and I am 16¾," he said in as low a voice as possible. "I have just killed your friend Dr. Evil, but he will live."

He strode to the table and picked up the destroyer. Before he left the room he turned to the girl, well, woman, and said:

"You will get cold lying around with no clothes on, anyway it looks silly, whatever they say in books. I would get a dressing gown on if I were you."

Moments later there came the distinctive sound of Bond's super three-speed-gear Raleigh as he pedalled away down the drive.

LORD ARTHUR WENTWORTH'S BLACKBOARD

Oscar Wilde's first play
(age fifteen)

(The scene is a richly decorated room, hung with damask curtains, rich brocade and the finest tapestries, but if you cannot get this your mother's dresses would do. There is a pale scent of incense and also the furniture is sumptuous. It is the Fifth Form at St. Topaz's School. A young man is seated at a desk, which is Arthur, who is the pupil. Standing by the gem-encrusted blackboard is a young man, which is Basil, who is the teacher. As the curtain rises, Arthur is lighting a slim, delicate cigarette.)

Basil: You know it is against the school rules to smoke, Arthur.

Arthur: What is the point of rules if we do not break them?

Basil: You have just made an epigram. Do you know the derivation of the word "epigram"?

Arthur: Like most words in English, it comes from the classics. Without the help of the Romans and Greeks, Englishmen would be hard put to it to express their contempt for foreign languages.

Basil: I sometimes wonder who is giving this lesson—you or me. Now, where was I?

Arthur: You were trying to persuade me that a knowledge of Canadian wheat production will enrich my career as a poet and artist.

Basil: My dear boy, one does not have a *career* as a poet. Poetry is too important to work at. One must content one's self with devoting one's self to it.

Arthur: Exactly. I shall write a play and with the proceeds withdraw to an exquisite house where I shall dedicate my life to a poem.

Basil: It is a charming thought. What will your play be about?

Arthur: It will be about two wonderful young men sitting in a classroom talking about art, poetry and Canadian wheat production. One must show the public one has taste and also has done one's lessons.

Basil: And how will the play end?

Arthur: Suddenly, without any warning at all.

(CURTAIN)

Zing
Go the Strings
of my
Vas Deferens

By ALEXANDER FRATER

WHEN Michael Parkinson announced to a startled nation that he had recently had a quarter of an inch excised from his vas deferens duct, he gave the vasectomy the biggest plug it has ever received; what Ted Heath did for ocean-racing he has done for sterilisation and the operation could well, in time, assume the fashionable stance of a German duelling scar. I anticipate it becoming one of those topics, like smoking at the time of the Surgeon General's Report, that loom up at one from all directions: "Are you going to be done?" will be the question, just as "Are you giving them up?" used to be the question back in the gay old carcinogenous Sixties.

Undergoing the operation is, of course, a lot easier than giving up smoking. The hard part comes beforehand when, since the process is deemed virtually irreversible, you must come to terms with the fact that your child-siring days are behind you. Once over that hurdle you (and your wife) sign the appropriate chitty and you report either to the surgeon of your choice or to one of the Family Planning Association's seventeen vasectomy clinics where, for a flat fee of £15.50, you slip off your trousers, tuck up your shirt and surrender yourself to the knife.

The whole thing only takes seven minutes and must be a bit like giving blood; although they don't send you away with a cup of tea and a Band Aid, it is the kind of appointment you could easily make for your lunch hour. Last year the Family Planning clinics operated on 4,331 men, with a further 4,000 on the waiting list. It is also possible to have it done on the National Health, though surgeons have shown a marked reluctance to perform vasectomies: why concern yourself with such trifles when you could be busy hacking off somebody's leg?

Among the public there is resistance to the idea too. The subject is still one which inspires winks and nudges—and not only from the men. All those primeval bogies of malehood, energetically preserved and fostered by the modern woman, swim up through the murk, accompanied by the usual grinning references to gelded cats growing fat and doctored tenors with shrill voices. It doesn't follow the other way. The woman who has had a tubal ligature or a hysterectomy is not a stock joke figure. There is no particular stigma attached to her. On the contrary, she tends to be viewed with sympathy, rather like the recipient of a war wound. But any man who undergoes a vasectomy is infringing certain tribal laws. He is letting down the side. He is abusing himself and putting the male preserve at risk. He is venturing out with a blunt sword.

The only chap I know who had had one was an American I met on a plane one night who, with that endearing but reckless habit they have of displaying a life-time's scars within the first ten minutes of acquaintance, told me he had recently been done in London. We were crossing the Alps and the air was turbulent and I wasn't paying him too much attention but, as I remember it, my first question was whether it had hurt. He said it had not hurt at all. There was the slight prick of the local anaesthetic which effectively numbed the groin and then a laundered green cloth with a hole in it was placed over him and the surgeon bent to his task, murmuring, "Just a small incision in your scrotum and then we make a nip and tuck inside and Bob's your uncle."

"Sid, this is my boy. I'm introducing him to the booze culture."

The plane dropped sixty feet and I spilt my whisky. "Hole in it?" I said.

"To effect entry."

"Ah."

"I felt like a mole on a tennis court," he said and, with the ardour of the newly-converted, proceeded to sell me the idea as the salvation of mankind. A decade from now, he said, all responsible adult males will be having it done. He may well be right though, probably for selfish reasons, I remained unconvinced. I was reminded of a *Panorama* programme on birth control in India which was shown some years back. One scene—a small, lonely peasant marching stoically up a long hall towards a brace of doctors who stood pointing eagerly as gun dogs—still rings my withers and I tend to identify with that fellow rather strongly.

I'm not sure why. Perhaps I still harbour grandiose illusions of siring another Shakespeare, or the man who will discover the cure for the common cold, or the first woman to play for Arsenal, or maybe it's the old matter of intimations of mortality and the wish to have plenty of progeny to support me in my old age. I'll probably need that. I'm not making the kind of money that Parkinson makes.

But as the operation grows in popularity—and that seems inevitable—there may be a kind of semantic spin-off. Most English euphemisms for penis are aggressive and faintly threatening: we liken it to a crowing male bird or a sharp instrument for felling trees, while the sex act itself has acquired the kind of terminology normally associated with carpentry or do-it-yourself activities—bang, screw, lay—all of which emphasise efficiency and functionalism, a job of work. Perhaps as the vasectomy gains ground there will be a shift of emphasis. A softer, more pleasurable note may creep in which might be reflected in the words we use. To joust, perhaps? To tilt? To dove? To float? To fiddle? To fly?

I don't know. The future looms and eventually decisions will have to be made. One has one's responsibilities. In the meantime, you can only gird up your loins and make sure she keeps taking the Pill.

Sympathetic Father (to son returning to school): ' I KNOW THE FEELING, OLD MAN.   I USED TO FEEL JUST THE SAME WHEN MY LEAVE WAS UP AND I HAD TO GO BACK TO FRANCE.'
Son: ' YES ; BUT THEN YOU HAD A REVOLVER.'

[1921]

Darken My Door Again by HANDELSMAN

"Ronnie is working toward a doctorate in astrology—the very first since the Dark Ages."

"You want my advice? Take the job with the napalm people. A clear conscience isn't everything in life."

"Bang! And another faculty sniper bit the dust."

"Inhale deeply. In a few minutes you'll be having beautiful thoughts."

"So Hume said that if A causes B, B is
caused by A? And that's how Hume made
a living?"

"We won the right to hire and fire teachers,
and you know what, dad? It turns out that
hiring and firing is my true vocation."

"Holy smoke, the Dean! He's still locked
in his office!"

"Why should I con-
tinue my studies? I
have taken acid, and
the secrets of the
cosmos have been
revealed unto me."

The Molesworth Saga

The brethtakingly beautiful Nigel Molesworth, as he was wont to describe himself, ran riot through the pages of Punch in the 1940's, closely followed by his chronicler GEOFFREY WILLANS, and into legend. Legends require homage, and the following six pages are, in consequence, Nigel's

Molesworth Excelsior

Contains: Diary of tuoughery, bullys, sloshes, ouches and skool pig.

May 8. Hols end skool weedy skool chiz. We rub our eyes as it haf been camooflaged but still conspikuous to enemy owing to mrs trimps (headmasters wife) new pink hat. Also enormous new bug who is a tuough and wear long bags (swank). molesworth 2 is a fule and sa you haf face like squashed turnip. He forget to rune away and new bug twist ear slowly. He will present some problems. Charge on big field with criket bat and slosh mightily. Score wizard near miss by skool dog and tuough wam on deaf masters moter bike. Deaf master sa bravo good shot sir so do not think he see.

May 12. Ferce air rade and wizard bombs drop. Germans all tuough and detmined to extermanate mrs trimps pink hat which important milertary objective. mr. trimp sa Take courage all no danger and all house maids faint including Lily (fat cook). Deaf master apply first ade to cook who scream and sa she never so insulted in her life. molesworth 2 larff like anything (conduc mark—Precocity). Skool pig unhurt but in high nervous condition. Give it bubly gum and chesnut leafs. Mr trimp sa germans make peace any moment: also hitler haf been murded and only an actor in his place.

May 13. Vilage constable peer over skool hedge.

May 20. Tuough new bug do not like skool pig he sa pigs poo gosh poo. He buzz conkers at pig but i trip him and he chass me. Hide in rodendron bushes and sa Ya boo swankpot. Unfortunately deaf master hear

(miracle?) and give me conduc mark (Tendency to impertnence). Chiz he haf down on me ever since unckle bingo wink at new misteress.

May 24. Suck up to deaf master. I sa show me how to ride your moter bike sir o you might. He visibly gratified and point out sparking plug. molesworth 2 who hapned to be by. sa gosh bet the old grid doesn't go. Deaf master start bike rattle rattle roar roar lamps drop off sparking plugs fly into air and all boys take cover. Mr trimp sa ah a heinkel could tell it anywhere and dash out with a duck rifle. He then fire furously at a wood pigeon he is bats.

June 4. Pla wizard criket match against staff. Do tuough bowling 90 m.p.h. charge grit teeth ground shakes and all boys tremble. Release ball but only hit skool dog who leap into air and bite new criket coach (long stop) and skool pig chiz. Camooflage skool pig with leafs against new bug, nazis and skool dog. New bug sneke and I get 6 chiz cruelty to animals. mr trimp sa germans giving eggs to noewegans.

June 8. Vilage constable lean over bicycle watching skool.

June 10. Draw wizard face on blackboard but new bug write under drawn by molesworth I chiz. Peason and I decide to tuough him up. Make tuough oath that we will fight in the streets and on the beeches until he is destroyed. Amen. Practise on Isaacs.

June 11. Decide to tuough new bug up tomow.

June 12. Decide to tuough new bug up tomow.

June 13. Decide to tuuogh new bug up tomow.

June 14. Argue with Peason who to strike first blow. Peason sa Fains chiz. Stork new bug stealthily through rodendron bushes but molesworth 2 come up and sa i sa what are you doing lying on ground chiz he is a fule. Crawl further but skool dog bite me in ear. New bug look very tuuogh but very cunning wait till he not looking then charge. He get me down and Peason just stand by and sa go it he is a funk. After sa to Peason cowardy cowardy custard but postion generally unsatisfactory. Draw wizard invention viz Tankplane on library book.

June 20. Wizard singing lesson minstrel boy to the war haf gone. All boys sing so beatifully that fotherington-tomas burst into tears. I sa whats up and he reply good thorts ascend like larks chiz he is wonky. Meet new misteress with scent bath poo gosh. Tell matron new misteress loved by all boys: she snort and give me two wopper pills. Coo.

June 21. fotherington-tomas disappear. Grate confusion and deaf master look at me chiz. All to big skoolroom. fotherington-tomas last seen picking rose and pressing to his heart. molesworth 2 sa he see three bearded men with vilainous xpressions storking him. They all had gats but noone belive him. Then vilage constable apear and all boys cheer as half holiday for funeral but super chiz as constable only sa Careless talk costs lives and warn mr Trimp against Rumours. Deaf master find fotherington-tomas on fairy cycle outside PUB (significant?) he sa he going to the war like minstrel boy. Not even kane chiz.

June 24. New criket coach (long stop) is fussy old man. He make me keep strate bat chiz. He sa he pla criket with W.G. and take bat to show me. Bowl tuuogh donky drop which descend on his nut and all boys congratulate me as no algy or geom for a week

cheers cheers. molesworth 2 still sa he saw three men storking fotherington-tomas. I ask him where they go and he sa he sprang upon them and routed them which is a fib. I then sa good thorts ascend like larks and molesworth 2 is stupified. mr trimp declare that we shall beat st. Ethelreds hollow—

June 25. V. st Ethelreds—lost 10 wkts.

June 29. Sports weedy sports. Tuuogh parents arrive and mrs Trimp wear new pink hat. Rune mightily puff puff but always last. New bug swank he win everything chiz but hundred yards Isaacs rune like billyo and beat him holow cheers cheers. Boo to new bug. mrs fotherington-tomas bring air gune. I sa let me haf a go o you might and take wizard pot at mrs trimps new pink hat. Feathers fly in showers cheers cheers. New bug come up who hapned to be by and sa bags and pinch gun but mr trimp arrive incensed about hat and he get 6 cheers cheers cheers cheers cheers. Isaacs blub as he only get criket bat (wally hammond) as prize. He thort the prize was money or he would not have rune so fast.

June 30. Criket coach recover consciousness. Deaf master console him and they go off to PUB to hatch plots.

July 1. Term plod like ploughman. All boys weary of lat french algy conkers matrons and all education. Get tuuogh deten write out amo, mono rego audio and decide to rune away like fotherington-tomas. Sa goodby to boys in dorm. Peason say good luck and fotherington-tomas blub quietly. Make cunning rope from sheets like Caveman charlie in boys mag. Goodby goodby noble molesworth. Make super speech from window ledge but fall backwards into cucumber frame chiz moan drone. Boo to everything.

the end.

Molesworth's Jolliest Term

Contains: More girls skools, flower monitors, prees, tuuoghery, headmisteresses and fruit.

July 6. Mum arive at st. cypranes cheers cheers she bring us wizard SWEETS inkluding whipped cream wallnuts. Chiz as molesworth 2 is suspious viz he sa Are not these the walnuts laid down for Armistice night? Mum blush chiz and blow fall i.e. Pop on embarkation leave agane and we to go to st. ethelburgas (girls skool) gosh chiz. mr trimp (headmaster) sa i am loss to eleven: chiz feel he is insincer as last match i make duck, blow 8 wides and stun long stop. Tell peason i am finishing term at eton to get feel of it. This is fib but molesworth 2 come by and swank he is a girl so cat is out of bag. Sell all dead maybugs at controlled price.

July 7. Find large DOLLY on bed chiz. Strongly suspeck deaf master who wink heavily at matron over korn flakes. No normal man would do this unless plotting. Hope to sneak away in skool taxi but alas all boys yell yar boo doris, farewell sno white ect. chiz and peason sa he haf always been struck by my beauty. Funny? mr trimp sa Order order do not rag them, fellows and all stop except deaf master who ask to be my valentine and skip weedily in front of taxi. i do not think he can haf heard.

July 8. Definite boos to all girls.

July 9. First day. Tuuogh headmisteress take one look at me and mutter gosh what i will do for money. Weedy bell go tinkle-tinkle: all girls, prees, flower monitors and other weeds asemble for Morning

Meeting viz singing skool song and tuough gigling. This is big morning aktually as miss fish (games misteress) haf leaped higher over horse than any other games misteress in england and win prize. Feeble feeble dora spatchworth (senior pree) sa Come on, st ethelburgas, lets give our heroine skool yell. All weeds then sa as follows: Q. Whats the mater with miss fish? A. she's all right. Q. Whos all right? A. miss fish is all right. Consider this perfecktly feeble so do head-misteress who pat all girls on head including dora spatchworth who she pat rather harder than neces-sery. She haf right idears.

July 10. Q. What's the mater with molesworth 1? A. he is entirely browned off.

July 12. Day dawn fine and bright chiz it is morning of tuough match v. st. cynthias. All girls haf but one topick viz outcome of this grate game. They sa Won't it be spiffing if spatchworth caries her bat? Bat is so big aktually that it is miracle if anyone can carry it and i sa so fearlessly i am even more browned off i.e. becos am in Wren patrol and haf to cry Chirup-chirup if in difculty or catching spy. Tuough team arive but super chiz as dora spatchworth bowl them all out. Headmisteress sa you can't help taking wickets with a face like that and rap girl smartly with sun-shade who sa d. spatchworth is the top. *Will st. ethelburgas do it?* molesworth 2 sa as a mater of fact he do not care brass button one way or the other and buzz small stone at miss fish. No prep on account of winning match and regret to state pla tuough game of tag. Gosh.

July 14. Peason write letter. He sa his admiration haf turned to something deeper and write poem viz

Hearts afire, hearts so true
betty darling i love you.

A joke in poor taste.

July 16. Small fat girl is still at skool you kno the one who is tuough and chew pen, scratch head also carve beta thomson is soppy on desk. She wish to let us in on RASBERRY RACKET viz pinch rasberries from skool garden and sell to ma timmis (pakenham gar-dens produce of the soil, Ltd.) Chiz rember all ser-mons, pijaws, kanes and shake head. molesworth 2 sa why not guzzle rasberries gosh? In the end give fruits as present to skool staff with compliments. Top in scripture. Significant?

July 17. molesworth 2 zoom by with trowel. He swank he is digging for defeat and all small girls are impressed.

July 18. Anual Pagaent. All girls pute on white dresses and tuough headmisteress haf new hat she stare in mirror and is aghast at what she sees. Pagaent begin viz HUMAN WHIST we are all feeble cards and haf to skip weedily chiz. molesworth 2 swank he is two of clubs cheers cheers he get dealt into wrong hand and trump dora spatchworth (ace of hearts). Small fat girl suggest we bag bunch of grapes from head-misteress hat as would never be missed among so much fruit but i refuse. Hand round ices i.e. moles-worth 2 sa May i tempt you to an icecream, moles-worth 1? and i repli allow me to press you to one of mine. Do 9 strawberry 3 vanilla affect boys?

July 19. Yes.

July 21. Pop's embarkation agane cancelled and he is to sit in barn near bognor and give all solders fatigues chiz. No real sign of end of term hols bombs or more rasberries. Weedy weedy all girls swot, bees place long noses in flowers and birds sing feeble songs. Buzz criket ball at dora spatchworth, brick at blak-bird and small pellet at miss fish. All miss. That is life.

July 22. Chirup-chirup and boo to von bock.

the end.

Molesworth : Man or Beast ?

Contains: Diary of mothers, bording houses, parots, tuough boys and weedy peoply.

August 2. Sumer hols cheers cheers we leave with mum for seaside. Arive at tuough bording house called mon repos (french) chiz as it is full of old lades including mrs furbelow (prop) and many canares which are not tuough and sing weedily. mrs furbelow look askance at parot which come with us and sa he will be EXTRA including boots baths lights and best sauce yum yum also molesworth 2. Mum sa gosh what a face but mrs furbelow hear and mum prertend she speaking of me chiz.

August 3. Very tuough bed so wake early. Healthy healthy take deep breaths and whole house tremble 3 old lades leave beds and zoom for air-rade shelter

hem hem i don't think. Dash on beach but sea is ten miles out. Cheers as jolly freezing. Also no destroyers or battleships only saucy sue. Read wizard book tarzan of the apes. Determin to be tuough leap on piano and beat chest. Unfortunately mrs baxter (old lade) come in and afterwards eye me closely chiz.

August 4. mrs baxter ask mum if i quite as i should be. Mum sa obviously no. chiz.

August 7. Tuough solders guard beach. molesworth 2 is a silly ass he stroll up to gun and sa bet it doesn't fire. He sa it is an old grid and no more use than a nanny gote. Tuough solder who is an old gentleman and haf red tabs sa indeed and molesworth 2 sa my father is head of army he captain molesworth. Old gentleman sa he will rember name he is only a genral. Tell mum who do not seem pleased. Slide down bannisters with tuough jungle crys.

August 8. Now i am EXTRA to chiz.

August 10. molesworth 2 is weedy he buy 2 windmills and zoom about with parot. He sa he twin engine fighter and parot is rear guner. Dive bomb mrs baxters bath chair and parot fall off scoring near miss on parrasoll. molesworth 2 sa bath chair is unlikely to have reached home. Walk along front and meet DEAF MASTER gosh chiz you can never get away from skoolmasters. He visibly shaken to see me but invite me to tea with his old mother adress sea breezes chiz chiz chiz.

August 11. Tuough tea with deaf master and deaf masters mother who is very ancient. She call him Cecil (n.b. must tell Peason) and give me rock cakes baked with her own hands. She sa Cecil was a lovely baby and when he was 5 he strike nurse gosh tuough. Silence try to eat rock cake crackle crackle bits fly in all directions gigantic raisin narrowly miss dresden sheppherdess. Place rock cake in pocket it will do as a bomb. Deaf master show me buterfly colection weedy unfortunately take out hankerchief (nose) and rock cake fly out badly damaging flertilery.

August 12. Gun still in same place but still as weedy as all solders pla foopball insted of fighting.

August 14. Wist Drive at bording house and all old lades very excited they pute on weedy dresses and sa feeble things e.g. clubs are, mrs furbelow molesworth 2 pla he sa it is pappy and do tuough trumping of partners ace. He sa he trumped trillions of aces in his time he is a swank. Mum is absolutely feeble she haf always to move to the left and mrs baxter swank she haf 53. Mum get booby prize (penny stamp in hat box ha ha) then sa Phew and take stiff drink out of toothmug in bedroom.

August 15. Rain and haf to stay indoors chiz. Fat lade miss boothroyd aktually read us weedy poem worse than gran's chatterbox e.g. there are faires at the bottom of our garden and rabits stand about and hold the lights. molesworth 2 sa there is a dirty old rubish heap at the bottom of his and miss boothroyd severely browns him off. Alone practice tarzan waddle like goriller and bite cushion with fiendish cries. In middle see mrs baxter looking at me chiz she seem somewhat

apprerhensive and grasp parrasoll tightly. Parot (rude bird) sa wot you doing sattiday ma and assault all canares. Parot is tuough.

August 16. Desine wizard yot with sails from bit of garden seat. At model boat pool it turn over and boy cyril who haf moter boat sneer in konsequence. Challenge him to race and molesworth 2 pute in his toy monky spinach also monkys son as tuough crew. Grate tragerdy bote and monkeys sink also cyril who overbalance in excitement so snubs. Meet deaf master in blazer and white flanels gosh posh. He is with young lade sylvia shriveham soobrette of peerots aktually you know the one who sings weedy songs viz just a song at twilight and no one clap. Walk along prom with them but deaf master do not seem keen on my company.

August 17. molesworth 2 and me are norty e.g. sa boo to mrs baxter. Mum sa she will send us to deaf master for punishment next time. Gosh tuough threat. Good deed we take mrs baxter for airing in bath chair that is i push and molesworth 2 ride in front. Unfortunately wizard spitfire pass and i let go handlebars. Bath chair zoom down slope 240 m.p.h. dogs bark policemen faint bath chair sweep across sands with grate destruction. Moan drone find bath chair stationery in sand castle. molesworth 2 sa absolutely wizard and mrs baxter also enthusiastick she always was one for spills and tumbles. Jolly sporting but do not want another go.

August 18. Grate activity round gun. Solders move gun up and down then round and round. Genral highly satisfied and solders all go to sleep they are exorsted.

August 20. Hols end chiz and mum pack trunks. All spades bukets and windmills dispear chiz and we shake sand out of shoes. Canares sing sad songs and parot weep. mrs baxter zoom up in bath chair and give us fruit pastille not bad acktually also deaf master on moter bike. He sa he haf decarbonized bike and she rune smooth as a bird. molesworth 2 sa i don't think and deaf master start bike. Record exploshon mrs baxter shoot into air and all solders wake and rush to gun. BONK they fire tuoughly and mrs furbelows greenhouse colapse cheers cheers cheers. Boo to jeraniums and zinnerareas.

the end.

Molesworth Goes Rustic

Contains: Diary of harvesting, loonies, aples cows seeds farmers and fruit.

Aug. 28. i sa gosh all plans upset i.e. Pop should not haf been on embarkation leave at all as war ofice were thinking of molesworth c. St. J. A, major, r. sigs who haf already been in egypt two years. Pop sa it is scandalous disgraceful but later see him do hornpipe in bathroom and sa 8 weeks leave in bag and no foreign service hurra cheers cheers. Mum also do hornpipe but brake plate which will haf to be replaced as on inventory and not one she haf sneaked from locked cupbord. Situation leave molesworth 2 cold. He sa he haf long suspeckted impasse at the ministry and zoom away to inspeck plum harvest.

Aug. 29. molesworth 2 confined to bed. Plum harvest rather bakward (oficial).

Sept. 1. Complications viz Pop haf choice of joining unit in aberdeen or stationed next door to grans house. He dercid immediately for aberdeen and buzz small cherry stone at molesworth 2 who sa So you can't take it? from larder. Mum is browned off at this i.e. becos Pop always so nasty about mother but find 2 unladered stokings and ½ botle of scent poo gosh and cheer up at once. P.C. arive from gran who sa she going to the country to fite on harvest front and think boys should do bit also. Strong pi-jaw from Pop who sa all boys to help national effort and bend backs with will. Chiz as he sa to mum Now we can haf wizard last week in town. Hay-ho all boys are stooges.

Sept. 4. Cheers cheers arive with gran at tuough farm viz golightly court farm dainty teas cream camping ground plums in season. Cow chikens dog pig ect see gran and cry bitterly. Knock knock where is farmer? Enter super weed viz silas croker (farmer) he see gran and almost moo too. Eat tuough tea in parlor but chiz as molesworth 2 sa tea O.K. but what about cream plums and camping? All larff inkluding mrs croker, granny croker and granny croker's friend mrs posnett they sa molesworth 2 such a pritty child cheers cheers. All then look at me and words freeze on lips wot do they expect robert taylor?

Sept. 5. Chirup chirup rise with dawn but all animals sleeping chiz but not bad aktually as zoom through wood and pester all flies wasps and bluebotles. Return to farm which in confusion as dairy haf not called. Gran sa why not milk own cows but nothing doing as only one cow i.e. Poppy which haf not given milk for 3 years. silas croker sa he slowly coming to konklusion that cow no use. Gran then sugest slorter house but mrs posnett fante away she canot stand blud. molesworth 2 highly delited he swank blud daggers ect favorite subjeckts and granny croker fante too. Result 2 heavy bombers down. Pilot, molesworth 2 award himself v.c.

Sept. 8. Heavy rane storm. silas croker shake head.

Sept. 9. Thunder and hail. Croker in despair.

Sept. 10. More rane. Croker sa if this do not hold up he will be ruined. Gran leap to feet. She sa give her a rake and harvest will yet be saved. molesworth 2 agree, providing there sunshine and light drying wind and ooze off to bomb chikens out of drawing room. Gran now return to parlor with rake but croker repli no go as no harvest anyway. He only worred becos he haf left mack in vilage bus and canot do rounds for

insurance coy. He ask if he can intrest gran in life policy or burglary risk. Find molesworth 2 who lie in dog kenel he haf been shot down by chiken and is dead once more.

Sept. 11. Gran find PROSPECTUS in bedroom viz. nice quiet little company with firm dividends invest now.

Sept. 14. Take farm dog for hunt but feeble acktually as dog think he frend of man and only wish to pla with rabits like cristofer robin, poo and wendy. Pop into vilage for 2 oz. persnal rashion but meet Loony lil, vilage idiot, in honeysukle lane she is bats and sing feeble songs viz: Maying lads tie on your ribons and wheel empty pram what is the sense of it? Chiz aktually as she sa i am long lost son. Vilage oiks highly delited they cheer like mad so tuough up young george thomas also postman baines youngest. From all these operations two of our teeth are missing.

Sept. 15. croker ask gran if she haf ever studied comercial aspekt of mushrooms?

Sept. 16. Poppy (cow) go too far as she drink all milk rashion. Gran sa if not slorter house why not market? mr croker agree and borow traler from a.r.p. He haf only paid for half a Poppy but will raise rest on sale and that will make her all his. Auctioneer sa what am i bid for this remarkable beast and molesworth 2 swank as he think he refering to him. Make tuough repli i.e. i would not give d. for anyone who haf been shot down by chiken he is a fule. Farmers all shake heads at Poppy but cunning cunning croker run up bidding and finally buy for twenty pounds gosh. Gran sa is this wise but croker only wink. He sa slickest thing he ever done and have BEER in spotted dog.

Sept. 18. Find farm dog who gaze at weedy calendar viz:

> If mistress haf a walk for me
> A model doggy i will be.

Throw stone for dog but he only take refuge under cow. i wash my hands of him.

Sept. 19. a.r.p. come for traler as they think there fire on somewhere.

Sept. 22. Grate day viz gran throw down force spoon at brekfast and give stiring message Plough for victory. mr croker sa dang from state of market he will jolly well haf to but no plough. Gran sa Fidledee dee, make one. Cheers cheers all infeckted with enthusiasm mrs croker scrub dairy, gran croker knit furously and mr croker borow small plough from over to copleys place. Cheers cheers enter gran on tractor and zoom around field. Birds sing cows graze and chikens peck everbode. Read wizard story 9 chinese Murders to farm dog which promptly catch rat.

Sept. 23. All in bed with colds. That is life.

Sept. 24. Moo.

the end.

Molesworth of the Remove

Contains: Diary of oiks, headmasters, ow yarouch, crikey and various ungentlemanly cries.

Dec. 8. st cypranes is still evackuated at st. guthrums and all record weeds flourish i.e. 2 headmasters, skool dog, matron, deaf master etc. all enemy agents in that order. Toda tuough man arive to see mr trimp (headmaster) with record OIK (son) called cyril who haf close resemblance to dirty pete the vilage tuough. Tuough man sa look here old man how about me sending my nipper to yore place? Herr trimp look down nose (long) he sa "We are full." Tuough man then wink and sa I AM A BUTCHER HOW ABOUT IT NOW and cyril is instantly admited chiz. All boys sa jolly shame and swanky new bug you kno the one with the pork pie hat sa he must serously consider resigning. All aplaud this except molesworth 2 who sa good ridance to bad rubish and rune away.

Dec. 9. Gran write p.c. She haf seen a poster which sa go to it and intend to become lady porter. Gosh tuough.

Dec. 10. French class. Deaf master address oik he sa turner where is papa rat? Oik sa cor stone me how should i kno and go to top of class (flewency and good prunciation). Oik is super weed aktually and always wanting to pla jolly japes on masters. He sa i votes felows we do a merry prank i.e. pute buket of water on classroom door. He gets these idears from comicks he is keen on bob cherry, billy bunter etc. and read about them in prep he will get cobbed one day.

Dec. 11. Mum write letter about Gran becoming porter. She sa what a wonderful old lade Gran is dedcating herself to the countrys cause. Very sad chiz it bring tears to my eyes i am filled with noble visions. Unfortunately Pop add note "This ought to finish the old geyser off" and i larff synically over poridge.

Dec. 12. Toda there is weedy pla by plarstercene class chiz. They are all wee bunnies and gnomes. fotherington-tomas jump for joy he is a pixie but molesworth 2 absolutely browned off he is CHIEF GNOME cheers cheers cheers. He is a weed and i sa how about you swanking you are a spitfire pilot when you haf to sa Come elves let us do what we may to help the princess. Pla is record weedy being full of good deeds and noble thorts but OIK do good thing viz he bag Chief Gnomes trousis in interval. mr trimp sa unless trousis are returned imediately pla cannot go on and all boys cheer they do not want to watch it anyway. mr trimp then get batey and sa culpritt to own up or no half hol but swanky new bug point out that what the nazis are doing in paris and get conduc mark (superiority).

Dec. 13. Matron find Chief Gnomes trousis in my tuck box chiz. She sa she will let matter go no further if I promise not to rage or pilow fight in dormtories. i promise faithfully and she believe me (sap). Swanky new bug sa whole skool seethe with vice and coruption. He sa no beauty anywhere and seem to look at me chiz. Don't care so boo.

Dec. 15. OIK is absolute weed he is only keen on stink-bombs and weedy ink darts which do not fly and canot do the pappiest sums. Toda we haf algy fuste lesson in afternoon which is the one when mr dashwood (st. guthrums headmaster) always sa get on with xsamples and then go to sleep. Unfortunately he break rule and wake before bell executing wizard pincer movement on OIK with ruler. Oik sa yaroo ouch goshsir i meantersay sir cor sufering snakes and recive second blip which all boys watch with delite. mr dashwood also give him deten although Oik offer him three pork chops and a nice loin of lamb without coupons.

Dec. 17. Hatch plot with peason to tuough up OIK on account of Chief Gnomes trousis. Oik sa look here you felows you did ought to be reasonable how about three tins of spam and we are inflexible and sa we will tuough him up and haf tins as well. Oik then sa his dad can get us comisions in air force and fotheringtontomas highly excited he wish to be air cadet. molesworth 2 sa gosh you can't even ride your fairy cycle yet and bow 3 times he think he is witty. He then rune off to bomb skool dog and steal blackcurrant lozenges.

Dec. 18. Gran write she highly disgusted she canot be a porter on account of stationmaster sa he is out of trains and haf none under the counter. Gran declare she strongly suspeck he pull her leg but will make xplosives instead.

Dec. 19. We haf weedy shepherds pie but mr dashwood tuck into pork chops. Significant?

Dec. 20. Toda there is jim comp and all boys do tuough things to the manner born we do record figure marching but molesworth 2 is weedy he forget to turn and march into tea room. All boys then hang upside down and pink cakes rane from molesworth 2's jersey he is a guzler. mr dashwood highly excited he dash into midle and sa gad a human pyramid magnificent and throw fotherington-tomas into air. parents screme mr trimp hide eyes but he do not break any bones chiz. Boys then clime on mr dashwood who sa all storms a rugged oak can bare. Wizard crash folow and great aplawse.

Dec. 21. Hurra for Xmas. Boys go mad in wizard rags and scrag all masters, dive bomb matron, hammer at bases of all latin books and suround skool dog in ring of steel. molesworth 2 is shot down in larder and fail to return to his base. Chiz. Ouch yaroo for Xmas.

Dec. 22. Good ridance to skool.

the end.

Meanwhile, in Angry Test-Tubes at Many A. I. D. Laboratories...

By BASIL BOOTHROYD

Student militancy by undergraduates and, more recently, sixth-formers, has attracted ample news coverage. But what of the tide of extremism among junior age-groups? A report from Surrey on the nursery school revolution

I SPOKE to Miss Judith Bince, attractive-sounding headmistress of "Merrytots", Godalming, through the keyhole of the pupils' toilet. where she was in her fourth hour of an enforced sit-in. She granted the interview on the understanding that I would send back a locksmith from Haslemere, my next port of call.

"Unfortunately," she explained, "both the local ironmongers have their little girls here at Merrytots, Jacqueline and Bunty: they went home as soon as they'd dropped the keys in the pond, and they'll have forbidden their fathers to come and get me out, on pain of being sick. The rest are round the back damming the paddling pool with abacuses and Class Three raffia. I wouldn't go out there, if I were you, because they're throwing horse manure. Felicity's pony——"

"How did the trouble begin?"

It appeared that two seniors, Reginald, seven, and Dominic, six, newly enrolled that day after their own school, in the next road but one, had been set fire to, had lost no time in heading a deputation demanding that the No Playing With Matches rule, long a tradition at Merrytots, should go. "I understood their feelings, but was unable to agree, even though they argued that they could run the place without help from me, and threatened to send their parents round to hit us—myself, that is, and Wendy, who is locked in the music-room, you might mention to the Haslemere man."

"What was your next step?"

"It wasn't mine, it was theirs. During milk-break they must have set up a revolutionary student body and roughed out a policy. They came back in an apparently orderly fashion to the first class after break, Wendy's Music and Movement, but when the radio asked the usual questions, 'Are you sitting comfortably?' 'Are you wiggling your fingers as *hard* as ever you can?' Reginald and Dominic began shouting back simply terribly rude answers, and naturally the smaller ones were soon joining in——"

"Not knowing what they were saying, presumably?"

"It's very dangerous to make assumptions with youth today. Perhaps some of the very youngest didn't, but it's hard to be sure. I heard the disturbance from the next room, my cutting-out class, and found them all throwing Noddy books and modelling-clay, tearing up art work and pushing pieces of jig-saw through cracks in the floor-boards. As for the noise, it sounded like an Enoch Powell meeting. They'd already locked Wendy in the music-room by then, gagged with a blackboard-rubber, and Reginald and Dominic and a big strong six-year-old called Barbara, very easily led, rushed at me and——"

"Yes. Did they seem to have any definite reforms worked out, anything you could make concessions on, as a basis for liberalising the attitude of the faculty?"

"The attitude of the——?"

"You and Wendy."

188

"Oh. They sent some demands round, yes. Coming under the door, if you can get hold of it." A crumpled paper appeared near my shoes. "I'll just sit down while you read them." Miss Bince's voice receded a little. "It's all been rather a strain."

The writing was in red crayon, and seemed to have started as some official scholastic exercise.

A, B, C, E, G, J, L, Z, 1, 2, 3, 4, 11, 12, 20.

At the zoo the animals eat buns.

DEMANDS

1. Gloves not to be on strings for over age 7s.
2. Stop silly morning pray and hymns.
3. No more daft kurb drill on walks.
4. Can bring mice.
11. Aloud to eat paints from pain boxes also lick building brick colours.
12. Wipe own noses, etc.
20. Mrs. Pringle stink of coff sweets.

"Of course," said Miss Bince, "I know it's the education policy to—are you still there?"

"Certainly. Are you?"

"Yes. I know it's the——"

"Who's Mrs. Pringle?"

"Our piano teacher, until she saw the Demands. But she was going in any case. The children kept cracking her over the knuckles with a ruler."

"Please go on."

"I know it's the modern education policy to make all the concessions you can, with the young people all maturing earlier and knowing as much as the teacher—more, in Wendy's case. They asked her during flower-pressing last week if she'd ever had an abortion, and when she covered her ignorance by saying, 'Oh, yes, lots,' we had seven pairs of parents round with the assistant education officer, asking whether she was a fit person."

"Would you feel able to concede any of the present demands?"

"It depends a lot on which ones the parents are backing. I wouldn't mind giving in on tying the gloves together, for instance: they can lose all the gloves and get all the chilblains they like; but then it's not *my* idea to have them anyway. They've put Gillian in the water-butt."

"I beg your pardon?"

"They're all going now. I'm looking out of the back window. She's got out again and she's going with them. It's a protest march. You'll see them go past, through the little window over the shoe-pegs. That's Dominic in front, with the toddlers' blackboard."

They passed down the side of the building towards the road, a bobbling straggle of woollen hats and slovenly gaiters. It said "VOTES AT 9" on the blackboard, and there were one or two other crayoned slogans, apparently on banners of torn wallpaper: LOWER JAM SHELVES, MORE POCKET MONEY NOW. A fat boy in spectacles jumped up at my window with a rude gesture and a cry of "Knickers to Miss Bince".

"That was Reginald," said Miss Bince. "Are any of them on fire?"

She seemed relieved when I said no. "Good," she said. "For their own sake, you can only let them do exactly what they like up to a point. You feel a responsibility. I'm wondering whether I could concede on that no more kerb-drill demand, for example. They seem so absolutely sure that they know better than we do on everything, you begin to come round to wondering if they're right. Usually, of course, Wendy and I see them to the bus, but—" There was a squeal of brakes and some confused shouting from the direction of the road. "What was that? Did you hear something?"

"No."

I thanked her very much for talking to me, and said I'd be off to Haslemere now, and St. Christopher's Mixed Infants. She seemed to think I should get some useful material there, as the children had been occupying the school since Tuesday, protesting against a ban on eating poisonous berries.

"I'll send you a locksmith," I said, snapping the elastic round my notebook. "If there's one free."

*"Look, Timothy, if I give you the two bars of chocolate **and** the ten new pence, will you tell Mummy that Daddy's on the telephone?"*

189

TOYSHOP

"We'll think it over."

"I hope he likes it."

"It's for the wife, actually."

"Let's club together and buy one for mummy."

"Two bathrooms?"

"Oh come along dad!"

"It's a tree son . . . a tree."

Missing My Daughter

THIS wall-paper has lines that rise
Upright like bars, and overhead
The ceiling's patterned with pink roses.
On the wall opposite the bed
The staring looking-glass encloses
Six roses in its white of eyes.

Here at my desk with note-book open
Missing my daughter makes those bars
Draw their lines upward through my mind.
The blank page stares at me like glass
Where stared-at roses wish to pass
Through petalling of my pen.

An hour ago there came an image
Of a beast that pressed its muzzle
Between bars. Next, through tick and tock
Of the reiterating clock
A second glared with the wide dazzle
Of deserts. The door, in a green mirage

Opened. In my daughter came.
Her eyes were wide as those she has,
The round gaze of her childhood was
White as the distance in the glass
Or on a white page, a white poem.
The roses raced around her name.

STEPHEN SPENDER

192